BEST PRACTICES

FOR EQUITY

RESEARCH

ANALYSTS

Essentials for Buy-Side
and Sell-Side Analysts

JAMES J. VALENTINE, CFA

New York   Chicago   San Francisco   Lisbon   London
Madrid   Mexico City   Milan   New Delhi   San Juan
Seoul   Singapore   Sydney   Toronto

The **McGraw·Hill** *Companies*

2 3 4 5 6 7 8 9 10   QFR/QFR   1 9 8 7 6 5 4 3 2 1

ISBN   0-07-173638-7
MHID   978-0-07-173638-1

This publication is designed to provide accurate and authoritative information in regard to the subject matter covered. It is sold with the understanding that neither the author nor the publisher is engaged in rendering legal, accounting, securities trading, or other professional services. If legal advice or other expert assistance is required, the services of a competent professional person should be sought.

—From a Declaration of Principles jointly adopted by a Committee of the American Bar Association and a Committee of Publishers and Associations

Library of Congress Cataloging-in-Publication Data

Valentine, James J.
    Best practices for equity research analysts : essentials for buy-side and sell-side ana-lysts / by James Valentine.
        p. cm.
    ISBN 978-0-07-173638-1 (alk. paper)
    1. Investment advisors. 2. Investment analysis. I. Title.
    HG4621.V35 2011
    332.63'2042—dc22   2010032041

To Emma, Laura, Alice, and Robert for their loving support.

If we knew what it was we were doing, it would not be called research, would it?

—*Albert Einstein*

Contents

List of Exhibits

Preface

I thoroughly enjoyed my career on Wall Street. I couldn't have asked for more thoughtful clients, talented team members, or supportive research management. But during those 16 years, I became intrigued by the criticism surrounding the quality of equity research, often coming from within the industry. There was no shortage of intelligent, hard-working individuals. So why wasn't there an abundance of world-class research? I'm not sure that I solved the entire mystery, but I did reach one major conclusion: There are few, if any, quality control processes. Furthermore, there is minimal professional training provided to equity research analysts.

Think about it: An experienced portfolio manager is relying on internal buy-side and external sell-side analysts to provide accurate, insightful information to make decisions that can impact millions, and possibly billions, of dollars of return over the life of an investment. And yet most of these analysts never received professional training beyond what they picked up on the job and classes they *may* have taken in college. Instead, our profession relies on the medieval master–apprentice approach, which results in training only as good as the master. Our society doesn't allow this in the medical, legal, or accounting professions, or even for licensed plumbers or electricians. Those fields require that certain best practices be learned, and that mastery be validated by a certification process. The closest thing we have is the CFA certification, which is highly credible, but not required for the profession. (Only a fraction of equity analysts are CFAs.)

So how bad is it? Let me first say, I've met more talented buy-side and sell-side analysts than I can count—individuals who produce impressive alpha-generating research. But unfortunately, this has been the exception more than the rule. As an analyst who worked at four of the largest sell-side firms in the United States, I witnessed too many inexperienced analysts making poorly constructed stock calls, often based on unsubstantiated theses (including me, during the first few years of my career). Worse yet, often in instances where the sell-side analysts produced good research, they couldn't effectively manage their franchise to get recognized by clients.

I didn't sense it was substantially better on the buy-side. Based on the 100 to 150 conversations I had with my clients every month, it was clear that there were too many buy-siders struggling in their roles, specifically failing to identify the factors most likely to drive their stocks. Occasionally, when I would get off the phone with a buy-side professional discussing a stock his or her fund owned, I'd wonder how the person could fail to understand some of the more basic elements of the story. To illustrate my point, here are some real-world comments I heard during my career:

- "I don't want to touch that stock because I'm concerned about a labor strike" (even though the company was non-union and would *benefit* from a strike at its unionized competitor).
- "We sold the [transportation] stock because oil prices are likely to rise" (even though this company's adjustable fuel surcharge was so lucrative that margins *expanded* when fuel prices rose).
- "I'm recommending this stock because we're bullish on ethanol" (even though ethanol was less than 1 percent of the company's revenue, and under an ultra-bullish scenario would go to no more than 3 percent of revenue over five years).

If these individuals were investing their own money, I could easily accept their misunderstanding of the company's fundamentals. But it was *other people's* money—people who were entrusting them to fully understand the investment case for a stock, which clearly wasn't happening. A buy-side analyst, with more than 10 years of experience at a firm managing over $ 100 billion in assets highlighted the impact this has had more recently, when he said, "Wall Street is shrinking because a generation of investors are alienated with equities." To help remedy the credibility problems he believes, "Anyone who wants to be successful in this business needs to follow best practices." (His thought was an inspiration for the book title.)

In 2006, after having been a sell-side analyst for 14 years, I decided to do my part to help improve the industry's quality issues by taking on a newly created role to develop a global training program for the one thousand employees in my firm's equity research department. Based on my experience as an analyst and holding this role, I began to formulate best practices for equity research analysts, which I later refined further through interviews with practitioners from other sell-side and buy-side firms.

There may be seasoned practitioners who consider my recommendation that analysts strive to follow these best practices as too ambitious, remarking, "There's no way an analyst could do all this." I agree; for many practicing analysts, such as those on the buy-side who are asked to *closely* follow well over 50 stocks with no support (or over 20 on the sell-side), it will be a challenge to implement many of the best practices, for sheer lack of time. These individuals are attempting to put out a high-rise fire with a garden hose. If there is cynicism about implementing best practices, I'd question if it's coming from the same population that underperforms the market each year. The industry has massive performance issues, and nobody seems to know how to fix them. (According to Standard & Poor's most recent data, 60 percent of U.S. equity funds underperformed their benchmarks over the past five years, which drops to a still disappointing 56 percent over the past three- and one-year periods.) I have one remedy: Reduce the amount of stocks an analyst covers. I'm not diminishing the need for generalist analysts, but let's call them what they are: portfolio managers or assistant portfolio managers. The best practices found here will likely help any type of equity analyst, but many are designed for those who look at their stocks from a bottom-up perspective and, most importantly, *don't cover an excessive number of stocks.*

If you're not sure how to prioritize the material that follows, new analysts should first focus on Part 1 because the topics are central to everything an analyst does. Experienced analysts can potentially jump to some of the most pressing challenges they face by focusing on (1) identifying and monitoring critical factors (Chapter 8), (2) forecasting scenarios (Chapter 18) and (3) improving their stock calls (Chapter 20 and 21). Alternatively, first read all of the book's exhibits labeled "Best Practice" and then go back to the chapters where you have the greatest interest.

The material attempts to solve problems that are typical for buy-side *and* sell-side roles, and drills down with more detail when it's clear a solution for the buy-side role is different than for the sell-side. It's important to note that all of the best practices were used by one or more of the practitioners interviewed for the book or by my team during my career. I've provided the practitioners' names when referring to their quotes throughout the book, but unfortunately a number are restricted by their firms from being identified for attribution. (Morgan Stanley allowed its analysts to be quoted, which explains why they appear more featured than other firms throughout the book.) Some of the best practices may appear ambitious to implement, but others have done it. Be mindful of the adage, "You don't achieve goals you don't set."

This book wasn't written simply to help analysts improve, but also to give them the competitive advantage to move to the top 10 percent of their peers. This isn't a textbook; the intent is not to repeat concepts already learned in college, but to provide what's required to get the job done successfully for buy-side and sell-side practitioners. When I set out to create these best practices, the goal was to get as much concentrated material into one place as possible, but space constraints prohibit in-depth discussions in many topics. The goal was to identify the skills and the body of knowledge required for success, but it's unrealistic to think that everything an analyst will ever need to know will be in one book, especially for complex subjects such as accounting, statistics, valuation, and technical analysis. Hopefully, after reviewing these best practices an analyst will at least know what he or she does-n't know. From there, the challenge will be to become proficient in those skills or gain greater knowledge. The best-practice exhibits are intended to be stand-alone tools that an analyst can quickly review to help master that task, and thus the content in the exhibits is often found elsewhere in the text. Due to space limitations, supplemental information can be found at AnalystSolutions.com. Furthermore, I encourage you to visit www.AnalystSolutions.com/book to provide your best practices or additional input to make these best practices bet-ter. It's my expectation that this body of knowledge will evolve as more practitioners contribute *their* best practices.

When I was an analyst, I was a big believer in being transparent to my clients so they could see my potential biases. In this spirit, it's important to disclose that during the writing of this book I haven't received compensation from any of the companies or vendors men-tioned in this book, other than the use of FactSet's database to com-pile data for the book (to whom I'm thankful) and a diminutive dividend from unvested Morgan Stanley stock I don't yet control (awarded as compensation when I was an employee).

I can't think of a better job than the role of an equity research ana-lyst. If you do your job well, you're essentially your own boss, deciding how to spend your time, with almost full control over your career suc-cess. There's frequent interaction with some of the sharpest people you'll ever meet. No two days are ever the same. And if you like to travel, there's often no limitation on the number of places you'll see. Oh, and did I mention the pay isn't too bad? To anyone who complains about the profession, including those who say it's "no longer fun" after Regulation FD and the Spitzer Settlement, I challenge them to find a more rewarding career. Hopefully, the material that follows will help make this career just a bit more rewarding.

Acknowledgments

I'd like to start by thanking those friends and colleagues who spent considerable time helping draft and edit portions of the manuscript, including Lauren Bloom, Chad Bruso, Dorris Dolph, Hunter DuBose, Chris Gowlland, Elmer Huh, Bob Jones, Barbara Lougee, Kurt Moeller, Quentin Ostrowski, Judy Sheehan, Barry Sine, Emma Valentine, and Chris Wright.

I would also like to thank all of the friends and colleagues who helped provide insight for the book as well as those who had a significant influence in shaping my view of the profession and many of the best practices in this book: David Adelman, Ajit Agrawal, Christine Arnold, Reena Bajwa, Jay Bennett, Rich Bilotti, Michael Blumstein, Bob Brizzolara, Celeste Brown, Nathan Brown, Zach Brown, Jeff Burton, Mayree Clark, Doug Cohen, Jim Crandell, James Crawshaw, Christina Dacauaziliqua, Darius Dale, David Decker, Ridham Desai, Christian Drake, Michael Eastwood, Jason Eiswerth, Robert Fagin, Simon Flannery, Casey Flavin, Phil Friedman, Steve Galbraith, Steve Girsky, John Godyn, Rory Green, Bill Greene, Michael Griffiths, Gem Guiang, Ian Gutterman, Phil Hadley, Nick Harness, Trevor Harris, Tony Hatch, John Havens, Shora Haydari, Matt Hedrick, Alison Henry, Marvin Hill, Allison Hirsch, Dickson Ho, Barry Hurewitz, Vlad Jenkins, Drew Jones, Rupert Jones, Hani Kablawi, Jane Kamneva, Jeff Kanter, Ronny Kaplan, Allison Kaptur, Ed Keller, Evan Kurtz, Michelle Leder, David Lee, Chris Leshock, Mark Liinamaa, Steve Lipmann, Dario Lizzano, Adam Longson, Steve Madonna, Mike Manelli, J. P. Mark, Gerson Martinez, Mike Mayhew, Brian McGough, Mary Meeker, Greg Melich, Ron Monaco, Suzanne Morsfield, Jack Mueller, Todd Neel, Peter Nesvold, Matt Nielsen,

Matt Ostrower, Robert Ottenstein, Vikram Pandit, John Pastorelli, Howard Penny, Steve Penwell, Juan Luis Perez, Ken Posner, John Quackenbush, Glenn Reicin, Lauren Rich Fine, Alan Richter, Jack Rivkin, Jim Runde, Mike Ryan, Joe Saiz, Eli Salzmann, Menno Sanderse, Alice Schroeder, Carl Schweser, Wes Sconce, Alkesh Shah, Stephanie Shaw, Dennis Shea, Jay Sole, Matthew Spahn, George Staphos, Josh Steiner, Joe Swanson, Naoki Takemoto, Gerry Tavolato, Jim Tierney, Bill Van Tuinen, Jeanette Ventura, Mike Vitek, Steve Volkmann, Jim Voytko, Marcus Walsh, Nelson Walsh, Bill Wappler, Guy Weyns, Greg Whyte, Byron Wien, Joe Wilkinson, Frank Wilner, Will Wrightson, and Dennis Yamada.

I would also like to thank Morgan Ertel, Leah Spiro, and Jennifer Ashkenazy for their help in making this book a reality.

Introduction

No man was ever wise by chance.
—*Attributed to Seneca the Younger*

Need for Best Practices

There are plenty of obstacles to learning best practices. As I've spent time studying the training profession since leaving Wall Street, it's become clear that there's one major difference between the learning we do in our profession and the learning we did in college: The what's-in-it-for-me factor is much higher for professionals. Without a clear incentive system, most professionals don't see the point in continuing education. Further raising the bar for professional learning, many corporate training programs are not learner-centered, but instead built around the needs of management. This is similar to how the computer industry failed to deliver user-centered solutions until Apple came along. I can't say the material in this book will be as exciting as a new iPhone or iPad app, but it has been assembled with the learner in mind, enabling quick access to the knowledge and skills required for success.

Some analysts may ask, "Why do I need to learn how to be an analyst when I can just learn it on the job?" Their competitors are glad these analysts have this view, because it increases their odds of failure. This was echoed by the director of research of a large hedge fund who said, "We like that there are a bunch of people doing mediocre research, because it gives us more opportunities." Here's why there is a significant need for best practices within the profession:

- Most on-the-job training for equity analysts follows the master–apprentice model, which has some notable flaws. Most new equity analysts work for senior producers who have little time to train new hires. After all, portfolio managers and senior sell-side analysts get paid to identify mispriced stocks, and when they fail in their primary role, it can lower their compensation (by six or even seven digits). This often distracts from their secondary role as trainer. Their intense focus on getting stock picks right often leads to a sink-or-swim environment for the new hires under their wings.
- Those producers who rightly make the time to train new hires may not have a style of conducting research worth emulating or the patience required to train others. The ugly truth is that the majority of money managers underperform their benchmark, which means there's a good chance the mentor is passing along poor practices (or lacks the best practices).

Here are some of the more pronounced situations where equity analysts go wrong, which could be avoided by adopting best practices:

- Cover too many stocks or fail to effectively manage inbound information flow, which reduces the likelihood of identifying unique insights required to generate alpha.
- Fail to understand the critical factors likely to drive a stock, which leads to spending too much time on factors that won't move a stock and too little time on those that will.
- Don't develop the unique industry contacts and information sources required to make differentiated stock calls.
- Don't understand how to interview a management team or industry contacts in a manner that extracts unique insights.

- Fail to understand how companies and the media can deceive through numbers, thus missing opportunities to avoid "the blowups."
- Generate financial forecasts with no basis other than an inexperienced gut feeling or company management guidance, leading to earnings and cash flow forecasts well above realistic levels.
- Apply premiums or discounts to valuation multiples on an arbitrary basis.
- Communicate stock messages ineffectively, either by being too verbose or failing to identify how the analyst's work differs from consensus.
- Make poor ethical decisions due to a lack of understanding of how to spot and defuse conflicts of interest.

The Road Map

The best practices that follow are intended to help analysts avoid these mistakes as well as overcome typical challenges more easily. They've been divided into the five primary areas of the equity research analyst's role, as highlighted in Exhibit I.1.

1. Identify and monitor critical factors
2. Create and update financial forecasts
3. Use valuation methods to derive price targets or a range of targets
4. Make stock recommendations
5. Communicate stock ideas

Before an analyst can jump into any of the five areas, it's important to develop organizational and interpersonal skills, such as time management, setting up an information hub, and influencing others. These topics are covered in Part 1. Once this foundation is established, we discuss the best practices for generating *qualitative* insights in Part 2. These best practices help analysts identify the critical factors and information sources necessary for better forecasting. Part 3 explores the best practices for generating *quantitative* insights, such as utilizing statistics, accounting, and Microsoft Excel to create a better set of financial forecast scenarios than consensus. Then, we move on to Part 4 to cover the best practices for valuation and the all-important stock picking. And the job doesn't end there; analysts need to effectively communicate their message if they are to be rewarded for their efforts. We explore this topic in Part 5. We conclude by highlighting best practices for making critically important ethical decisions in Part 6.

Exhibit I.1   Primary Tasks of an Equity Research Analyst

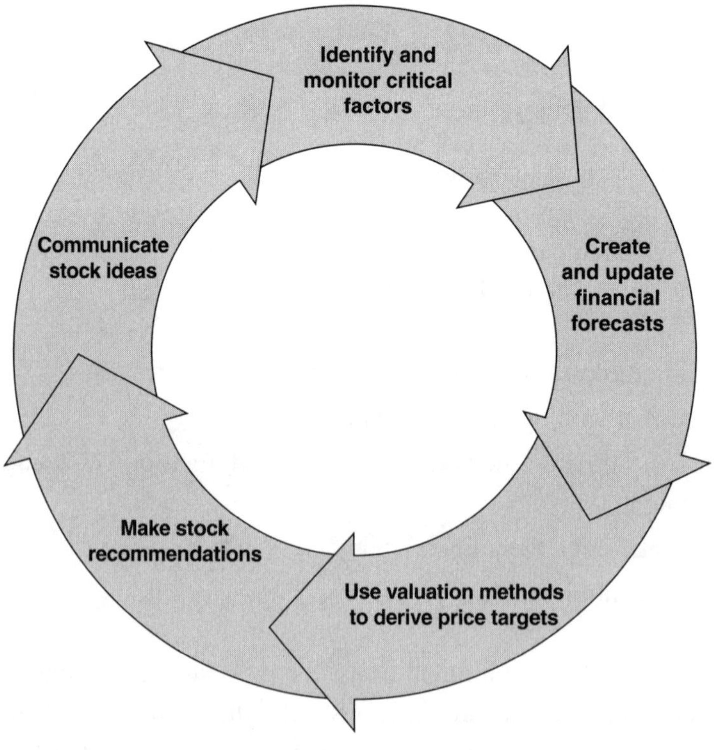

Just a Few Truisms

In general, I believe each problem should be solved with its own unique tool, and as such, I'm hesitant to offer sweeping advice about how to be a successful analyst. But as I was assembling the book, it occurred to me there were a number of themes that transcended more than one best practice. Here are some beliefs I subscribe to that were reinforced from the research conducted for this book:

- Be skeptical, very skeptical, and even more skeptical. Great analysts *rarely accept anything at face value*. Douglas Cohen, who has spent 16 years at Morgan Stanley as both a sell-side analyst and a portfolio manager, focused on using the best ideas from equity research put it well when he said, "Good analysts always challenge what they've been told or given." Over time, if a source of information proves accurate, let it into your circle of trust. If we include the financial press and everything distributed by companies, I'd say at least 75 percent of the information out there for consumption by financial analysts is misleading or omits an important piece of information relevant to the topic. Herein lies the challenge: You need to determine which 25 percent is reliable and then, which portion of that is critical to your investment thesis. Very often, less than 2 percent of the available information will help make an investment decision that creates alpha. And that 2 percent of the information today won't likely be found in the same place as the 2 percent you'll need in six months.
- Beyond sheer intelligence, properly prioritizing your time is the single biggest factor that separates the good from the great. We all have the same 24 hours per day to find the 2 percent of information that matters, but some have figured out how to use the time better than the rest.
- It's tough to beat the market. In doing so, don't look for shortcuts or quick answers as a substitute for thorough

research, because they don't work—at least not consistently. If they did, capital would be attracted to these "easy money" strategies until all of the alpha was captured.

- Fear is more powerful than greed, but they are both important to watch. When you see others becoming fearful, look for opportunities. When you see others becoming greedy, look for an exit.
- When it comes to the investment process, *simplicity* trumps *complexity*. The more complicated the model, catalyst, thesis, etc., the greater the likelihood something will go wrong.
- Forecasting is not as much about getting the exact EPS or revenue figure correct, but determining that expectations need to be raised or lowered materially (e.g., if your marquee reads, "XYZ Likely to Earn $3.00" when consensus is at $2.50, you have a winner, regardless of current valuations).
- For the most part, company management is not good at telling investors:
  - How well the economy will perform *in the future*, because their macro crystal ball is rarely better than anyone else's.
  - When their company's revenue growth rate will slow or margins weaken, because management rarely spots the negative inflection points. (They will argue their bullish view with investors and sell-side analysts as they're driving off the cliff.)
  - Where the directions of commodities or currencies are headed. (There's an entire industry of professionals dedicated to this 24/7, who are routinely challenged to get it right.)
- Don't mistake news for research:
  - The media tends to hype things; don't forget that they get paid by advertisers who want to maximize eyeballs, not objectivity. To this end, data can be, and often is, misconstrued to meet the needs of the journalist.
  - Experts in the press often aren't; they may simply be the person who had time for an interview.

Hopefully, these truisms can serve as helpful guiding principles, but the challenges most analysts face also require thorough and often very specialized solutions. The material that follows has been developed and organized in an effort to help analysts efficiently reach those solutions by following the best practices of other successful practitioners.

Chapter 1

Do You Have What It Takes to Be a Successful Analyst?

This best practice isn't intended to tell analysts if they are guaranteed to be a success, but rather to make them more aware of their strengths and areas for development. I've recently built an assessment tool for research analysts in conjunction with a consulting firm that specializes in this area. It's still a bit early to draw sweeping conclusions, but my preliminary findings help show how experienced buy-side and sell-side analysts differ from novices and how the degree of experience for sell-side analysts impacts their perspective of the job. *Spoiler alert: Don't read this section if you intend to take the online assessment (www.AnalystSolutions.com/assessment), as it will undoubtedly bias your responses.*

As part of the ongoing assessment development, I survey successful, experienced buy-side and sell-side analysts asking them to respond to questions that ultimately help me understand their perspectives about qualities and skills necessary to be successful as an analyst. As the control group, I'm surveying individuals new to the industry or starting a career in finance. Based on my work to this point, I can draw the following conclusions, ranked in order of greatest statistical significance.

When compared with novices, senior analysts:

- Thoroughly understand inputs to their company's production or creation of their service and the primary markets to which the company sells.
- When recommending a stock, place more focus on the factors where their view is distinctly different than consensus.
- Are more comfortable articulating the strategies of all the companies they follow and how they differ from their competitors.
- When their price target materially differs from the current price, they know where their assumptions differ from the market's.
- Fully understand the peak and trough valuation levels for their companies going back at least 10 years.
- Are more realistic in appreciating that even the best stock pickers don't have 100 percent of the information necessary to make a stock call.

When compared with novices, senior analysts self-assessed themselves to be:

- Less likely to have a calm disposition.
- Less willing to find common ground in times of conflict.
- Not as good at developing and maintaining relationships.
- Less likely to encourage feedback from others.

I've also looked at just the senior analyst population to identify relationships between years of experience and responses to each question. For both buy-side and sell-side analysts, as experience increases, so does agreement with the following statement: "When recommending a stock I like, I focus primarily on the factors where my view is distinctly different than consensus." If you take away only one concept from the book it should be this. Generating alpha is all about determining where consensus is wrong, a concept that often gets overlooked by less experienced analysts.

Among the sell-side analyst population, as their experience increases:

- They gain more job satisfaction from speaking with clients.
- The more they *disagree* with these statements:
  - I build only the bare essential financial model necessary to uncover anomalies and trends.
  - I have a generally calm disposition.
  - I'm exceptional at finding common ground in times of conflict.

While I continue to learn as more analysts take the assessment, the initial mosaic shows successful, experienced analysts as determined to identify where they differ from consensus, which they do by understanding their companies (and how those companies differ from their competitors) as well as how current valuation differs from the past. When making stock calls, rarely do they have all the information needed. In terms of personality, they tend to be headstrong, independent, and easily roused. This picture is fairly consistent with my observations of successful analysts. I was initially surprised by the solitary qualities that emerged, but upon further consideration, this job isn't a team sport. Although there may be investment committee meetings, most of the work typically conducted by analysts is independent of colleagues (e.g., most firms don't have two telecom analysts), which probably wouldn't set well for someone seeking high interaction with her coworkers. I'm not saying all great analysts are introverted, but rather they need to work and think independently to generate alpha.

While the assessment above helps paint the broad strokes of a typical analyst, interviews with dozens of professionals and a career working with sell-side and buy-side analysts helps to fill in more detail. Here are some attributes of great equity research analysts:

- Intelligent: You don't need to be the smartest person in the room, but given the intense competition, great analysts need to have above-average intelligence. Those analysts who retain what they learn, and can recall it at a later point when needed, are likely to generate more alpha than those who can't.

- Innately inquisitive: As children, their parents may have complained that they were asking too many questions or taking apart things that weren't broken. Friends ask, "Why do you want to know that?" Great analysts are always asking *why* in an effort to determine where consensus could be wrong.

- Self-motivated: There are tens of thousands of other professionals all looking for the same alpha-generating ideas, which means the winners need to be naturally motivated to jump out of bed before 6 a.m., be at their desks by 7:30 in preparation for their morning meetings, and willing to work evenings and weekends to develop an edge.

- Self-directed/resourceful: Akin to reading all of the books in the library, the daily tasks of financial analysis can go into infinitesimal directions, most of which are dead ends. Great analysts don't wait for their managers to tell them the next steps to take or to notify them when they've reached a dead end.

- Focused: There are many distractions in the world of equity research that can consume an entire day but add nothing to the pursuit of alpha. Learning to stay on task and ignore distractions is a big part of the job.

- Risk-taker: All great stock calls require the analyst to be out-of-consensus, essentially telling the rest of the world it's wrong. Waiting for a more comfortable situation, when additional information becomes available, is usually too late because it immediately gets incorporated into the stock price. Great analysts are not uncomfortable when their well-researched thesis is in disagreement with others.

- Influential: We spend a lot of time on spreadsheets but being an equity research analyst isn't just about the numbers. It's also about the people behind the numbers. Much of financial analysis is obtaining good information to make future assumptions, which is facilitated by having an extensive network of contacts. The three areas where it's needed most are (1) getting information from management, (2) getting information from industry sources, and (3) conveying stock ideas to portfolio managers (PMs) (and clients and salespeople for the sell-side). In general, the more influential (charismatic by some definitions) an analyst is, the broader his or her network is, leading to better analysis.

PART 1

MASTERING ORGANIZATION AND INTERPERSONAL SKILLS

When I was designing a global training program for research analysts and associates of a large Wall Street firm, it was relatively
easy to identify the required *technical* skills and knowledge for the job,
such as creating forecast models and conducting thoughtful valuation.
But after all of this was cataloged, there were clear deficits, specifically
in important nontechnical areas such as the following:

- Selecting the optimal universe of stocks
- Time management
- Influencing skills
- Managing information flow
- Buy-side only: maximizing the benefits of sell-side
  relationships

It's important to understand that seasoned practitioners may not consider the aforementioned skills as critically important to master because they weren't in any of their formal training. But as I learned from my experience as an analyst and manager of analysts, these foundational skills are some of the most important in helping accelerate analysts' careers, and should be mastered early.

Chapter 2

Take Control to Optimize the Coverage Universe

There are modern-day farmers and ranchers in the western United States who owe some of their success to the luck of their ancestors who took part in land rushes during the 1800s. Similarly, long-term career success and failure for some equity analysts are dictated by the universe of stocks they are initially assigned to cover. Early in their careers, most buy-side and sell-side analysts accept whatever they're given, because they're thrilled to have the responsibility. If you're asked to provide input in defining your stock universe, make sure to seize the opportunity because it's usually short-lived. Be mindful that the managers of research analysts, portfolio managers (PMs) on the buy-side and directors of research on the sell-side, are not in the trenches looking at every stock in a given sector, which means they may not be in a position to provide constructive guidance beyond noticing a broad gap in the organization's coverage that needs to be filled. Having worked in sell-side research management, I had a general idea of what needed to be covered for each sector, but not the expertise to provide a detailed list with justification for every name on it. If possible, try to get ahead of the process and proactively ask your manager for some time to determine the best sectors and companies to cover before being assigned the equivalent of a rocky, barren lot in your land rush.

Here are questions that should be answered in an effort to cover the ideal sectors and stocks:

- Does the analyst have any say in the matter?
- How important are the available sectors and stocks to the firm?
- How many sectors or stocks can be realistically covered and still add value?
  - What are the firm's requirements, formal or informal, for covering a sector and individual stocks?
  - Will any help be provided by colleagues or outside resources such as off-shore personnel, either now or in the near future?
  - How homogeneous and volatile are the potential stocks to be covered?
  - Are any sectors complementary or driven by similar factors?
- Where are the analyst's interests?

It's rare for analysts to be given a clean sheet when it comes to selecting a universe of stocks. But that doesn't mean they should just accept what's given. Clearly, they need to work within the confines of their firm or fund (e.g., an S&P 500 fund is limited to those 500 stocks), and avoid picking up anything that's currently covered by a colleague (one of the fastest ways to make enemies is to encroach on another analyst's coverage territory). Beyond that, analysts should assume that their manager doesn't have the assigned coverage fully etched in stone. Taking the bull by the horns and proactively requesting a pre-defined universe of stocks is somewhat unconventional, and so some or all of this preliminary work may need to be completed during evenings and on weekends to avoid the appearance of wasting time on something that normally occurs on its own. The objective is for an analyst to present a list to a manager that meets the firm's needs while maximizing the analyst's probability of success.

If it appears that the analyst can influence the decision process, the next question should be, "How important are the available sectors and stocks to the firm?" After all, this is the criterion the manager will be using. Some analysts make the mistake of looking only at stocks that interest them; remember that the manager needs to sign off on the list. Buy-side analysts should look to see how often the available stocks and sectors have held an out-sized position in the firm's portfolios. Sell-side analysts should determine how much trading volume and investment banking are done in the available stocks. Although investment banking cannot request that a specific stock be followed by a particular analyst, it can request certain sectors be covered by research.

Now comes the toughest question of all: "How many sectors or stocks can be realistically covered by an analyst and still add value?" Optimally, an analyst wants the largest universe of relevant stocks so as to get noticed without taking on so many stocks that it's difficult to proactively generate alpha (don't forget that each analyst is competing against thousands of others who are all looking for the same alpha). It probably goes without saying that most sell-side analysts cover fewer stocks than most buy-side analysts because sell-side analysts spend a significant portion of their time marketing their ideas and responding to client requests (by some estimates over 50 percent), which takes time away from their research activities.

The question above can't be answered without defining success. What are the firm's requirements, explicit or implicit, for covering a sector and individual stocks? Buy-side analysts are often evaluated only on the alpha generated, while others are expected to provide comprehensive financial forecasts in their firm's system for every company under coverage. This level of requirements needs to be appreciated to determine how much time it will take to properly cover a universe of stocks. Many sell-side analysts are expected to be servicing clients at least 50 percent of their time, while others are allowed to share some of this activity with specialty sales.

Because the role of an equity analyst can be widely varied, for the purposes of this discussion, I'll focus on sell-side and buy-side analysts working for firms with at least five analysts, and who are expected to always have a fair valuation for every stock under coverage. There are plenty of shops with fewer than five analysts, but in these situations the analysts are often expected to cover a third or even half of the S&P 500, which essentially puts them in the category of a portfolio manager. There is a hybrid of these two models: those shops that assign their analysts a large universe but only expect them to focus on a handful of opportunities. Many smaller buy-side shops will ask their analysts to use a funnel approach by starting with a large universe, such as 100 assigned names, and through a screening process, expect that their analysts will self-select a more manageable list, such as 25 names.

Be careful not to cover too many stocks, especially when new to a sector. Based on my experience, the primary reason so many buy-side and sell-side analysts underperform their benchmark is because they're covering too many stocks. I saw this time and time again when I would receive calls from buy-side clients who were asking questions about issues that were no longer truly important to the investment thesis (or never were), illustrating the "day late and a dollar short" adage. This has also been substantiated with academic work (Ramnath, Rock, & Shane, 2008). One study showed that buy-side analysts who covered fewer than 40 stocks, which was the mean for the sample group, did a better job in identifying risks than those covering more than 40 stocks. In a study of sell-side analysts, those in the bottom 10 percent for forecasting accuracy covered 21 more firms than analysts in the top 10 percent (Clement, 1999: 300). And more recently, a study found that sell-side analysts' forecasting accuracy improved between 1984 and 2006, due in part to a general trend during that time period of analysts each following fewer stocks and fewer sectors (Myring & Wrege, 2009).

For analysts who just landed the job of a lifetime, it may be tough to tell their boss that they have been assigned too many stocks, but conversely, if they're being asked to research too many, it's a recipe for failure. There are a number of stock- and sector-specific issues that affect the amount of stocks that can effectively be followed (discussed later), but as a general rule, limit it to 35 to 50 *closely covered* stocks for an individual buy-side analyst and 15 to 20 stocks for a three-person sell-side team. Analysts new to a sector or the investment process altogether should cut these figures in half. There are certainly exceptions to this rule, but based on my experience, the top 10 to 20 percent of buy-side analysts who knew their stocks well enough to be ahead of the crowd and generate alpha were closely covering fewer than 50 stocks. From my perspective as a research manager, the best sell-side analysts were those covering 5 to 7 stocks per team member.

The guidelines above need further refinement with these qualifiers:

- *Closely cover* means the analyst is expected to have a price target (or fair valuation range) derived from a thoughtful earnings or cash flow forecast in order to maintain an edge over the market. If the firm doesn't expect this of the analyst, then more stocks can be covered, but this approach causes me to wonder how the analyst develops an edge. Buy-side analysts who are expected to always have current, fully integrated financial forecasts for every company under coverage, or to publish regularly to an internal system may struggle to cover 35 to 50 stocks, especially when new.
- Many buy-side firms will expect their analysts to *watch* a large number of stocks, but only *cover* a small subset of that figure. If *watch* means to have a view only when there is a major news event, then more names can be covered.
- When stocks are more homogeneous, a greater number can be followed. For example, oil stocks generally move as a group due to one factor: oil prices. Whereas biotech companies move almost completely independently of one another due to the

unique patents and FDA approvals for each company. To test for this, conduct a correlation analysis of the daily or weekly closing prices for individual stocks within a universe over an extended period of time. Those with high correlation are likely being driven by a common factor and thus likely easier to cover.

- Similarly, if stocks all belong in the same food chain, more can be covered than if they are completely unrelated. Following handset manufacturers, their parts suppliers, and wireless carriers will produce more synergy than having an analyst covering an unrelated basket of cyclicals such as forest products, autos, and chemicals, where few factors run through all of the stocks.

- The levels of trading volatility and news flow for a sector will dictate how challenging a sector is to follow. When I was asked to add airlines to my coverage, I declined each time, in part because the news flow and volatility are so much higher than the rest of the transportation sector that it would have led to weaker coverage.

Unless matched up with a sector(s) that has the exact number of stocks an analyst is capable of covering, more work will need to be done to determine which names within the sector(s) are worthy of attention. Using the earlier discussion as a guide, find the names that appear to be most important to the boss or clients. Once past the list of obvious candidates (e.g., after McDonald's and Yum! Brands there is a big drop to the next publicly traded restaurant), find stocks that have these qualities:

- Best match the requirements of the firm or clients, such as investment style or market capitalization.
- Are less followed and have the possibility of surprising on the upside (studies show companies that are tougher to follow have fewer analysts, which arguably leads to more alpha opportunities).

- Offer a broader window into the sector because they are a customer or supplier to the larger companies, or because they offer more disclosure. Food chain analysis is one of the best ways to develop unique insights.
- If there are still too many stocks to cover, analysts should satisfy their personal curiosity by following stocks of interest, because they'll dig deeper into stocks they find intriguing.

It may seem counter intuitive, but covering too few stocks can actually be a problem too. It's relatively rare and so not worth much discussion, but for analysts who find themselves covering only a few names in one sector, they run the real risk of missing the forest for the trees. This was especially problematic during the tech bubble, when the explosion of new companies created the need for analysis in new, very narrowly defined sectors. Unfortunately, many of these analysts were so focused on their small niche that they failed to see the strain on overall valuations before the tech party ended in early 2000. Analysts with a limited universe of stocks should periodically take a step back and look at it in a broader context compared with its larger sector and the overall market.

In situations when there are more potential sectors to cover than an analyst can possibly manage, look for sectors that complement one another but are not followed that way by other buy-side or sell-side firms. For example, early in my career one of my competitors covered the railroad and coal sectors, which was unique, and likely a contributing factor to his #1 rank with clients (at the time, railroads generated almost 40 percent of their profits hauling coal to utilities, but no firms thought to combine coverage that way). Covering aircraft manufacturers and the airline sector or the machinery and agriculture sectors will likely provide a competitive advantage to the analyst and thus potentially more alpha to capture. Just because MSCI Barra (owners of the GICS sector classification) or Standard & Poor's has group subindustries within a larger sector doesn't mean it's the optimal way to discover alpha.

Having a discussion with a manager about coverage should be handled delicately because managers want to feel in control of the decisions and as though their input is integral. The proposal should have options other than just the analyst's wish list.

Exhibit 2.1 Best Practice (Skills): Take Control to Optimize the Coverage Universe

1. If you know (or suspect) you'll be given responsibility for a new universe of stocks, proactively create your wish list in advance, likely on your own time.
2. Determine how much influence you have in the process. Unless clearly stated, assume you have enough influence to be worthy of making a recommendation to your manager.
3. Starting with a list of stocks not covered by other analysts in your firm, rank their importance based on your firm's metrics (e.g., trading volume or investment banking revenue for the sell-side and amount of holdings or a stock's style appropriateness for the buy-side).
4. Determine how many stocks you can cover and still add value. Look within your firm for successful analysts to determine the number of stocks that can be *closely* covered. A realistic range is 35 to 50 stocks on the buy-side and 15 to 20 for a three-person sell-side team, but these figures should be lower for analysts new to a sector. To help gauge the number of stocks that can be successfully covered:
   a. Identify the minimum requirements for success as defined by the most seasoned analysts at the firm (e.g., do they have updated models for all of their companies or only for the names where they have strong conviction?).
   b. Assess if you'll likely have any colleagues or outside resources helping you.
   c. Conduct a correlation of the stocks in your proposed sector and compare with stocks covered in other sectors to determine their homogeneity (i.e., do they trade similarly or very independently?).
   d. If you're looking at more than one sector, determine if there is any synergy in covering both, such as a food chain relationship or factors that influence both. To be of value, information you learn in one sector should give you a competitive advantage in following the other.
   e. Conduct a news search by ticker for the past few months to determine how many unique news stories are likely to be generated (and thus need to be read) in a given day.

5. For each sector under consideration, narrow down the individual stocks from each sector into the following categories. If this list of candidates is still too long, narrow it down further by the stocks that are the most intriguing.
   a. *Must cover* and *not expected to cover* due to size or appropriateness for portfolio or client base.
   b. *Potential candidate to cover* driven by factors such as potential for upside surprise, number of sell-side analysts covering the stock, or the information the company provides in helping cover other stocks in the sector.
6. To avoid making enemies with colleagues, try to assess whether they have aspirations to pick up the firm's uncovered sectors so this information can be incorpoated into your final conclusions. Your desire to pick up a sector may need to be weighed with how much of a problem you'll have with a colleague in doing so.
7. Present your ideas to your manager before a final decision is made so that you can influence the process. Provide your manager the work you've done and a few recommended options, but make it clear that it's the manager's decision.

Chapter 3

Prioritize Time for the
Most Valuable Activities

Everything analysts do during the day should help achieve the primary objective of identifying mispriced securities, or in the case of sell-side analysts, helping clients identify mispriced securities. If the activity doesn't meet this objective, stop doing it. For the buy-side, stop taking calls and reading e-mails from those who don't help the stock picking process. For the sell-side, don't focus on minutia such as attending a plant tour in Iowa for a company that isn't likely to perform substantially different than the rest of the sector.

Here are just a few areas where analysts often use their time ineffectively:

- Reading news feeds or e-mails that don't add value to generating alpha (i.e., there's nothing new). As one senior analyst put it, "If you chase all of the news flow and data points, you may miss the critical data that will actually drive a stock."
- Watching stock screens beyond a cursory look.
- Attending sessions of an investor conference that aren't likely to yield new insights.
- Sell-side only: speaking with clients who ultimately aren't paying for the analyst's time.

Good and Bad Time Management

Time is an analyst's most valuable resource and will be the weapon to provide competitive advantage. During my career, I had the opportunity to watch hundreds of buy-side and sell-side analysts conduct their jobs. Over time I could put the analysts into one of two categories: *offensive* and *defensive*.

The *defensive* analyst attempts to digest all incoming information, regardless of its importance in generating alpha, primarily out of concern that something will be missed. While this is a great CYA strategy, it doesn't give analysts time to find ideas that separate them from the pack. Richard Bilotti, an analyst with 27 years of experience on the buy-side and sell-side, reinforces this view with, "Most analysts on the buy-side don't have time to be creative in terms of exploring unknown areas."

The analyst who is on the *offensive* learns to ignore most, if not all, of the noise, so as to explore unique avenues that may lead to great stock picks. These types of analysts have enough confidence so as not to be embarrassed when they don't have an answer to more esoteric questions that may come up from their portfolio managers (for buy-side analysts) or salespeople and clients (for sell-side analysts). Don't forget that in order to maximize wealth on the buy-side or sell-side, an analyst must become a stock analyst, not an industry analyst. If someone asks you if a company is buying six-axle or four-axle locomotives, say you'll look into it. Nobody is going to fire an analyst for not knowing this, and time will be better spent trying to determine if the stock is going to outperform or underperform.

A Day in the Life of an Analyst

No two analysts work the same way, so it would be impossible to pin down an optimal formula for how time should be spent. But for analysts who wonder how their time usage compares with others, the following is a general breakdown based on interviews I've conducted and my personal experience. The numbers have purposely been left off

Exhibit 3.1 Time Allocation for Buy-Side and Sell-Side Analysts

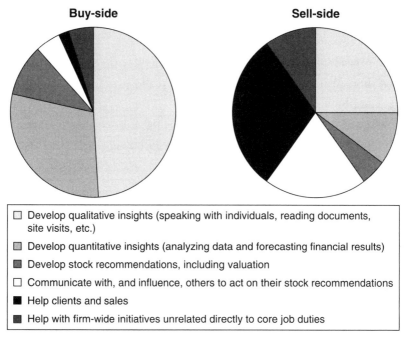

□ Develop qualitative insights (speaking with individuals, reading documents, site visits, etc.)

▨ Develop quantitative insights (analyzing data and forecasting financial results)

▨ Develop stock recommendations, including valuation

□ Communicate with, and influence, others to act on their stock recommendations

■ Help clients and sales

▨ Help with firm-wide initiatives unrelated directly to core job duties

the chart because these are estimates and shouldn't be misconstrued as precise measurements (see Exhibit 3.1).

Be on the Offense

Successful analysts spend as much of their day on conducting research *offensively*, specifically focusing on activities that help discover unique insights about critical factors. (Refer to Chapter 8 for a complete discussion of this topic.) Some people might call these activities the proprietary aspect of research or the core to developing an edge. Examples include the following:

• Making outgoing calls to information sources to get updates on critical factors

- Reading industry journals for ideas and to find names of potential new information sources
- Comparing spreadsheet data in a manner or format not easily available to the financial community
- Forecasting earnings based on observations not readily available to the broader markets
- Reading company regulatory filings for a specific issue in an effort to come up with a unique perspective on a critical factor (not just read filings to check the box)
- Attending an event not marketed to the financial community that is "target rich" with investment-significant insights about critical factors
- For the buy-side, calling key sell-side analysts for updates on critical factors

No matter how much one might try to minimize it, there will always be parts of the job that are conducted *defensively*, but these should be minimized because they're being done by thousands of competitors; finding a substantially new insight from these activities is relatively low. Learning the basics about a company is important early in the process, but the way an analyst works should evolve over time. As one senior analyst put it, "When I want to learn more about a new topic, I'll ask myself 'Is this going to add any value to an investment thesis?' Specifically, will it drive a company's top or bottom lines?" If not, eliminate or at least minimize it. Once an analyst knows a company, there shouldn't be a need to read everything that's published.

Tactical Advice

I've provided a list of time management tips for equity research analysts in Exhibit 3.4. Within this list, there's one time management technique that deserves special attention: *turn off pop-up e-mail and instant message alerts.* Unless you're in a trading environment, they only serve as a distraction. A study by Microsoft shows that it takes up to 15 minutes to refocus on a task after you've been distracted, which is what potentially occurs every time you click on a message alert. According to Basex, an IT consulting firm, the typical desk employee loses 2.1 hours of productivity each day due to these distractions. *Entrepreneur* magazine identified this problem in an articlc on the topic (Robinson, 2010: 61):

> As workers' attention spans are whipsawed by interruptions, something insidious happens in the brain: Interruptions erode an area called effortful control and with it the ability to regulate attention. In other words, the more you check your messages, the more you feel the need to check them—an urge familiar to BlackBerry or iPhone users.

Understand that you're fighting a natural temptation because it's human nature to get excited or feel good when you've received a message. But each time you stop concentrating on your current research project to see something another person wants you to read, you shift from offense to defense, which requires recovery time to get back to offense. It's important to have the ability to multitask, which is switching between two or more tasks quickly, but it's impossible to simultaneously conduct two tasks that require serious concentration. The solution is to check e-mails periodically throughout the day, with a frequency dependent on expected response rates from others within the firm (or from clients, for the sell-side). Some may say this is a crazy strategy that disconnects the analyst from the markets, but how is an analyst going to identify information not in the market if he or she is always reacting to others? If responding to news flow is the analyst's primary responsibility, then the analyst's title should be changed to "trader."

As part of good time management skills, analysts should plan their upcoming week in advance, at a time when there are minimal distractions such as end-of-day Friday or Sunday evening. This can be facilitated best by creating a recurring weekly calendar appointment for preparing for the upcoming week. It may seem like overkill, but it's these little steps that bring discipline into the work flow, which is missed by many in the financial community who fail to add value. Here are some activities the analyst should consider for that recurring event:

1. Review and block out time for upcoming obligatory appointments (ones where the analyst is required to attend) including travel. RSVP to those requests that require a response.

2. Spend a minute or two reflecting on, "What unique insights did I proactively find this past week that will help generate alpha?" If the answer is routinely "none," then more discipline needs to be put into the schedule.

3. For analysts who discover in hindsight that all they do on most days are defensive activities, they should try blocking out time in their calendars for conducting proactive proprietary research. This should be scheduled during the times of the day when the analyst is most productive, whether that is due to personal preferences or fewer distractions. The frequency of this activity should be increased over time, especially as the analyst gets to know the sector and companies better. When possible, the analyst's phone should be set to forward calls to voicemail in order to reduce distractions; for those working in a space without walls, put on a headset so people walking by think you're on a call. At a minimum, screen inbound calls and only answer those individuals returning calls or with a proven track record of helping to produce insights.

4. For those managing a team, ensure the team members are following a similar process.

Analysts who have additional resources, such as an assistant or offshore help, should consider delegating, automating, or outsourcing lower-valued activities. Many analysts I met in my career live by the well-know adage, "If you want something done right, do it yourself." But this can ultimately drag down their productivity. The amount of resources provided will dictate how much flexibility an analyst has here, but in general, if an activity doesn't *help to understand critical factors* but is required to do the job, attempt to do one of the following: delegate, automate, or outsource.

The most common reason analysts conduct low-valued activity is to ensure high-quality output. While this is a valid concern, it can be overcome by spot-checking the output done by others. "Don't expect what you don't inspect" is an appropriate adage that helps reinforce the point that as an analyst, you're required to inspect other people's work when it impacts your analysis. It may be necessary to spend an extra 5 to 10 minutes spot-checking a historical spreadsheet updated by somebody else, but the analyst will save hours over the long-run by not having to build them from the ground up. It's imperative not to skip this quality control step, because if others' work is not spot-checked, an analyst will typically get burned and then take on the task, which is a bad career move. Note that it will require a significant investment of up-front time before those who you delegate or outsource to understand your requirements and quality standards. There are some additional considerations for making this decision that can be found in Exhibit 3.2. Specifically, if the task involves proprietary information or a quick turnaround time, it should stay in-house. Otherwise, it can likely be outsourced to a vendor. If the activity is often conducted by equity analysts at other firms, such as building historical financial models, there are vendors who can provide the service.

Exhibit 3.2   Automate, Delegate, or Outsource Decision Tree

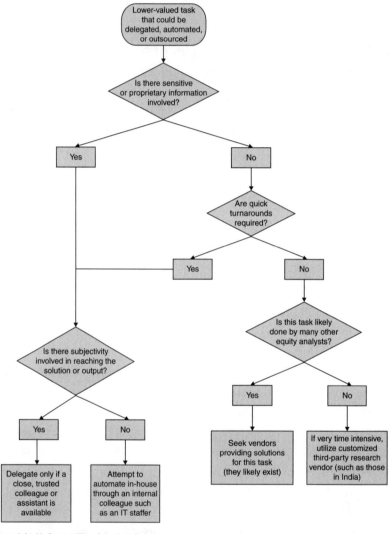

Set Parameters around Communicating with Others

Speaking with industry sources and company management to obtain new insights and speaking with portfolio managers and clients to convey your stock ideas are critical elements of the job. But they can also become a time drag if not managed properly. To stay on the offensive in managing communications, set a time limit before you start. Live discussions, especially one-on-one, aren't scalable, and so it's important to set a realistic time limit before you begin. While no two communications are identical, Exhibit 3.3 has some guidelines to help budget your time. If you're spending significantly more time on these activities, you may not be managing your time wisely.

Exhibit 3.3   Best Practice (Knowledge): Time Parameters for Conversations and Meetings

Participants	Purpose of Discussion	Typical Time Limit
I. Buy-Side and Sell-Side Roles		
Outgoing call to company management	A few follow-up questions about the most recent quarter.	10 to 30 minutes
	Conference call with management to discuss a topic in detail (where preparation is required).	45 to 60 minutes
	Meeting with management at its headquarters.	45 to 60 minutes per executive
Outgoing call to information source found on your own	Initial call.	15 to 30 minutes
	Follow-up calls.	5 to 20 minutes
Outgoing call to information source provided by an expert network	Simple question.	5 to 15 minutes
	Detailed discussion that includes preparation.	15 to 60 minutes
II. Buy-Side Only Role		
Inbound call from your portfolio manager	You are responding to a question(s).	1 to 10 minutes (Some might say spend unlimited time with your boss, but the reality is that you need to get back to your job to generate alpha.)
Meeting with sell-side analyst (who has proven value)	Sector and company update.	45 to 60 minutes
Meeting with sell-side analyst (who has been shown to not add much or any value)		0 minutes (Don't accept meetings with people who don't add value.)

(Continued)

Exhibit 3.3 Best Practice (Knowledge): Time Parameters for Conversations and Presentations *(Continued)*

Participants	Purpose of Discussion	Typical Time Limit
Unsolicited call from helpful sell-side analyst	Analyst has new insight about a stock or sector you cover.	5 to 10 minutes (Ask for the conclusion, follow-up questions, and move on.)
Unsolicited call from unhelpful sell-side analyst	Some sell-side analysts believe calling you will result in votes, even if no insight about a stock or sector you cover is offered.	0 minutes (After an analyst has done this to you once, let these go to voicemail until the voicemails begin to add value.)
Outgoing call to sell-side analyst for help	Ask 1 to 5 questions about a company or sector.	5 to 20 minutes
	Ask 5 or more questions about a company or sector.	45 to 60 minutes (Set up a conference call so that the analyst can prepare and neither of you feel rushed.)
III. Sell-Side Only Role		
Meeting or call with an important buy-side client for the first time	Learn about the client's needs and convey your insights about the sector(s) and companies you cover.	60 minutes (There will likely be more time required, but don't overwhelm the client in the first meeting; the human mind needs a break after 60 minutes.)
Routine outgoing call to important client	Convey new insight about a stock or sector of interest to the client.	5 to 10 minutes (You'll likely get voicemail at least 75% of the time, and so it will actually be a 30- to 60-second voicemail.)
Inbound call from important client	You are responding to a question(s).	5 to 30 minutes (Some might say spend unlimited time with a client, but the reality is that you need to get back to your job so you can service other clients.)
Inbound call from an institutional salesperson	You are responding to a question(s).	5 to 10 minutes
Outgoing call to unknown client per the request of a salesperson	Often unknown	0 to 10 minutes*
Meeting or speaking with a junior team member	You are responding to a question(s).	5 to 10 minutes (If it's likely to take longer, try to have the team member read something on the topic and then discuss.)

*Note for the sell-side analyst: Your salespeople can be very important, but some of them feel they're at a Las Vegas all-you-can-eat buffet and your time is the featured offering. They will request your time to ensure their personal profit and loss (P&L) looks good at year end; make sure a client is likely to make the firm money before picking up the phone or conducting a one-on-one meeting.

Copyright McGraw-Hill and AnalystSolutions

Here are some tips for breaking away from a conversation that's going on for too long:

"I have another meeting/call I have to attend."

"I have to get ready for a meeting later today/tomorrow."

"I have a deadline I'm up against on a project."

"I want to move quickly on getting your answer, and so I need to jump."

"I have to leave soon if I'm going to catch my 7:08 train home." (Buy-siders can use this with sell-siders, but not the other way around.)

Remain Balanced

To avoid burnout, analysts should strive to have balance between their professional and personal lives as well as a realistic timetable for achieving career goals; don't expect to become a star overnight. I've seen too many talented, type-A individuals work too many hours, become their worst critics, and eventually burn out. This problem is more prevalent on the sell-side but I've also seen it on the buy-side.

Long hours are okay for those who are fresh out of college and who have few outside interests or relationships. But as personal interests develop, these long hours can become toxic. I've seen very talented 25- to 30-year-old sell-side research associates decide not to become full-fledged analysts because they've burned out. I've also seen plenty of newly minted research analysts leave the sell-side after only a year or two in the role, often due to burnout. To illustrate this point, of the 1,080 ranked analysts by *Institutional Investor* from 1996 to 2008, 41 percent were ranked for two or fewer years. These were analysts who worked their tail off to get ranked (which is an exceptional feat), but didn't stick around long enough to get ranked more than twice. Based on my experience, it's this lack of work-life balance that drives them out of the business.

The key to avoiding burnout is to be aware of balance. It's more difficult than it sounds, and often requires self-reflection or input from close friends. Here are some of the questions that should be periodically asked:

- Are you enjoying activities outside of work?
- Do you find yourself regularly in conflict between professional and personal goals?
- Are you becoming annoyed with your job?
- Do you genuinely celebrate personal and professional victories?

Time Management Programs

Whenever I hire new team members I encourage them to take a time management program, to which I receive a bit of skepticism. After all, won't it be boring and just cover commonsense topics? But each time they come back with something along the lines of, "That was the best training I've ever had." I recently received an e-mail from a colleague who left my team years ago, commenting on how valuable the class was to her long-term career success. There are dozens of time management classes out there, but the two gold standards are Getting Things Done and FranklinCovey's FOCUS program. Each offers a one-day seminar (for a fee) to master its unique time management system.

David Allen's book *Getting Things Done*, along with his public seminars and private coaching sessions, have created an almost cult-like loyalty among his followers. His system, commonly known as GTD, consists of a five-part workflow: *collect, process, organize, review, do.* It starts by working with what's on your desk, in your inbox, or on your mind. If any of these items can be addressed in two minutes or less, GTD dictates to just do it. But if that's not possible now, or if it needs more than two minutes, *collect* it into a leakproof container—paper or digital. Everything that comes in gets collected—an intriguing e-mail arrives in your inbox or you see something worth exploring further in a 10-K. Once you've collected it, you need to *process* it, or put more simply, think about it. Processing includes asking two key questions—What is the desired outcome? What is the next action? By taking the time to fully define the desired outcome for any project, the way forward becomes much clearer.

The *organize* phase is the area where GTD sets itself apart. Allen encourages replacing the simple to-do list with a series of context-sensitive action lists, specifically: calls, errands, at home, at computer, agenda, waiting for, anywhere, someday/maybe. If the action requires online research or a call to a portfolio manager, organize that task according to its appropriate category. Included in all of this are the tasks where you can't yet act—*waiting for* and *someday/maybe*. All of these lists are intended to live in one location, such as your Outlook tasks, Google Tasks, or Lotus Notes. Externalizing all tasks and projects to one system is intended to free up the mind to think creatively, innovatively, and freely.

Perhaps the most challenging phase of Allen's work is the *review*. Here, he recommends pausing and reflecting on our lives, at least once a week. The weekly review helps to maintain a clear head and update all of your action lists. And finally, of course, you have to *do* the work at hand. If you have collected everything you need for a particular research project, processed it so that it makes sense, organized it so that it can be utilized (and retrieved in the future), and reviewed it so that you are up to date, you're in a good position to come up with a sound answer.

FranklinCovey takes an entirely different approach (the company's co-founder, Stephen Covey, is the author of *The 7 Habits of Highly Effective People*). It starts by asking each individual to create a personal mission statement from which everything else emanates. For those who want to be a great dad, it's necessary to weigh potentially conflicting goals like being among the top 20 percent of analysts within the firm or finishing in the top 50 percent of the Boston Marathon. It can be quite a challenging exercise because it forces the individual to realistically think about how time will be allocated during a typical week. From there, specific goals are created that help achieve the mission statement.

For example, for analysts wanting to improve their professional rankings, they might set a goal to derive at least one out-of-consensus idea worthy of putting into the portfolio per month. From there, tasks are created that are more tactical in nature, such as being at your desk by 7 a.m. and having all inbound e-mails and research scanned by 8 a.m. Each goal may have multiple tasks, some that recur every day while others occur on an as-needed basis (such as, "Meet John Smith next week to develop insights about regulatory risks for my sector coming out of Washington."). Each day, tasks are prioritized, which ultimately helps to create the analyst's schedule. For those who find they fall short of accomplishing their scheduled tasks, it forces them to determine whether they're using their time wisely or have too many ambitious goals.

From my perspective, it doesn't matter which system you use, as long as you have a proven system that helps to prioritize and keep you moving toward predetermined goals. I strongly encourage you to take a day out of your life to participate in one of these programs (or read a book on one of them). Don't assume that time management will take care of itself. Time is the most valuable resource an analyst has, and how it's leveraged will have a long-term career impact.

Exhibit 3.4   Best Practice (Skills): Time Management Tips for Equity Research Analysts

- Implement the prioritization skills taught in time management classes. (GTD and FranklinCovey are two of the better ones offered nationally.)
- Plan your week in advance. (It will never play out exactly as planned, but having no plan puts your valuable time at risk of being wasted.)
- Prioritze the types of events to put on your calendar, choosing more *offensively* focused events over *defensively* focused events.
  - Offensively focused events are those where proprietary insights are most likely to be found:
    - Private or small group meeting with industry expert
    - Visit with company management
    - Industry conference where few analysts are in attendance

- ○ Defensively focused events are those that likely provide background but not alpha-generating insights:
  - – Quarterly earnings conference calls
  - – Sell-side-sponsored investor conference (assuming no one-on-one meetings with management)
  - – Site tour, especially when no senior management are present
- • Plan travel intelligently:
  - ○ Once the companies are understood, attend only the portion(s) of events that are likely to help you identify or understand the critical factors.
  - ○ Leverage time on a trip by trying to accomplish more than one goal. (If you're going to be traveling, try to have more than just one meeting.)
- • Use time out of the office wisely; commuting and travel time can easily comprise 20 percent of the work week. Make sure to use this time for more than just reading the financial press.
- • During offensively focused research time, send all calls to voicemail, shut the door, or if in a common area put on headphones (or a headset) to make it clear to you and others that you don't want to be disturbed.
- • Screen all in-bound phone calls, only taking calls from those who add insight or are responding to your questions.
- • Turn off pop-up e-mail and instant message alerts.
- • Unless in a trading environment, look at your stock screen only a few planned times per day (e.g., at the open, lunch, and near the close or every hour).
- • When possible, skim conference call transcripts rather than listen to the entire 45-to 60-minute event.
- • If a regular daily task is required to conduct research or communicate your message, but is of low value, consider delegating, automating, or outsourcing.
- • Periodically self-reflect to ensure that you're not on a road to burnout.
- • Be smart about setting up an information hub to maximize insights and minimize noise. (Refer to Exhibit 5.3 for an in-depth discussion.)
- • Don't spend time speaking to the press unless:
  - ○ The journalist provides insights
  - ○ Your ego badly needs gratification
  - ○ It will improve your year-end review (which in most cases, it won't)

- Buy-side only:
  - Avoid attempting to read every sell-side report on every company and instead find the two to three analysts who meet your needs (Bloomberg, StarMine, and FactSet have features to identify sell-side analysts who are the best at forecasting earnings and stock picking). Watch for ratings changes or other big think pieces from the rest of the sell-side.
  - Unsubscribe from information services and analysts' distribution lists if they don't add value.
  - Avoid taking calls from those with an unproven ability to add value. (Let them go to voicemail until they begin to add value.)
  - Routinely remind sell-side salespeople of your interests and how they can add value.
  - Utilize sell-side or third-party financial models when it doesn't compromise accuracy or insights (see discussion in Chapter 17), such as:
    - Creating the model architecture in terms of what's important
    - Building historical data
    - Updating quarterly data
- Sell-side only:
  - Return all non-time-sensitive calls at one block of time during the day (e.g., from 2 to 4 p.m.), delegating some of the less important calls to a junior member of the team.
  - Learn how to say *no* diplomatically (e.g., telling a salesperson you're not doing lunch with a small client).

Chapter 4

Influence Others to Accumulate Insights and Get Heard

Introduction

The U.S. Department of Labor has an exhaustive list of skills describing the financial analyst, ranked in order of importance from highest to lowest (U.S. Department of Labor, 2009). It's a respectable list except that influencing skills ranked quite low (*social perceptiveness* ranked fifteenth, while *persuasion* came in at seventeenth). The list furthers a common misperception that being a successful analyst is primarily about understanding companies and their financial results. What I learned as an analyst and then as a manager of analysts, is that the most effective analysts are *those who can influence others*.

In almost any action where an analyst is communicating with somebody, there is an influencing element involved. The best analysts routinely use their influencing skills to be more effective. To illustrate this point, here are just a few common examples where influencing skills are critical to the role:

- A buy-side or sell-side analyst influencing:
  - Industry sources to obtain needed information through one-on-one conversations or more broad-based requests such as surveys.

- Internal colleagues to obtain important information from other sectors.
- A portfolio manager to take the analyst's advice or reward the analyst for providing helpful insights.
- A sell-side analyst:
  - Writing a persuasive report or leaving a persuasive voicemail to motivate clients to take action on the recommendation.
  - Influencing the salesforce to make investment recommendation calls to clients.

Don't confuse influencing with coercion or manipulation; they are very different concepts. Coercion and manipulation are about getting a desired behavior from another person regardless of their needs or desires. Since most analysts don't have direct authority over most of their stakeholders, they'll need to rely on influencing.

Skills Required for Successful Influencing

There are a number of important skills required for all types of influencing, whether speaking to superiors one-on-one or e-mailing an information source. It's critical to possess these skills (Dent & Brent, 2006: 28):

- Self-awareness
- Communication skills (both speaking and writing)
- Awareness of others' needs
- Listening skills
- Adaptability
- Network building
- Confidence
- Credibility

Self-Awareness. Unless you're superhuman, you'll likely have deficits for some of the important influencing skills. The first step in correcting these shortcomings is being aware they exist. It's for this reason you should regularly be asking friends and trusted advisors about your performance. After you've made an important presentation to a group of people, contact at least one from the meeting and ask for advice. To ensure you get useful advice don't just ask, "How did I do?" but rather, "Rank me on a scale of one to five on these areas:

- Ability to be understood and heard
- Logic in my thought process
- Information to support my points
- Body language, such as eye contact and posture."

Sell-side analysts should always ask salespeople who participate in their presentations to provide feedback afterward. Being specific is also helpful here: "What could I do to be more like [insert the name of a successful analyst at your firm who has mastered the skill]?"

Communication Skills (both speaking and writing). Do you speak and write the language of your stakeholders as though you were raised in their culture? I've met successful analysts who didn't meet this criterion, but the quality of their work had to be well above average to get noticed. If you can't be understood, you'll have a tough time influencing others. As with many of the other areas discussed in this section, make sure to get candid feedback about your abilities so as to correct deficits. In a case like this, there are speaking, language, and writing coaches who can help cultivate one's ability to be understood.

Awareness of Others' Needs. Based on my experience, this is the secret ingredient for being a great influencer. Throughout my career

I would regularly see highly intelligent analysts miss opportunities to gain insights because they plowed through discussions with almost no regard for others' needs. Before beginning a discussion, the analyst *must* have in his or her head the answer to these two questions in order to influence the other person:

- What's in it for them (WIIFT)?
- What are their concerns?

If you are meeting one-on-one with a company executive and ask, "Do you think you'll hit your quarterly target of 10 percent revenue growth?" what do you think is going through that executive's mind? Here is a likely scenario:

- I want this analyst to think more highly of our firm so we'll get a more positive stock recommendation, but . . .
- I don't want to risk losing my job by violating Reg FD (Regulation Fair Disclosure).

So, he or she answers the question with a generic response that adds no value such as, "We have not made any changes to the guidance we provided a month ago."

The executive would likely provide a more insightful answer if the question was asked in a way that was sensitive to his or her motivations and concerns. For example, it could be asked as, "Could you discuss some of the factors that would lead your company to exceed or fall short of its 10 percent revenue growth target?" In this example, the executive has much more latitude to answer the question without being concerned of violating Reg FD. It's the analyst's job to note how much emphasis and time the executive spends discussing positives versus negatives in order to provide a better indication about the company's progress.

Beyond WIIFT, also be aware of political sensitivities, such as the biases that each person may likely have. Company managers are not going to run down colleagues or an important product line, so don't ask direct questions that will be in conflict with these biases. It's for this reason that I always tried to speak to company management or my industry contacts one-on-one so as to isolate the biases and keep them from conflicting with others in the room. When visiting with one of the larger companies I covered, management would always parade in their five or six most senior executives who would collectively sit there for the three-hour discussion. This caused problems because these executives, all of whom had ambitions for the CEO's job, were not going to question one another or their own program over fear of making a misstep. I've also seen problems when sell-side analysts invite company executives to a dinner with the company's customers (such as at a conference); this is less than ideal for extracting unbiased information since the company will hesitate to explain how it's taking up price and dominating the market, and the customer will be hesitant to criticize the quality of the product or discuss the company's competitors. Understanding WIIFT is the primary reason analysts should try to "divide and conquer" when seeking information from individuals who are likely to have conflicting motives.

Listening Skills. Analysts can't possess skillfulness in being aware of others' needs if they don't hear other people's concerns. While being inquisitive is important for an analyst, are you doing significantly more than 50 percent of the talking when having a conversation? Do you find you interrupt others to help finish their thoughts or to interject yours? If so, you're probably not a good listener, which will ultimately hurt your ability to influence others. It's not only that the analyst misses part of the message, but there is a decreased sense of control from the other person's perspective. As control is lost, so goes the desire to provide helpful insights. There are numerous programs available to help assess one's ability to listen and make improvements if necessary.

Adaptability.   If you're going to do field research, be prepared to adapt. Individuals are more likely to open up to those who are similar to them. When I would travel to a conference of truckers I was much less likely to wear a tie or cufflinks than when meeting the CEO of a large company. And adaptability goes way beyond appearance. Get in the mindset of the person you're trying to influence. You'll regularly come across company middle managers who are reluctant to speak to Wall Street analysts because they're concerned about not being smart enough about the topic at hand. So adapt to the situation by sharing an anecdote on a common industry topic that they'll likely be comfortable discussing. For example, if I met a grain shipper at a conference, I'd open by saying something like, "I hear there's been quite a shortage of railcars for grain this year." It's something so basic and universal to the industry that it's likely to bring down anxiety the other person might have about speaking.

Network Building.   One of the primary reasons analysts with more experience are better than those with less, is the vast network of contacts they've developed over time; and I'm not just talking about industry information sources. The network includes other people in their firm, such as those who don't work in their department, clients, salespeople, traders, and friends. Don't lose sight of the fact that you need information to develop unique stock insights, and the best way to get this information is through word-of-mouth; in this way there's a better chance it's not already in the market. (If you could build a mosaic by speaking with four colleagues in your network or learn about a new concept by reading the *Wall Street Journal*, which is more likely to help generate alpha?). Keeping in mind that time is your most valuable resource, and that you can't possibly get to know everyone, cultivating opportunities to make connections is crucial. If you've been invited to a meeting, internal or external, make an effort to get to know the individuals well enough that you could follow up with a phone call at a later point if necessary. Make sure to add them to your contact list when you get back to your desk. (Refer to Chapter 5 for a full discussion about how to set up a contact database.) Don't dismiss any contact as too insignificant. I made a contact with a frontline employee during a tour of the Port of Los Angeles who later was very helpful in confirming port congestion problems, which I used to help support a big stock call for the railroads that haul the containers from the port.

Confidence.   People are more likely to follow those who demonstrate confidence. If you want to take someone down the path of a discussion or try to convince them to act on your stock recommendation, you'll need to do so with confidence. Some of the ways to demonstrate confidence include:

- Be prepared. (Know the topic you're going to discuss.)
- Demonstrate interest by being enthusiastic, and have a high degree of energy.
- Appear relaxed.
- Be an optimist when discussing challenges you might face.

While confidence is important, don't take it to an extreme by becoming blindly confident. There were times in my career when I sensed an analyst was becoming more confident in his thesis as the stock was going the wrong way, all in an effort to convince himself it would come true. Just because you say something with confidence doesn't mean it's going to happen; do the research to increase the probability you're right. One senior sell-side analyst told me, "I believe analysts who express a high degree of confidence in any recommendation or forecasts are usually naïve. Being aware of the counter arguments for any recommendation and being ready to change your view when the facts change is a key criterion in being a balanced analyst."

Credibility.   People will avoid being influenced by those they don't trust. As such, you'll want to develop trust with individuals you seek to influence. Unless you walk in the door with 10 years of experience on the topic at hand, it will likely take time to develop credibility with those you want to influence. *It usually takes much longer to establish credibility than to lose it.* As such, be calculating when opening your mouth or putting a thought in writing, ensuring it's helping you move toward establishing credibility rather than away. When I would have my initial meeting with a new client, the client would often take me on a test drive by asking questions to which he or she already knew the answer, just to see if I knew what I was talking about. Some sell-side analysts are offended by this type of questioning because they want meetings with the buy-side to be all about selling their new ideas, but it's important to understand that the road to developing that client relationship often needs to be paved with trust before getting to other topics, like favorite stock picks. (Dent & Brent, 2006: 157).

Exhibit 4.1 Best Practice (Knowledge): Understand the Key Skills Required for Influencing Others

Influencing skills are critical for developing information networks, obtaining proprietary information, and getting others to act on your stock recommendations. Here are the most important elements of influencing skills:

- **Self-awareness:** Solicit feedback from trusted advisors to know your limitations, and then work to improve them.
- **Communication skills:** Ensure that you can speak and write like a sophisticated native speaker in the culture of those you want to influence.
- **Awareness of others' needs:** Make sure to understand (1) what's in it for them, and (2) what their concerns are before attempting to influence them.
- **Listening skills:** Avoid dominating the conversation. If available, take training on how to improve listening skills.
- **Adaptability:** Adapt to those you want to influence by using terms and a level of discussion they'll be comfortable with.
- **Network building:** Use every conversation and meeting as an opportunity to expand your information network.
- **Confidence:** Demonstrate confidence to those you want to influence by being prepared, enthusiastic, relaxed, and optimistic.
- **Credibility:** Develop credibility with those you want to influence by providing accurate, insightful thoughts. It usually takes much longer to establish credibility than to lose it.

Chapter 5

Construct and Organize an Information Hub

As discussed earlier, I've heard it said that less than two percent of the information a typical analyst receives in a given day actually provides new insight—a figure I wouldn't dispute. The purpose of this best practice is to modify work practices in order to maximize this figure. We'll cover the elements necessary for increasing the flow of good information and reducing the flow of bad information.

To simplify things when setting up an information hub, an analyst should have a thoughtful strategy in response to these questions:

- What needs to be collected?
- Where will it come from?
- How is it best organized?

Without a strategy to approach each of these, the analyst risks getting too much or too little information.

What Needs to Be Collected?

In terms of figuring out what needs to be collected, remember that the endgame is to select stocks that are mispriced based on a current misunderstanding in the market. As such, the focus should be on the critical factors that are likely to drive a stock price, either up or down. (I'll discuss this in detail later in Chapter 8.) The key message here is that an analyst's job is *not* to collect all information on all topics for every company being followed. When collecting fundamental information on critical factors, think about organizing information in the areas found in Exhibit 5.1:

Exhibit 5.1   Best Practice (Knowledge): Key Information to Collect

Sector Information (to develop macro view)	Company Information
• Sector growth/demand/market opportunities • Major input costs • Sector threats/risks • Mergers and acquisitions (M&A) • Sector sources of information	• Management guidance, targets, strategy • Major product lines, services, customers • New growth opportunities • Cost inflation (or reductions) • Threats/Risks • Capital expenditures; property, plant, and equipment (PP&E) • Financing needs; free cash flow (FCF) • M&A

Where Will It Come From?

In making stock recommendations, there are basically two types of information: publicly available and proprietary. This best practice helps ensure an analyst gets all of the relevant publicly available information, whereas proprietary information is discussed later in Chapter 9.

The first step should be to create a list of all the services and applications utilized by your firm (e.g., Bloomberg, FactSet, Capital IQ, StarMine), because they are among the most useful weapons on the buy-side and sell-side battlefields. Access to good information and understanding how to receive/retrieve it when needed is critical to an analyst's success. Learning how to leverage market data vendor's applications is time well spent.

When looking for resources your first reaction might be to ask the person who sits next to you, which is probably a good starting point, but rarely will she be versed on all that your firm offers. After getting that person's perspective, speak to the operations manager for your department or whoever pays the bills, as individuals in this role will likely know the vendors well. In every firm at which I've worked, there were services available that most analysts didn't use because they weren't aware of them. The reality is that the operations manager isn't going to promote a list of everything available for every new hire because some of the services require a per-seat user fee. I'm not suggesting you consume everything at your firm's smorgasbord, but make sure you know what's on it before starting your research effort.

If you think there's even a slight chance you'll find value in a service, see if it has training, which most do (and there's rarely a cost to your firm for the training). You can't leverage a tool if you don't know how to use it. If you're not sure how applicable the service can be, ask the vendor representative (salesperson or training person) to explain how most other analysts leverage the service. If it sounds promising, take at least a 30-minute class on how to use it. Yes, this will require an up-front cost of your time, but you need to know about all of the tools in your arsenal if you want to beat the competition. Also, ask the vendor representative for quick reference cards (QRCs) or "cheat sheets" that summarize the most important functions of the application, preferably customized for equity research analysis. Make sure to put the service's help desk phone number in your contacts list because you might need it after hours in a crunch.

Among these services, one of the most valuable is the news service, or a news feed aggregator. In addition to news services, it can also be helpful to set up customized web-based searches such as Google Alerts and active blog searching (through services such as Google Blog Search, Blog Pulse, and Technorati). Now comes the important part: fine tuning *news filters and alerts*, which is arguably among the top five "killer apps" analysts can use to leverage their skills and be more efficient. At a minimum, have an individual filter/alert for:

- Each company
- Each sector
- Key words for all of the terms important to your analysis

Continually fine tune news (and e-mail) filters to deliver a concentration of relevant information. If you keep receiving content for topics of no interest, refine the filter. It may seem like a hassle to continually make these changes, but it will save hundreds of hours of wasted time over a career. You may also want to create pop-up alerts for only the very most important topics, but it really depends on how much of a trader mindset your constituents (PMs or clients) expect you to have. Similar to the problems with e-mail alerts, unnecessary news alerts can be distracting at best and a productivity killer at worst.

News feeds efficiently deliver a constant flow of information, which can be a double-edged sword. While many analysts rely too heavily on the press (or company management) for their insights, the financial press does a good job of providing much of the day-to-day information needed to develop a view about the macro environment, especially economic releases by the government and data points about companies in sectors not in the assigned coverage universe. But there is a darker side that a financial analyst should understand. First, the press reports on events occurring right now or that have occurred in the past. While the news may be interesting and provide new data points, it doesn't forecast the *future*, which is the job of an equity analyst. You can waste a lot of time reading stories that don't help pick stocks. Second, the financial press will often follow a herd mentality by having a party when the Dow Jones Industrial Average hits new levels and predicting the next Great Depression when the market hits a near-term low. Don't look for the press to take an out-of-consensus money-making stance, a position your employer expects of you. Third, the press does not always take an objective view toward the subject at hand because its primary motive is to increase readership or viewership (and thus advertising dollars). Learn to appreciate this difference because the press will often inflate an issue's importance or explore an angle of the story that has less investment significance than another, simply to attract more eyeballs.

News services are great at distributing company press releases, but they don't have *all* the information distributed by companies, and may distribute little for industry associations. Among buy-side and sell-side analysts, there are two very different schools of thought on how to stay in the flow for this information. One is to get added to every company and industry distribution list (and sell-side lists for buy-siders), and allow them to "push" the information to you via e-mail as soon as it becomes available. The other option is to remain as anonymous as possible and, "pull" information via the Internet from only necessary sources on an as-needed basis. The push system assures the analyst gets everything, but runs the risk of information overload. The pull system puts analysts in full control of the information flow and cuts down significantly on the noise, but there's a good chance they'll learn about something well after the fact because they're not entirely in the flow. This goes back to the offense versus defense discussion covered earlier. Personally, I prefer to play offense with the pull strategy by requesting information when I need it, but my experience helps me to know where to get information and the value of the source, which may not be the case for analysts new to the industry. In addition to experience level, this choice is also likely influenced by how many stocks the analyst covers. Someone responsible for a large number of stocks (e.g., 25 percent of the S&P 500), would be unwise to utilize the push method because a good part of the day would be dedicated to sorting through inbound information.

When making a decision between the push or pull, there are a few hybrid approaches to consider:

- If you select the push approach, set up e-mail filters to move specific e-mails to predefined folders, such as from certain companies or based on the filing type, so that the primary inbox doesn't fill up, causing you to miss an important e-mail. The problem here is that the filter needs to be updated every time there is a change to the inbound e-mail format, such as the way the topic is stated in the subject line.

- Buy-side analysts should consider using an aggregator of sell-side research such as TheMarkets.com or StarMine Professional to receive sell-side research. Approximately ten of the largest sell-side firms founded TheMarkets.com, which means research is delivered as quickly and in the same form as if it came directly from the broker (in addition to the ten owner-firms, the service supplies research from over 500 other sell-side firms). StarMine has a similar product that delivers sell-side research to an Outlook inbox. The benefit is that all research can be turned on or off, via Ticker or Analyst (no calling sell-side salespeople or analysts to repeatedly ask to be removed from e-mail distribution lists). It's not easy to get off of individual lists, as conveyed by a senior buy-side analyst who said, "Useless e-mails are one of the toughest things to eliminate." In addition, aggregators can provide access to the following:

  ○ Financial models
  ○ Sell-side earnings estimates
  ○ Regulatory filings (e.g., from EDGAR)
  ○ Transcripts (e.g., from Seeking Alpha and CallStreet)
  ○ Corporate events
  ○ Company overview (e.g., from Hoover's)
  ○ Deals (e.g., from DealLogic)

To get in the flow for industry information, start with the most important associations. If you don't know where to start, do an Internet search for "[sector name] industry association." When you're speaking with investor relations contacts, ask them for suggestions as well. If possible, avoid limiting yourself to just the three or four most commonly known industry associations, as it's likely that other analysts are also using them for information sources, which means the data isn't proprietary. Remember that you're looking for sources of information that will provide insights about the critical factors that drive your stocks. Some associations publish industry facts and even create content, but understand that the association is almost always funded by its members, and so you're more likely to see opportunities than risks. When you've identified a good association, look for the following:

- Trade journals or industry news (preferably available via an RSS feed or e-mail distribution list)
- Industry data
- Industry conferences
- Influential industry experts (often those who are asked to speak at industry conferences)

In general, try to have one good journal, magazine, or blog per sector. While these should provide useful insights, they have a major secondary benefit: the names of industry sources including those writing the content. If you're the only person in your firm with interest in the sector, sign up for the association's RSS feed so that it's easy to turn off if its information doesn't ultimately have value. If there are others in your firm with similar interests, such as associates in your immediate team or in other geographic locations, create an internal e-mail group and use it to sign up for the association's news or announcements. This will save you from needing to forward information to your colleagues each time it comes in and they can add themselves or be removed from the distribution list. (It also makes it easier for your assistant to manage subscriptions if they're part of the group.)

Review all of the industry conferences (not just those targeted to the financial community) to determine which are the most target-rich for finding good sources of information. *BtoB's* Vertical Insight is a good place to start because it lists publications by circulation and lists major trade shows and resources (www.btobonline.com/vertical). Keep in mind that the most senior executives of the stocks you cover, while very knowledgable, are also heavily advised by their legal departments not to speak with the financial community. As such, I found the best information at conferences attended by middle managers, rather than C-suite management. Try to attend at least one conference every year for each sector you follow.

If you feel that certain investment-significant topics won't be properly captured through a news or RSS feed, set up a Google alert to scan the Internet. It can be set up to send e-mails as information becomes available, daily, or weekly.

After you've made your choice for the pull or push strategy for receiving information, call the investor relations contact at each of your companies and do the following:

1. Ask if the company publishes anything that isn't widely picked up by the news services, such as a fact book or company-specific statistics. The answer to this question may help you decide if you want to be on the company's e-mail distribution list.

2. Request to be put on distribution lists for invitations to upcoming company events targeted for the financial community, such as a company-sponsored investor day.

3. Based on your strategy discussed earlier, be clear in requesting to be added or not added to the company's press release e-mail distribution list. (Their default is to add as many analysts as possible.)

4. You may want to ask for an intro package from the company, but you'll probably receive information that can be accessed from their website. My preference is to get information from the company's website because it's usually the most current and can be stored electronically for easy searching. But occassionally a company will provide information not on its website such as size or makeup of its operations.

5. If on the buy-side, ask if any sell-side analysts are coming to visit the company in the near future. If so, you may want to contact the sell-side analyst to see if you can attend.

6. If on the sell-side, request to get in the queue to visit the company. The larger the company, the more likely you'll have to wait for a slot to visit, similar to planes arriving at

LaGuardia during rush hour. Ideally, you don't want to visit a company until you've done your homework, but it may take two to six months to get a meeting with the company, which is why you should ask right away.

7. If you're on the sell-side, ask that the company not publicize your interest in the company, because it could lead buy-side clients to call you prematurely, before you're ready to launch on the name.

How Is It Best Organized?

In response to the question, "How is it best organized?," the key is to record information in a manner that can be easily retrieved when needed. If you have a perfect memory and can recall almost anything you've heard or read in the past, then you probably don't need a solution to organize your information, but for the rest of us there are primarily two systems: computer-based and paper-based. I'll get the paper-based out of the way first because it's relatively simple. As we're well into the twenty-first century, I'm a big advocate of computer-based systems, although there are still many analysts taking notes on paper. If you choose paper-based, get yourself one binder for each company and sector you follow and make sure to tape your business card right inside each binder so you don't lose years of work if you should happen to leave it behind somewhere. Ideally, you'll want a binder-based system that allows pages to be added and moved; spiral notebooks suffer this shortcoming but are easier to carry around. As highlighted in Exhibit 5.2, the problem with physical notebooks is that it's almost impossible to index or search for information quickly, impossible to store digital information such as websites or conference call transcripts, and tough to access when working remotely.

I highly recommend keeping as much information, including even hand-written notes, in electronic form. Based on my experience, one of the best applications for this is Microsoft OneNote, which was launched in late 2003; unfortunately, I find few equity analysts using it. The analysts I know who have adopted this application speak very highly of its capabilities. Not only can it store notes, but it allows almost any file type to be saved, such as a website, a company's PowerPoint presentation, or a specific version of an Excel model (or sell-side models if you're on the buy-side). There are alternatives to OneNote, such as Evernote, which is the most comparable desktop notetaking system. OneNote and Evernote have web-based options in addition to the desktop solution, which is helpful for collaborating with colleagues. Zoho and Ubernote are two additional options, but are web-based applications.

For this discussion, it's important to think about the two places analysts take notes: in and out of their office. When at your desk listening to a conference call or speaking with an industry source on the phone, try to use your computer for all of the benefits highlighted in Exhibit 5.2. The one downside is that some information sources you speak with on the phone may not be as forthcoming when they hear a keyboard clicking away every time they speak. Consider getting a quiet keyboard to overcome this; they sell for under $50.*

When not at your desk, there are fewer options for capturing notes. For example, when you're meeting with company management at its headquarters or in a conference room at your office, a laptop could be used for notetaking, but it's distracting and can raise a level of formality that may inhibit the speaker from opening up. To create a more informal setting, take hand written notes when face-to-face with the speaker. The trick is getting these hand-written notes into a digital format so they can be indexed for searching and summarizing. While handwriting recognition software is getting better, it's still far from perfect. As such,

---

* Having looked extensively for quiet keyboards, the best I've come across is the laptop-style keyboard by Lenovo. Not only is it quiet (something that I find more common in laptop keyboards than stand-alone keyboards), but it also has a built-in pointer mouse that speeds up moving around the screen.

there are no seamless options for converting handwriting to searchable text. Here are the options I've used, ranked from best to worst:

1. Take hand-written notes using a digital pen that integrates with notetaking applications.* OneNote will recognize handwritten text for searching purposes, assuming the user has clear handwriting (which isn't my situation).
2. Manually reenter the key points of hand-written notes as typed text.
3. Manually enter *all* hand-written notes as typed text. This ensures nothing is lost but is time consuming or requires delegating to an assistant who may not understand the notes.

Regardless of the option selected, make sure to scan and save all hand-written notes so they're saved on a network where they can be backed up and retrieved in the future. (In the first option above, they are automatically transferred to the computer in digital form.)

Saving all of these notes digitally can quickly become overwhelming unless the analyst has a method to separate key information from background information. This is solved in the more popular notetaking applications through user-defined tags. For example, for each company I cover I create a "management guidance" tag that I apply to any portion of my notes that pertain to such (including press releases or PowerPoint presentations I've saved in my electronic notebook). Then, as I'm preparing for a company's quarterly call, I'll pull up all my notes and files for the company that are tagged with "management guidance"; this way I can review how it's performing relative to prior guidance. Similar to paper-based systems, it's best to set up an electronic notebook for each company and sector under coverage, and create tags similar to those found in Exhibit 5.1. Analysts who don't

---

* Capturx is the only pen I've found that integrates with OneNote without the need of additional accessories.

tag electronic notes are destined to become overwhelmed, because unlike a college course or corporate project, most companies don't end, which means the information in each notebook will continue to grow every year, making it harder to find useful information unless its organized and prioritized.

Here are a few alternative methods used by buy-side and sell-side practitioners for recording notes electronically, although I would contend that they have shortcomings compared with dedicated notetaking applications discussed earlier (see Exhibit 5.2 for more details):

- E-mail: Create a blank e-mail for every conversation and then save it in a company or sector e-mail folder. It's likely accessible anywhere corporate e-mail is available and can be searched or forwarded.
- Word processing document: Create a file for each company and sector. While this approach has some benefits, why not just move over to a notetaking application that has all the benefits of a word processor plus additional searching and indexing options?
- Advent's Tamale Research Management Solution: An enterprise-level solution that allows for collaborative mark-up, storage, and retrieval of almost any file used in equity research. (To use this application, your firm will need to have already installed it.)

Refer to Chapter 10 for addition information about notetaking, including tips for taking notes during interviews.

Don't Lose Their Number

While we're on the topic of storing information, don't forget about your industry and company contacts (which can include internal colleagues who have knowledge helpful in analyzing the assigned universe of stocks).

Exhibit 5.2 Pros and Cons to Notetaking Options

	Note-taking application (e.g., OneNote or Evernote)	E-mail (e.g., Outlook, Gmail)	Word-processing document (e.g., Microsoft Word)	3-ring binder	Spiral notebook
Key word search	●	●	●		
Can be cut and pasted into other formats quickly	●	●	●		
Can be easily shared with and interpreted by others	●	●	●		
Likely stored and backed up on your firm's network, which provides safekeeping and allows for 24/7 access from any computer	●	●	●		
Can tag specific items for indexing and quick retrieval by topic	●				
Can capture and store other electronic files such as web pages, PDFs, PPT presentations, etc.	●				
Can easily change the system notes and organize (e.g., by topic or by company)	●			●	
Likely already familiar with methodology (don't need to learn new application)		●	●	●	●
Doesn't require technology to record notes				●	●
Likely doesn't need customized support by your firm		●	●	●	●

Copyright McGraw-Hill and AnalystSolutions

Experienced analysts learn that the difference between making a good call versus a great call can come down to one piece of key information. Proprietary information sources are arguably an analyst's most valuable tool, which is why you should have a system to manage contact information. (Refer to Chapter 9 for a discussion about how to cultivate these proprietary sources.) Each time you meet someone who might have valuable information, make it a point to record his or her professional details, including a cell phone and personal e-mail if possible; you never know when you may need to initiate contact outside of business hours, or how to contact someone who has left a firm.

Enter this information into a contact database that can be searched and accessed 24/7, even from the road, such as Outlook, a firm-wide CRM, or a web-based application such as Google contacts. When entering their contact information, include the following (set up a field for each of these if possible):

- Where you initially met and who introduced you, if applicable.
- The person's specialty.
- The types of critical factors this person can discuss. (You'll want this in the record so that you can search on these terms in the future.)
- Something personal (to use when opening your next conversation).

You'll want to search this database in the future, which will be worthless if you haven't entered notes to describe each contact. Entering contacts is a hassle and your natural instinct will be, "I'll do it later," but the reality is you won't. Take the extra initiative as you receive contact information or your database won't grow; you can also leave it for batch processing during your once-a-week planning sessions. Another alternative is to use LinkedIn, as the updating part takes care of itself. The problems with LinkedIn are that you're not likely to have access to phone numbers with this format, which can be critical when a speedy response is required, and many contacts aren't included in its system.

Your company probably synchronizes your contact information with your mobile device, but if not, figure out a method to have it accessible 24/7. If you're asked to put your contacts into a central repository for your firm, avoid allowing anyone to call the contact without your permission, because there's a trust factor that can be destroyed if an information contact feels like you're widely disseminating his or her private information.

Exhibit 5.3 Best Practice (Skills): Construct and Organize an Information Hub

1. Make sure to have a strategy for these three questions or run the risk of getting too much or too little information:
   a. What needs to be collected?
   b. Where will it come from?
   c. How is it best organized?
2. Focus on collecting information that covers critical factors and has investment significance. In setting up your collection, look for information in these categories (if using an electronic notetaking system, create tags for each of these):

Sector information (to develop macro view)	Company information
• Sector growth/demand/market opportunities	• Management guidance, targets, strategy
• Major input costs	• Major product lines, services, customers
• Sector threats/risks	• New growth opportunities
• M&A	• Cost inflation (or reductions)
• Sector sources of information	• Threats, risks
	• Capital expenditures, PP&E
	• Financing needs, FCF
	• M&A

3. Speak to your firm's operations manager to determine which services your firm subscribes to that provide data or information (e.g., Bloomberg, Capital IQ, FactSet, StarMine, TheMarkets.com).
4. Contact the vendor(s) for training and quick reference cards. Learn how each product can provide a competitive advantage.
5. Set up news filters (and possibly alerts) for the following, fine tuning them regularly:
   a. Each company
   b. Each sector
   c. Key words important to your analysis

(Continued)

6. Choose a *push* or *pull* strategy for company and industry information. If push, contact the companies within the assigned universe and industry associations to be put on their distribution lists.

7. Don't fall into the trap of reading too much news. Focus on the stories that help discover alpha, namely help forecast *future* events better than the market.

8. Contact the Investor Relations (IR) manager for at least three of the companies that are major players in the sector(s) being followed. (You can usually find their names on the company's financial-related press releases.) Ask the following questions:

    a. Which trade journals do the company's managers subscribe to?
    b. Which trade associations does the company belong to?
    c. Which conferences are attended by company management and the financial community?

9. Sign up for industry trade insights by subscribing to a journal, through an RSS feed, or through an e-mail distribution list.

10. Create a system to record, organize, and retrieve notes on a 24/7 basis.

11. Build a comprehensive contact database by entering information into a contact list for each industry or company person you meet. It should be accessible 24/7, including from a mobile device.

Chapter 6

Buy-Side Only: Maximize Benefits of Sell-Side Relationships

Buy-side analysts should have a strategy to manage their sell-side relationships because some sell-siders can be of tremendous value while others will waste their time. This may not be an issue for buy-side analysts at small firms, but for most, there will be enough sell-side research, phone calls, and events to fill every hour of the workday, leaving no time for proprietary research. While the sell-side can be very helpful in providing unique perspectives, especially on the market psychology surrounding a stock, much of what it provides is widely disseminated and therefore shouldn't be the sole justification for a stock call. Viewed another way, the sell-side should be used as a means to an end and not the end itself. As one senior buy-side analyst put it, "Don't allow the sell-side analyst or salesperson to push product. Instead pull what is needed."

For a buy-side analyst, the sell-side can be a double-edged sword.

- The sell-side can help the buy-side's efforts by:
  - Providing insights on topics buy-side analysts may not have time to explore. Quentin Ostrowski, CFA, vice president at Castleark Management, said it well with, "I leverage the sell-side to avoid getting stuck in the weeds."

- ○ Identifying critical factors earlier than buy-side analysts may have discovered on their own.
- ○ Providing access to management or industry experts.
- ○ Knowing the consensus view of the buy-side.
- ○ Creating detailed financial forecasts that would be time consuming to replicate.
- ○ Providing a more accurate and objective assessment of a company's management than any other source.
- • The sell-side can interfere with the buy-side's efforts by:
  - ○ Calling or e-mailing buy-side analysts about stocks that are not within their investable universe.
  - ○ Raising concerns about factors not large enough to move a stock.
  - ○ Making assertions in writing or in forecasts that are not well grounded.
  - ○ Creating financial forecasts that have flawed logic or are riddled with mistakes.
  - ○ Not updating their earnings estimates to reflect reality, which results in an unreliable consensus estimate.
  - ○ Writing about a topic of interest that the buy-side analyst feels compelled to read, only to discover there are no unique or investable insights.

Successful buy-side analysts stay close to those sell-side analysts who add value and reduce distractions from those who don't, all the while not offending any given firm. As one senior buy-side portfolio manager said, "There's no upside in offending the sell-side because you might need them some day . . . for information or possibly even a job lead." So here are some thoughts on managing your sell-side relationships:

1. As quickly as possible, identify the most helpful sell-side analysts *and* salespeople.

a. Determine which analyst(s) meet your needs. Some of their specialties include understanding the sector and companies, superior financial modeling, strong industry or company contacts, a solid historical perspective, and insightful writing skills. Unfortunately, some analysts don't provide any of these while others provide all, which requires ferreting out the good from the bad.

b. To more quickly identify some of the better analysts:

   (1) Reference the most recent year's October issue of *Institutional Investor* magazine. It's a bit of a popularity contest, but almost anyone who makes the top three or four spots should have at least one specialty to offer.

   (2) If your firm participates in the Greenwich Associates poll, attempt to get the results for your sector(s). As a sell-side analyst, I found this poll more representative than the *Institutional Investor* poll regarding client commissions earned by a given analyst.

   (3) Review sell-side analyst accuracy statistics for your sector (stock picking and earnings forecasts), which are available from StarMine (owned by Thomson Reuters), FactSet, or Bloomberg.

   (4) Ask for input from company investor relations contacts, although their views can be heavily biased based on the rating an analyst has on the company's stock. For this reason, it can be more constructive to go through each analyst's name, asking about specific strengths.

   (5) Ask experienced buy-side counterparts at industry events.

   (6) Ask the brokerage firm's salesperson. To avoid putting the salesperson in a difficult position, ask the question this way, "Would you put [name of their analyst covering your space] in the top 20 percent of analysts within your firm?"

    c. Sell-side salespeople should be your filter for information coming out of their firm. Great salespeople only call or e-mail on topics that matter to you. If you find a salesperson regularly leaving messages or sending e-mails on topics of no interest, send a message back to reinforce how you need to be served.

2. Request to be added to sell-side analysts' blast voicemail lists. It's a quick, passive way to determine which analysts may add value. If you get bombarded by too many useless voicemails from a particular analyst, send an e-mail to be removed, but explain that it's nothing personal—you're taking yourself off all lists.

3. Decide if you want to be in the analyst's blast e-mail system. Going back to the discussion in Chapter 5, if you get on an e-mail list for every broker who covers your sector(s), it will take a considerable amount of time to be removed if you change your mind or sector coverage. An ideal situation would require asking the analyst to e-mail only invitations to special events, and then get all of their regular research through an aggregator such as TheMarkets.com or StarMine, which makes it very easy to turn on or off research from any particular analyst.

4. Have an initial meeting with the three to six sell-side analysts who appear to provide the most value in terms of their prior written work, voicemails, or phone calls to decide on your core two or three analysts per sector. Most successful buy-side analysts say it's inefficient to have more than three core analysts per sector. *In advance* of an initial meeting or conference call with the sell-side analyst:

    a. Ask for his or her best stock call or think piece in the past year. Review it to determine if it's proactive, thought provoking, or just following-the-herd.

b. Check the analyst's rankings for stock picking and earnings accuracy. One year does not make a trend. Look for a three- to five-year track record, when available.

c. Take the most complicated company in your sector and review the analysts' models to see who captures the important elements best.

For the initial meeting (or conference call) with a sell-side analyst, cover the following ground:

1. How long has the analyst followed the sector? Each stock?
2. Ask about alternative valuation methodologies.
3. Ask questions on topics you've already researched and that are indisputable, such as the sector's (or individual company's) historical growth rate or peak return on invested capital (ROIC). This will help assess if the analyst has a handle on the sector's big picture and understands the numbers.
4. Ask for the analyst's best stock idea(s) and put them into your notebook. Before meeting next time with the analyst, review the stock pick performance.

One of the brokerage firms I worked for would regularly note that it published over one million pages of research each year. So if you're a buy-side client at the receiving end of 15 to 30 brokers, you can see how you might become overwhelmed. If you request that sell-side analysts use the push methodology in distributing their research to you, developing a screening process will be imperative; otherwise, you may start receiving 50 to 500 sell-side reports each day, depending on the size of your coverage and number of brokers used. As highlighted in Exhibit 6.1, as new research comes in, assess it on the following two dimensions:

1. Impact the topic likely has on your stocks (i.e., is it a critical factor)
2. Proven quality of the sell-side analyst

Exhibit 6.1 Best Practice (Skills): Buy-Side Only—Screening Sell-Side Research

		Quality of Sell-Side Analyst Based on Your Prior Experience		
		New and Unknown	Experienced and Bad	Experienced and Good (or Great)
Impact the Topics They Discuss Have on My Stocks	**Critical to My Stocks**	Scan for key points in less than 2 minutes. If warranted: • Speak with the author to assess thoroughness of research. • Speak with more well-respected sell-side analysts; or • Investigate on your own.	Scan for key points in less than 2 minutes. • Send an e-mail to a well-respected sell-side analyst asking for his or her opinion. • File in a manner that can be easily retrieved by key word in the future.	Read ASAP. If likely to materially impact your investment thesis: • Speak with the author to assess thorough-ness of research. • Investigate on your own if warranted.
	Could Be or Become Critical	Scan for key points in 2 minutes; if warranted: • E-mail the analyst to assess the thoroughness of research. • If it seems credible, send an e-mail to a well-respected sell-side analyst asking for his or her opinion. • If warranted, add the key points to your "potential critical factors" list. • File in a manner that can be easily retrieved by key word in the future.	Scan for key points in less than 2 minutes to understand his or her perspective.	Read for less than 10 minutes. Add the key points to your "potential critical factors" list.
	Not Critical	Send directly to recycling bin.	Send directly to recycling bin.	Read on your own time if you find it interesting or amusing.

Once you've identified the two or three sell-side analysts who add value, utilize them for insights that can't be obtained elsewhere, such as the following topics:

- To understand the market psychology around a stock, ask these types of questions:
  - What are other clients calling you about?
  - What types of clients (e.g., value, growth, momentum) are calling you about stock XYZ?

- To gauge conviction in a stock ask, "What would need to occur to change your view on the stock?"
- To evaluate management, ask them to rank management on a forced scale from best to worst within each sector based on an important criterion, such as use of cash or focus on shareholders.
- To understand more about the critical factors for the assigned universe of stocks, make proactive calls to the analysts who can provide insights. Be careful not to tip your hand unless you've already taken your position in the stock because if your questioning provides a new line of thinking for a sell-side analyst, it may become his or her next big call.
- To understand the importance of an industry or company event you can't attend (e.g., conference or quarterly call), call a sell-side analyst immediately after the event has ended (you may need the analyst's mobile phone number in advance). Be clear that you're not trying to front run his or her view, but rather don't want to be blindsided by new information that comes from the event.

While the sell-side and buy-side analyst roles have many similarities, there are also significant differences, especially in how success is defined. This was put well by Richard Bilotti, an analyst with 27 years on the buy-side and sell-side, who believes, "A sell-side analyst can add value by providing industry insights, whereas a buy-side analyst needs to have investable ideas." Occasionally, there are debates about how a sell-side analyst can provide value to buy-side clients. To approach the debate from an objective perspective, I took buy-side feedback used in the *Institutional Investor* and Greenwich Associates polls, as well as private surveys, to derive a short list of where buy-siders find the most and least value from sell-side analysts. The findings are outlined in Exhibit 6.2.

Exhibit 6.2   Sell-Side Skills and Knowledge as Prioritized by Buy-Side Clients

Most important:
- Understands key sector factors, including secular changes
- Understands a company's competitive advantages and drivers of growth
- Conveys integrity, professionalism, and trust
- Is accessible and responsive
- Provides access to company management
- Provides insightful and accurate written product and financial models
- Provides a sound basis for stock recommendations

Moderately important:
- Provides frequent calls and visits

Not important:
- Provides superior stock selection
- Provides superior earnings estimates

Copyright McGraw-Hill and AnalystSolutions

It's worth noting that many new sell-side analysts (and even some not-so-new ones) tend to be surprised that buy-side clients have higher expectations from the sell-side than just receiving frequent inbound calls. If you find you're getting too many calls from an analyst, politely tell the analyst that he or she doesn't need to call you so much. Also note from the list above that financial modeling is ranked high, while earnings estimates are ranked low; this conveys the importance of a sell-side analyst's thought process more than simply a single-point estimate.

Do sell-side analysts' ratings matter? After participating in countless debates on this topic, it's clear to me that buy-side analysts and portfolio managers don't act on a sell-side analyst's ratings, but they're needed to assess the analyst's conviction level, which would be tough to do without ratings. Matt Ostrower, CFA, an analyst with 15 years of buy-side and sell-side experience put it well with, "The buy-side won't pay the sell-side for stock recommendations, but they do care because it's the starting point to have a meaningful discussion."

Sell-side analysts tend to have a positive bias in their ratings, which can be explained in a few ways. The press often cites "for banking reasons," which has some legitimacy but also gets over-played. There were probably times in my career when I was less likely to downgrade a stock after the company had just done a big deal with my firm, but it was never used as a consideration for proactively changing a rating or for my valuation framework. I'd contend the biggest reason analysts have more buys than sells is that the stock market tends to go up. If you were asked to put a buy or sell on the S&P 500, you'd find the buy worked best over almost any 3-, 5-, and 10-year period (in absolute terms and relative to cash). Also, sell-side analysts tend to pick up companies they like and avoid the ones they don't, which creates an automatic positive bias in terms of ratings.

Another reason analysts don't put a sell rating on a company is that it upsets management and clients. Analysts need management access, even if only for one meeting a year, and they need institutional clients to pay the bills. Analysts who routinely put sell ratings on their stocks find it more difficult to access management of those companies and get meetings with clients who own the stock. Don't get me wrong, the analyst shouldn't cater to company management when it comes to stock ratings but you can't completely avoid management either. Some of my earnings projections and stock calls were controversial because they went against company management's view, but I didn't get put into the penalty box unless I put an "underweight" on the stock. As much as I'd like to think I didn't need company management to help me objectively follow the stock, the reality is that you have to have some form of communication if you're expected to have credibility.

Exhibit 6.3 Best Practice (Skills): Maximize Benefits of Sell-Side Relationships

1. Have a strategy in how you'll manage sell-side analysts and their research.
2. Quickly and proactively identify the most helpful sell-side analysts and salespeople.
   a. Review external polls, such as those by *Institutional Investor* or Greenwich Associates, and performance statistics (provided by Bloomberg, FactSet, and StarMine) to find the analysts who have done well in your sector(s).

(Continued)

b. Ask company management and other buy-side counterparts for input.

c. Ask the brokerage firm's salesperson, and to keep the salesperson honest, make it a forced ranking of all their analysts, not just the one you're discussing.

3. Clearly tell your salesperson how to serve you best. Reiterate this point regularly if you're being served incorrectly.

4. Ask to be added to the blast voicemail systems of sell-side analysts you meet.

5. If you have chosen to have brokers use the *push* strategy, ask to be signed up for their research via e-mail. If you select the *pull* strategy, be very clear with the analyst and salesperson that you do not want to be on research distribution lists.

6. Meet (or have a conference call) with the three to six analysts who appear to provide the most value in terms of their written work, voicemails, and phone calls.

7. Utilize the two to three best sell-side analysts for insights that can't be obtained elsewhere, such as the following:

a. Understanding market psychology around a stock

b. Evaluation of company management

c. Identifying the most likely critical factors and competitive advantages for a company or sector

d. Providing unique opportunities to meet with company management or industry experts

e. Understanding or creating a detailed financial forecast

8. If you receive sell-side research via e-mail, dedicate the appropriate amount of time per piece based on these two dimensions: (1) impact the topic likely has on your stocks, and (2) proven quality of the sell-side author.

PART 2

GENERATING
QUALITATIVE INSIGHTS

One of the biggest mistakes made by new equity research analysts is their overcommitment to mastering the *quantitative* aspects of the job at the expense of the *qualitative* elements. After all, for most left-brained thinkers, it's easier to sit at your desk fine tuning the most intricate discounted cash flow (DCF) model than it is to get out and interview unknown industry contacts or company management on unfamiliar topics. Fortunately, the better analysts start to understand that the qualitative insights are often the key ingredients to generating alpha. This isn't to say the quantitative elements, such as building a forecast, aren't necessary, but rather those forecasts are far less accurate without good qualitative insights.

This section's best practices explore the softer elements necessary for building an understanding of sector and company fundamentals. It starts with some of the more traditional steps found in sector analysis, but then makes an unconventional turn by foregoing much of the process found in traditional company analysis. This intentional detour is to help avoid being pulled into the black hole of becoming a "company expert," rather than the more rewarding role of stock picker. Given that buy-side analysts are evaluated more heavily on their stock picking than a typical sell-side role, I find this is often more of a problem on the sell-side. A common complaint from sell-side salespeople is that their analysts are too focused on companies and not enough on the stocks. I steer clear of this problem by directing analysts' attention to seeking insights likely to drive the critical factors of the company, rather than a more traditional, detailed bottoms-up SWOT (strengths, weaknesses, opportunities, and threats) analysis. The section concludes with methods for obtaining proprietary sources of content in order to help quantify the likely critical factor outcomes, including a best practice on how to interview effectively.

Chapter 7

Identify Factors that Impact a Sector's Valuation and Performance

Great analysts are those who work on a more macro level. Most equity analysts are expected to look at stocks from a bottom-up approach. Those who can also look at them from a top-down approach have a competitive advantage.

—*Drew Jones, former Associate Director of Research at Morgan Stanley*

Introduction

When you hear the quote, "Those who cannot remember the past are condemned to repeat it,"* it likely conjures up historical images such as war and famine, but it also has relevance for security analysis. During my career, clients would call daily asking for *company* details, but it was rare to get a request for *macro* or *sector* information, which was an indication of the lack of work being done at that level. In the 1990s,

---

* From George Santayana, philosopher, novelist, and poet (1863–1952).

the limited investors who conducted historical work on the railroad sector quickly realized that it hadn't earned its cost of capital in 50 years, primarily because of (1) powerful labor unions extracting above-market wages and benefits; (2) fierce competition from trucks that received indirect government subsidies in the form of low highway taxes; and (3) a dying industrial customer base. Those who didn't fully appreciate these secular factors, which included many sell-side and buy-side equity analysts, were likely to miss the overriding factors that would eventually separate successful company strategies from those destined to fail. For example, at the time, Illinois Central had unique strategies to leverage its unionized workforce better than the competition, and to focus on hauling freight in sectors that were less truck-competitive, enabling it to overcome two of the three secular problems mentioned above. Its stock more than doubled between the end of the '91–'92 recession and early 1998 (before being purchased by Canadian National), substantially outperforming its major peers. It's critical to conduct *sector* analysis in order to put *company* performance in perspective. Reena Bajwa, equity analyst, UBS Global Asset Management, makes this point when she says, "Understanding the industry and understanding the stocks are two different skills."

After an analyst has been assigned a sector(s), the most common mistake is to immediately start researching companies. In doing so, one fails to look at the sector as a whole, which is necessary to put the companies and their performance in perspective. It would be similar to a pilot who has a clear understanding of his or her destination, jumping into the plane without first checking the weather. Companies don't operate in a vacuum; they compete within a sector. More importantly, the largest factor in explaining a portfolio's performance relative to its benchmark is usually sector selection. As such, equity analysts must understand when their sector tends to historically outperform and underperform the market, something missed by many analysts. This critical step is advocated by many successful practitioners, including

Drew Jones, who believes, "As the first step of an industry analysis, new analysts should develop a strategic view about the industry." Portfolio managers want to see this to help frame the discussion. It also helps raise your game in terms of the types of discussions you can have with company management.

While this is an important part of the research process, your boss or clients generally aren't paying you to pick *sectors*, and so analyzing macro factors should be isolated to the areas that impact stocks. Here are the most useful types of analysis to conduct at the sector level:

- Historical sector-level capacity and demand (and pricing, when available)
- Historical sector-level financial metrics
- Historical sector-level outperformance and underperformance compared with broader indexes
- Food chain analysis

It's worth noting that these historical analyses are only practical in established sectors. For example, some emerging subsectors within technology and health care may not lend themselves as well to this effort due to their limited history, but the number of sectors that fall into this category are relatively limited.

As you conduct the historical and food chain analysis discussed above, you'll undoubtedly come across *sector*-level questions that need to be answered. The immediate reaction is to start contacting qualified information sources, which isn't a bad strategy. But also be mindful that you'll likely need to contact these same individuals later when looking to answer *company*-level questions. To avoid "going to the well" twice, I advise getting through as much of the sector analysis on your own, while also compiling unanswered questions; wait to have detailed discussions until you're well into the company-level analysis. It's for this reason that I hold off until Chapter 8 to discuss the best information sources for answering questions.

Capacity and Demand Analysis

The objective of conducting a capacity and demand analysis is to determine the factors that cause the sector's valuation to change, especially relative to the broader equity market. Working backward, valuation is usually driven by the growth rate of cash flows, a function of a company's volume and pricing; volume and pricing are usually a function of sector capacity and demand. So we start by analyzing capacity and demand, all in an effort to forecast company-level valuation and stock prices.

At the risk of over-simplifying this, the supply (capacity) to create a product or service should, over time, match the demand by end markets. When building the sector analysis, get historical capacity and demand data going back as far as realistically possible, for a minimum of two economic cycles. (When I was an analyst, I came across railroad data dating back almost 100 years that helped tremendously in understanding the impact of recessions.) If there is a common metric for price, such as an average sales price (ASP), it should be collected as well.

Measuring capacity and demand can be challenging because the data isn't always available, and it's not always clear how to define either factor. For example, how would you define the most important capacity measurement for the freight railroad sector—number of track miles, locomotives, rail cars, rail miles, or number of employees? Each of these is a component that must be expanded when customer demand increases. Further complicating the issue is that the need for many of these resources generally declines as train speeds increase. If the average network speed increases by 10 percent, the effect is more available capacity (but it also gets more difficult to run the network). This isn't a hypothetical example; I spent years trying to come up with an ideal metric for sector capacity, but the problem was that the railroads were improving their velocity, which freed up capacity to satisfy demand. At the risk of complicating things further, even when you identify a capacity factor it may not be homogeneous throughout the sector. Having 500 extra refrigerated box cars doesn't help the sector meet growing coal customer demand (hauled in hopper cars), and having 200 miles of idle track in Washington State doesn't help when business is growing in Southern California. In the end, I focused mostly on locomotives and employees because the companies were very thoughtful about growing or shrinking these figures, and to some extent they could be moved around the system to meet changing demand.

One way to prioritize the more important capacity factors is to ask yourself, "Which factor has the most impact on changes in sector pricing?" Looked at another way, when sector returns start to improve, what is the first thing the companies expand to grow their businesses? Often, it's a key piece of equipment or a certain type of employee being hired (e.g., sales, engineering). Once the capacity factor(s) has been identified, it may require obtaining capacity data from foreign companies; for example, assessing U.S. auto production includes volume from foreign producers.

When looking at demand, try to keep it as simple as possible by segmenting only where a unique perspective will later be needed to forecast company results. For example, the parcel sector can be divided by domestic versus international, and then the domestic market is divided between air express and standard ground. The railroads get a bit messier due to their many end markets, such as coal, grain, chemicals, autos, and intermodal, but it's necessary to look at the historical trends in each category because the factors in one may have no impact on another. Conceptually, all of the units or sales from the demand analysis should match up with the capacity analysis, but this isn't always a perfect science due to the lack of available data.

When possible, overlay ASP onto the capacity and demand analysis to determine how it reacts to changes in these two factors. Many sectors aren't selling a homogeneous product or service, which makes it tougher to get a meaningful ASP for each segment. This is where the analyst needs to either make some educated adjustments to the data, or make the decision that historical pricing can't be properly analyzed. At a minimum, make sure to understand how pricing has changed for the major sector players over time. Understanding the volatility and elasticity of pricing will be critically important when it comes time to develop financial forecasts.

It's common to encounter many challenges in building capacity and demand models, sometimes so many that it requires more time than is available for the task. Considering this, start by looking for others who may have already simplified the data to make your analysis easier, such as industry associations, industry-specific consulting firms, and trade journals. Furthermore, if you're on the buy-side, it's likely that a sell-side analyst has done some form of this analysis. If you find yourself getting bogged down trying to get all of the data to fit into one uniform spreadsheet, take a step back and remember that you're attempting to understand how changes in capacity and demand cause fluctuations in the sector's valuation. In the end, you may have to compromise and just take data from the sector's three or four biggest companies, which may not provide an air-tight analysis, but it should help to meet your objective. If you decide to aggregate company data to create a sector composite, try to incorporate companies that have failed and are no longer trading as long as it's not too challenging; otherwise, you'll be missing historical capacity and demand of those companies.

The historical capacity and demand analysis has these important benefits:

- It serves as a source of information to identify when the compound annual growth rate (CAGR) of sector capacity is growing at a materially different rate than sector demand, potentially resulting in a big impact on pricing, margins, and returns, which in turn impacts stock prices.
- If you're fortunate enough to have an air-tight analysis that includes all of the sector players, it can be an extremely helpful tool in:
  - Understanding historical shifts in market share.

○ Creating company-level revenue-forecast reality checks by ensuring that the volume and sales growth rates for all of the companies adds up to a realistic sector growth rate. I've come across numerous examples where growth rates in individual company forecasts summed up to a sector growth rate $1.5\times$ to $2\times$ faster than the sector average. Adam Longson, an analyst at Morgan Stanley with a CFA and CPA, believes analysts should "approach a problem from top down as well as bottom up, not just to sense-check your analysis, but also to uncover implicit assumptions or errors that may come from using a single approach. This additional analysis helps you better assess what the Street may be missing."

Historical Analysis of Financial Metrics

Before you can apply the capacity and supply data to stock picking, you need to understand how these factors impact the sector's financial metrics. Where possible, compile the historical sector-level financial metrics below as well as macro-economic data. It's not that common for industry associations to compile a sector's financial ratios (e.g., return on equity), and as such, you'll likely need to collect the individual company data and aggregate it to a sector level. There will be holes where private company data isn't available or some of the sector players are global and don't break out their financial data on a geographic basis. This effort is as much art as science, but it's required to understand how the sector's financial health changes over time. As with the analysis above, attempt to include companies that have been sold or have gone out of business to ensure that you have the entire picture. Here are some of the sector-level data that will be helpful in building this analysis:

- Revenue
- ASP for each major product or service
- Earnings before interest and taxes (EBIT)
- Pre-tax income

- Net income
- Free cash flow
- Dividends
- Net capital expenditures (including acquired leases)
- Return on invested capital
- Return on equity

Analyze the historical data to identify when growth rates and returns peak and trough as well as the length of time when stability exists (if it exists at all). Determine when the sector earns or exceeds its cost of capital. Going back to your earlier capacity and demand analysis and using historical macro-economic data (e.g., GDP, industrial production, retail sales), identify if there is a relationship with the sector's financial metrics. It's critical to identify the difference between cyclical and secular trends.

Historical Analysis of Sector-Level Stock Performance

Now that you've reviewed the impact that capacity, demand, and macro economics have on the financial health of your sector, it's time to see how they impact the sector's valuation. You first need a time series of data points that's representative of the stock prices for the sector's universe of companies. Your universe of assigned stocks may fit nicely into one of MSCI's Global Industry Classification Standard (GICS) sectors, which should make it relatively easy to get historical stock data, while less-defined sectors require building an index of appropriate companies. If you're building your own and there is one company in the sector that dwarfs all others, consider creating the index on an equally weighted basis so that the large company's performance doesn't overly distort the sector's performance. Try to include companies that have gone out of business or have been acquired in order to eliminate a survivorship bias.

To derive useful valuation multiples, you'll need some form of forward-looking consensus expectation for all the historical points in time, such as consensus earnings per share (EPS) or cash flow. Usually, when you download historical EPS or cash flow from a third-party service, you'll get actual data. But stocks don't trade on actual data; they trade on forward expectations. It's unlikely that you'll find *sector*-level consensus expectations, and therefore you'll likely need to build the index by compiling all of the individual companies' forward-looking consensus EPS and cash flow. For my team, we manually collected 12-month forward consensus expectation data for the 20 stocks in our universe going back 20 years, which was very helpful in understanding consensus expectations for the stocks at any point in time.

When collecting this information for the broad market or your benchmark, note that there is a significant difference between the top-down and bottom-up approaches when it comes to the S&P 500 forward earnings expectations; the top-down is forward-looking consensus estimates from sell-side strategists, whereas the bottom-up is adding the forward-looking consensus EPS estimates for the 500 individual stocks. There are reasons to focus on one over the other; just make sure you're consistent over the historical time period and for the forecast period.

The overall goal of this analysis is to:

- Identify periods of *sector* outperformance and under-performance. (Don't be tempted to start looking at individual companies just yet.)
- Isolate whether the relative performance is due to changes in the forward-looking valuation mulitples or changes in the consensus earnings and cash flow.
- Identify the lead or lag time between changes in relative sector performance and changes in sector fundamentals.

Review the historical market data to determine when the sector index substantially outperforms or underperforms the broader index or your fund's benchmark. For these periods, ideally you want to identify how much of the relative performance was due to changes in the valuation multiples (e.g., price-to-earnings [P/E], price-to-cash flow [P/CF]) versus changes in the financial metrics (e.g., earnings, cash flow) in an effort to isolate the psychology (i.e., expectations) from changes in the results. (Refer to Chapter 19 for a more detailed discussion of this topic.) If valuation multiples tend to react 6 to 12 months before the financial results change trajectory, then you have a better understanding for how early you'll need to be at the next inflection point. One of the most talented individuals I've had the pleasure to work with explained it as, "To make money, it's critical to understand the psychology of the market, sector, and stock."

Food Chain Analysis

As discussed earlier in Chapter 6, one of the most important skills expected of an analyst is the ability to understand sector factors, including secular changes, as well as a company's competitive advantages. It's difficult to develop this knowledge if you don't understand how the sector operates. As such, one of the most useful exercises is to create a food chain analysis, which is a map of all the suppliers and vendors required for your company to create its product or service (see Exhibit 7.1). The map helps the analyst understand how an upstream or downstream event can impact a company. For example, in the past, investors looked to RF Micro Devices to gain insights into Nokia because it generated a large portion of its revenue from the handset manufacturer.

Companies that sell basic materials from their company-owned asset base (oil, gold, lumber, etc.) will likely have a more simplistic food chain than the manufacturer of complex products reliant on

Exhibit 7.1 Food Chain Analysis for U.S. Railroad Sector

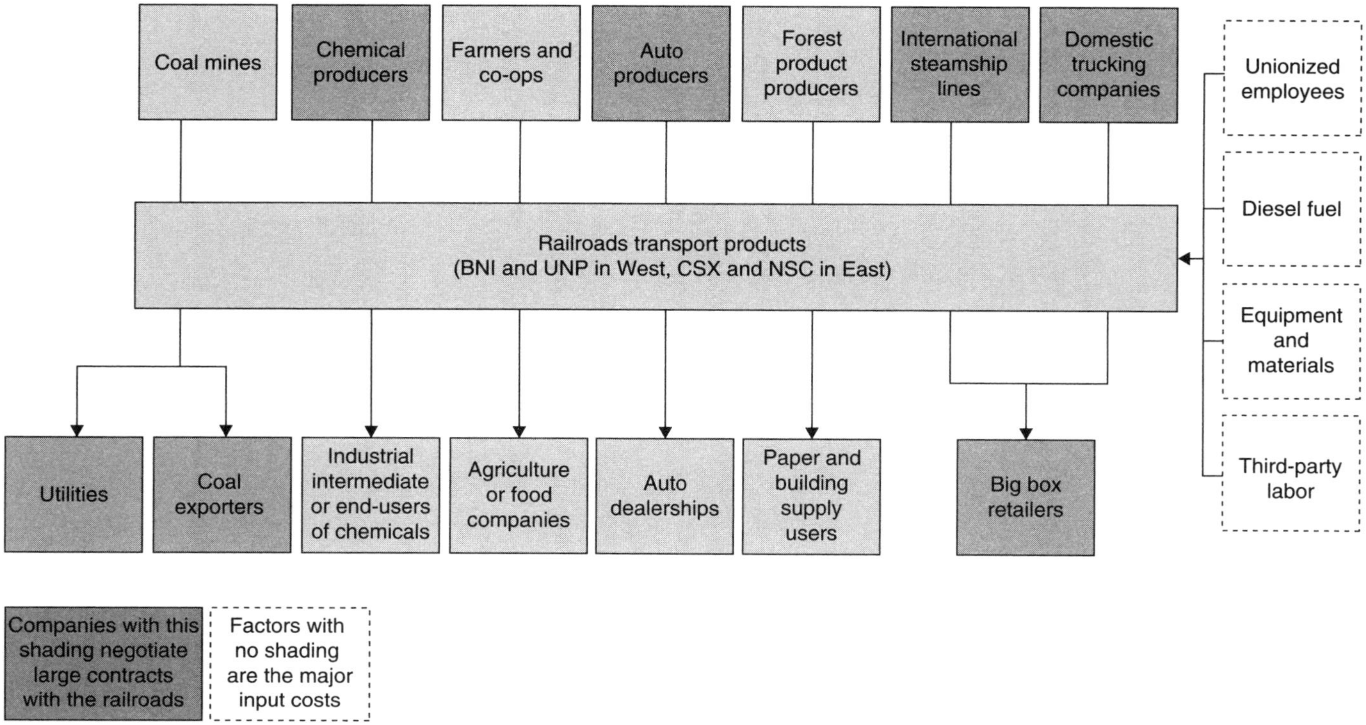

Copyright McGraw-Hill and Analyst Solutions

outside suppliers (e.g., aircraft or computer manufacturers). In general, the more vertically integrated a company, the more simplistic the food chain.

Before building your own food chain from scratch, see if you can find one created by others. If you're new to the sector, ask the company investor relations contacts if they've seen the work done by others. Check with a trade association to see if it has the elements of the analysis; the association may not call it a "food chain," but it may show the major suppliers and customers for the sector. If you're on the buy-side, ask sell-side analysts for food chain analysis or macro factor analysis they have already conducted.

Follow these steps to build your own food chain analysis:

1. Identify the products or services that are major inputs to your sector. To find specific names, look to see which companies sponsor industry trade shows or run ads in industry trade journals. Many associations will have a buyer's guide listing the companies that sell into your sector. While I'm on this point, it may be helpful in building your information hub to create news filters for the largest publicly traded companies that sell into your sector.

2. Identify the sector(s) that purchases products or services from your companies. It may be obvious from looking at the revenue line items, or it may be found in the company's 10-K (search for *customer*).

3. For a reality check, run it by colleagues who have followed the sector in the past, including a few of the most seasoned investor relations contacts. If you're on the buy-side, ask the sell-side for feedback. The goal is to make sure you understand the major suppliers and customers of the sector.

Exhibit 7.2   Best Practice (Skills): Identify Factors That Impact a Sector's Valuation and Performance

1. When you've been assigned a unverse of stocks, resist the temptation to start analyzing individual companies and instead conduct a sector analysis first. Avoid wasting time on minutia by focusing on these investment-signficant elements:
   a. Historical sector-level capacity and demand (and pricing, when available)
   b. Historical sector-level financial metrics
   c. Historical sector-level outperformance and underperformance compared with broader indexes
   d. Food chain analysis
2. Create a sector capacity and demand analysis:
   a. Define *capacity* as the factor(s) that causes the largest change in your companies' pricing (often the area of large capital outlays). You may need to include foreign capacity used to create imports if they impact your sector. Instead of looking for just the best data series, which may not exist, collect all series that mimic the sector's expansion or contraction.
   b. Define *demand* for your sector by looking for the consumers of the capacity identified in the previous step; this may include exports. Try to keep it as simple as possible by segmenting only where a unique perspective will later be needed to forecast company results.
   c. When possible, overlay ASP onto the capacity and demand analysis to determine how it reacts to changes in these two factors.
   d. Search for the best sources of sector capacity and demand data. Some places to look include:
      (1) Industry associations
      (2) Industry consultants
      (3) Industry trade journals
      (4) Sell-side analysts (for buy-side clients)
   e. Analyze historical capacity and demand because it has these important benefits:
      (1) Helps identify when the CAGR of sector capacity is growing at a materially different rate than demand, resulting in a big impact on pricing, margins, and returns, which in turn impacts stock prices.
      (2) If you're fortunate enough to have an air-tight analysis that includes all of the sector players, it can be an extremely helpful tool when it comes to the following:
         (a) Understanding historical shifts in market share among companies.
         (b) Creating company-level revenue-forecast reality checks by ensuring the volume/sales growth rates for all of the companies add up to a realistic sector growth rate.

(Continued)

3. Analyze the impact that changes in capacity and demand have on a sector's financial metrics, including the impact from macro-economic factors. Specifically identify when EPS or cash flow growth rates and returns peak and trough, as well as the length of time when stability exists. Collect or compile macro-economic data that is likely to affect the sector, as well as the following financial metrics at a sector level, going back as far as realistically possible (preferably at least two economic cycles):
   a. Revenue
   b. ASP for each major product or service
   c. EBIT
   d. Pre-tax income
   e. Net income
   f. Free cash flow
   g. Dividends
   h. Net capital expenditures (including acquired leases)
   i. Return on invested capital
   j. Return on equity
4. Using the information collected in steps #2 and #3 above, identify the metrics that cause the largest swings in the sector's stock price performance relative to the broader market or your fund's benchmark. Ideally, you want to identify how much of the relative performance was due to changes in the forward-looking valuation multiples (e.g., P/E, P/CF) versus changes in the forward-looking consensus financial metric (e.g., earnings, cash flow) in an effort to isolate the psychology (i.e., expectations) from changes in the results. If your assigned universe fits nicely into a GICS sector, use the index data, but if not, build your own. If one company dominates the index, consider assigning an equal weight to each company to ensure the index captures the movement of many companies. The objective is to:
   a. Identify periods of sector outperformance and underperformance. (Don't be tempted to start looking at individual companies just yet.)
   b. Isolate if the relative performance is due to changes in the forward-looking valuation mulitples or changes in the consensus earnings and cash flow.
   c. Identify the lead or lag time between changes in relative sector performance and changes in sector fundamentals.
5. Create a food chain analysis for each sector to thoroughly understand how upstream or downsteam factors impact the companies. Identify all of the suppliers of input required for the companies to create their product or service, as well as all of their major customers.

Chapter 8

Identify and Monitor a Stock's Critical Factors

The toughest part of the job is filtering out the material
information from the noise.
—*Celeste Mellett Brown, a Morgan Stanley*
analyst with more than 11 years' experience

The most distinguishing element of great analysts is that they put a
disproportionate amount of time into forecasting only a few of the
factors likely to move their stocks. This approach turns the traditional
company analysis on its head because they're not attempting to know
everything about their companies. The problem many analysts have
is that they approach company analysis similarly to college students,
highlighting all 300 pages of their textbooks to ensure that everything
is understood for the final exam. Great analysts focus their time on
only those questions that have been asked in prior exams or, due to a
change in the environment, are likely to be asked on the next exam.
A seasoned manager of analysts echoes this view with, "There's an
opportunity for analysts to do a better job pre-defining the drivers of a
stock and why investors own the stock."

   Because this best practice requires that work be done on every stock
within the assigned universe, it lends itself best to analysts who have

a manageable number of stocks (e.g., *closely* follow 50 or fewer on the buy-side or 7 or fewer per team member on the sell-side).

What Makes a Factor Critical?

Identifying mispriced stocks requires information not widely understood or accepted by the financial market. When this information will likely move a stock during the analyst's typical investment time horizon, we call it a *critical factor*. The best analysts focus the majority of their time on identifying and monitoring these critical factors to develop an edge. After all, there are many more factors that *will not* move a stock than *will*.

It can be a challenge to identify critical factors, especially for someone new to a sector, which is why I've created the criteria below. For an issue to be a critical factor, it should meet both of the following standards:

- Occur during the investor's typical investment time horizon.
- Have an associated catalyst that, when triggered, will cause the factor to become a greater opportunity or risk in the view of market participants. In most instances, this factor causes one or more of the following:
  - Material changes in earnings or cash flow growth.
  - Material changes in returns.
  - Material changes in the probability:
    - The company makes an acquisition.
    - The company is purchased by another entity.
    - There is a change in senior management.
  - Material change in the volatility profile of the stock.

Analysts will have different thresholds for measuring materiality based on their fund's objective, time horizon, and the sector being analyzed. We use 5 percent and 50 basis points as starting points to help illustrate this best practice. If the factor impacts the financial statements, determine if it will likely cause the market's expectations of:

- Earnings per share (EPS) or cash flow per share (CFPS) to change by more than 5 percent
- Return on invested capital (ROIC) or return on equity (ROE) to change by more than 50 bps (e.g., cause a company's ROIC of 10 percent to move to 9.5 percent or 10.5 percent)

If it doesn't explicitly result in a change to the near-term financial forecast, will it change:

- Investor confidence
- Any implied control premium

Identifying *materiality* is often a complicated and time-consuming process, but it's imperative in narrowing down the list of factors to those worth monitoring. Some level of research is usually required to determine if a factor meets the materiality threshold. Here are some examples of factors that could easily be mistaken by the broader market as critical even though additional research would prove otherwise:

The market believes:	Which is true if:	But is not a factor if:
All airlines will be negatively impacted by higher fuel prices.	An airline doesn't hedge fuel and can't pass along fuel inflation to customers.	An airline successfully passes along fuel inflation in the form of fuel surcharges.
A coal company will benefit substantially when coal prices suddenly increase 10%.	The company has coal to sell in the spot market.	The company has locked up all of its sales for the next two years with long-term contracts.
A global technology company will be hurt when it's forced to divest its subsidiary in an important developing country.	Revenue from that country is profitable and makes up a material portion of the company's EBIT.	The company loses money within that country, with no sign of improvement over a reasonable investment time horizon.

Throughout my career, a significant portion of the questions and concerns raised by investing clients initially appeared to them as critical factors, but upon more thorough research, did not meet the materiality threshold. For those who spent time being concerned with these noncritical factors, they were taking time away from efforts to forecast the real critical factors.

To illustrate this point further, here are common examples of factors that often don't meet the critical threshold and yet investors spend significant time analyzing them:

- A company makes an acquisition that is neither accretive or dilutive and doesn't change the company's long-term earnings power.
- A company shuts down or opens a plant, all part of a long-term strategy that won't change consensus earnings expectations.
- A company expands into an international market that's too small to have a material impact during a typical investment time horizon.
- A company wins a new customer contract that's too small or is signed at such attractive rates for the customer that it's not likely to materially move earnings or returns.

Financial Metric and Valuation Anomalies Can Help in Finding Critical Factors

Your first step in identifying and monitoring critical factors should be to dedicate a portion of your notetaking system (electronic or paper-based) to *factors* (some of which will be labeled *critical* in a later step) and their catalysts. As each new factor is discovered, put it and its catalyst in this central location so they're all easy to reference in the future. You'll want to dedicate a place for factors specific to each company as well as those that could impact an entire sector. For example, if you're researching the auto sector, you'll probably want *unionized labor* listed both as a potential sector-level and company-level factor, because certain union issues impact all companies while others pertain to only one.

With a space set aside in your notes, start by going back to your sector analysis in the earlier best practice, and begin breaking out the financial data on a company basis, specifically look at how each company's *financial metrics* and *valuation levels* changed during periods of substantial outperformance or underperformance, relative to its peers and the broader market.

In this next step, it's important to note that there are two elements of financial metric and valuation analysis, *historical* and *current*. The historical element obviously lends itself better to companies with long track records, which due to the natural lifecycle of a business, often equates to value stocks. The current element of the analysis is important for all stocks, but especially for growth stocks because so many of their critical factors are driven by the factors surrounding the company's sustainable growth rate.

Review the key financial data for at least the past 10 years on an annual basis, and go back even further if you want to explore how the stock performs at the trough and peak of multiple cycles. (This may not be as necessary for growth stocks as it will be for value stocks.) Personally, I prefer to get financial information directly from the company's regulatory filings for each year because I'm assured there's been no manipulation of the data, which is done by some data providers, although this takes time that some analysts don't have. The human mind isn't very good at deciphering anomolies buried in a page filled with numbers, which is why it's often helpful to create a dedicated spreadsheet and graphs that show the compound annual growth rate (CAGR) of the key financial metrics, such as revenue; earnings before interest, taxes, depreciation, and amortization (EBITDA); EPS; CFPS, capital expenditures; and depreciation, depletion, and amortization (DD&A). It's also important to review the change in returns over the time period. Using the DuPont return on equity (ROE) analysis is a good way to see how returns have changed over time based on the three important factors. Also look for the accounting anomolies discussed later in Chapter 14.

Similar to the financial metric analysis, go back to your sector work on *valuation* to conduct a company-level historical valuation analysis. You're attempting to identify the typical valuation level the market has historically afforded each of your stocks, and how it has changed over time, relative to the market and its peers. An example would be to look at forward-looking relative price-to-earnings (P/E) ratios (based on consensus estimates) for each of your stocks going back at least 10 years, such as in Exhibit 8.1. Anomalies should be explored to ensure that they are fully understood. If time permits, conduct a basic statistical analysis of historical data to spot trends, as discussed in Chapter 12.

After analyzing the historical valuation data, do the same for the current valuation level in an effort to answer the question, "What's in the stock?" *This isn't intended to be an exhaustive valuation exercise*, but rather to help frame your quest for critical factors. The goal is to identify the key assumptions that have influenced valuation in the past and are necessary for the company to achieve consensus expectations for this year and the next (and possibly beyond for those with a longer investment horizon).

To help illustrate this effort, Exhibit 8.1 shows the relative P/E ratio for five major North American railroads on a forward-looking basis (e.g., the data point for January 2005 is the stock price from that month divided by consensus EPS expectations for the next 12 months all divided by the forward-looking P/E ratio of the S&P 500). Looking at this exhibit, a few questions should jump to mind:

- What caused CNI's significant discount to its peers to erode away over the 10 years?
- What caused NSC to lose the premium it commanded to its peers in the past?
- What caused UNP to trade at such a premium to its peers from 2004 to 2006?
- For the most recent time period, why are BNI and UNP trading at such a premium to CNI, NSC, and CSX?

Exhibit 8.1 Forward-Looking Relative P/E Ratios for Major Railroads Operating in the United State (relative to the S&P 500)

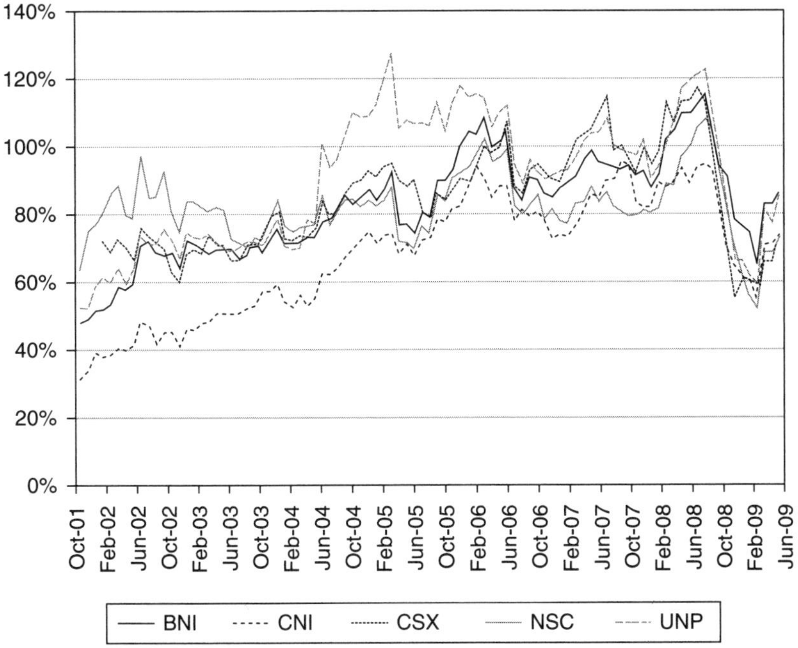

Finding the Answers

One of the fastest ways to get answers to questions surrounding *historical* financial metrics and valuation anomolies is to speak with someone who has closely watched the stocks during that time period. You'll need to prepare for these discussions by analyzing the historical data; avoid being ill-prepared, as it will show a lack of respect to the individual and you may have only one opportunity to speak regarding this line of questioning. Keep in mind that you're not trying to understand every aspect of the company but rather just the factors and catalysts that caused major changes to the company's financial metrics and valuation levels in the past; more thorough research into the company's future prospects will take place later. The best sources for *preliminary* information that should be reviewed before having any discussions include:

- Company documents. (There is likely to be information in the management discussion and analysis [MD&A] section of the regulatory filings to help explain major changes in its financial metrics.)
- Financial news written at the time of major stock moves.
- Trade industry journals or websites that include articles written at the time of major stock moves as well as year-end reviews or an annual outlook.
- Internal documents written by the analyst following the stock at the time of a major stock move.
- Buy-side only: sell-side reports written at the time of a major stock move.

While the company can provide a treasure trove of information, it comes from the company and so it's likely to be biased in its favor. As a general rule for any best practice, try not to rely solely on the company's perspective when looking for objective answers.

After conducting preliminary research, explore the information sources below to get responses as specific as possible regarding *financial metrics* and *valuation* anomolies that have taken place in the past, as well as why the stock currently stands where it does relative to its peers and the broader market. (See Exhibit 9.1 for the pros and cons of information sources.) The objective is to identify the *critical factors that moved the stock in the past* and *the current assumptions critical for the stock to achieve current consensus expectations*:

- Investor relations (IR) contacts are usually very good with the basics because their full-time job is to educate investors about their company. But don't use the IR contact as your sole source of information because you'll likely find the IR contact biased in the company's favor.

- For buy-side analysts:
  - Speak with portfolio managers, other analysts, or traders within your firm who were responsible for the sector or put the stocks in the portfolio in the past.
  - Speak with sell-side analysts and salespeople who have been familiar with the sector for an extended period of time.
- For sell-side analysts, speak with seasoned internal salespeople or traders. Salespeople may put you in touch with seasoned buy-side clients who can offer their perspective, but this should be done sparingly because as your firm's clients, they're doing you a favor.
- If you have the time and resources:
  - Speak with seasoned experts who would likely be familiar with the types of critical factors that move a stock, such as the company's competitors, seasoned executives who recently left their firm, and consultants who specialize in the sector.
  - Some financial journalists, individuals at forecasting services, and bloggers can be helpful if they've followed the sector for a long period of time and understand at least the basics of valuation.

Let's explore each one of these in a bit more detail. I cringe a bit when offering advice to call IR contacts, because they're not always on the pulse of market psychology. Unfortunately, some firms put individuals into the IR role as gatekeepers to provide the bare minimum of service, such as distributing company information and answering basic questions. These individuals often won't understand the factors driving their stock or current consensus thinking. But there is another breed of IR contact, who is actively engaged in the markets, speaking with some of the savviest investors and seasoned sell-side analysts on a regular basis. These individuals can be helpful in understanding the historical and current market thinking about their stock. They may try to sugarcoat the negative issues, but you'll likely see through this after asking a few pointed questions about your down-side scenarios. If every answer to your question results in a posi-tive outcome, you know the person doesn't have a balanced view. But the contact can still be helpful, especially if you ask direct questions such as, "What are the key assumptions in consensus for next year?" The speed and thoroughness of the response should give you an idea of how well he or she is plugged into the financial markets.

Experienced buy-side analysts and PMs who own the stock, or have owned it in the past, should have a good understanding of historical factors and provide the best feel for the key assumptions in current consensus thinking toward a stock. If you're on the buy-side, clearly you can approach your internal colleagues to answer your questions, but you might be surprised to know you can also approach buy-side analysts at other shops. They are often willing to speak because they want to expand their network of investors who traffic in their names, all in an effort to keep a hand on the pulse of investor psychology. The best way to make these buy-side-to-buy-side connections is to speak with a sell-side salesperson or make an effort to meet other buy-side analysts at investor events.

If you're on the sell-side, the challenge in questioning the buy-side is that they may not be willing to speak to you because they may have a proprietary view about the stock. For this reason, you may want to start with buy-siders who don't currently own the stock to get their view of the critical factors; they'll be less defensive about your motives. Sell-side salespeople are helpful in connecting you with the "smart money," namely, those investors who they believe are in the know on a stock.

If you're on the buy-side you also have the benefit of calling sell-side analysts to get their view about critical factors. Make sure to speak with seasoned analysts because the rookies will still be feeling out the factors. Also make sure to separate the analyst's view from the consensus view; sell-side analysts pride themselves on being out of consensus, and so you need to keep them on task if you're trying to identify "what's in the stock."

Sell-side salespeople are responsible for having at least a cursory understanding of all the stocks covered by their firm. Although this is sometimes over 1,000 stocks, each salesperson often has a number of sectors or stocks they know better than others. You can usually tell in the first few seconds when discussing a stock if the salesperson traffics in the name. If so, the salesperson should have a view in terms of what's in the stock, based on conversations with clients.

Sell-side analysts can openly speak with the internal trader of their stocks, which makes them a great resource when attempting to understand historical and current thinking. The limitation to speaking with traders is that they are often short-term thinkers, sometimes only looking out a few days or even just a few hours. For this reason, don't expect the typical trader to have a 12- or 18-month forward view. Due to the number of stocks they trade, they also may not have as much detail as you want.

When you're speaking with any of these market participants be careful not to tip your hand if you're beginning to develop a proprietary view on a critical factor. If your work shows that western coal pricing is likely a critical factor, and your forecast has it increasing 10 percent, don't ask them, "Do you think the production problems could lead to a 10 percent increase in coal prices?" Instead ask something like, "What is the current consensus thinking in terms of coal pricing for next year?"

Create a Short-List of the Best Critical Factors

Having discussions with these market participants, combined with your earlier research, should help identify the factors that have moved your stocks in the past or are most likely to do so in the future. The challenge now is to distill the list of factors down to a manageable size. When stocks substantially outperform or underperform an index it's often the result of just one factor; the trick is to determine which one, well in advance. In order to create an edge, analysts must narrow down their list of factors to those that have good catalysts. Bill Van Tuinen, a seasoned buy-side analyst, looks for catalysts that are big enough to overcome the risks. If a critical factor's catalyst is a broad-based macro event difficult to forecast, such as GDP or oil prices, it will be almost impossible to gain an edge over the market. As such, look for catalysts that can be identified and quantified through comprehensive research, such as determining the timing and likelihood of new industry regulations or the probability that a company's new product will be successful. Some of the more common places to anticipate catalysts include the following:

- Company-sponsored analyst meetings and calls
- Earnings releases
- The company's annual pricing, volume, or earnings guidance or projection
- Deadlines for new legislation, regulations, or court case outcomes
- Pre-scheduled announcements by the company's customers, competitors, or suppliers
- New product releases or significant product extensions
- Interim sales data for the company or the sector

Analysts should put dates for these events on their calendars and attempt to have a view on the event if it's likely to include a catalyst that impacts one of the critical factors.

Rank the list of sector and company factors collected to this point, using the following criteria:

- The level of materiality (e.g., impact on the financials or changes in the probability of a major corporate event)
- The likelihood that the catalyst can be forecast over the investment time horizon

The best two to four critical factors should be the topics of the analyst's focus.

Narrowing down a list of factors to only those that are critical is important for time management purposes as well as for picking stocks. For example, FedEx's stock dropped in late 2003 when it announced the Kinko's acquisition, even though it wasn't likely to impact the company's earnings power or returns over a typical investor's time horizon. Instead, the real critical factor was the company's effort to improve margins within its core operations, which ultimately allowed FedEx to beat expectations and caused its stock to outperform the S&P 500 and UPS substantially over the next one-, three-, and five-year periods. In isolation, the company paid too much for Kinko's, as evidenced by future write-offs, but it was a minor issue compared with improvements in the company's core operations in driving the stock's performance.

Optional Step: Meet with Management

By design, my process of identifying critical factors has yet to involve an in-depth company analysis because I don't want to get buried in the weeds researching issues that haven't impacted, and aren't likely to impact, the stock price. As Adam Longson, an analyst at Morgan Stanley with a CFA and CPA, put it, "The focus should be more on the stock than the company." For analysts who have the time and resources to meet with management (this is strongly advised for buy-side analysts and absolutely required for sell-side analysts), additional preparation is required, which involves a basic level of company analysis. It's important to meet with company mangement to understand if it's aware of the critical factors on the analyst's list and to determine if there's a plan to exploit or mitigate them.

By following the recommendations in Chapter 5, the analyst should be in the queue to meet with management (e.g., at its office, the fund's office, investor conference). To get the most from a management meeting, the analyst should conduct preliminary research to answer the questions highlighted in Exhibit 8.2. The level of research before a meeting is almost completely dependent on the analyst's time, but at a minimum, the strategy questions should be explored because they are so critical to almost every investment thesis. The information sources selected for each question in Exhibit 8.2 are considered the *best place to start,* but if an information source isn't selected it doesn't mean it can't help answer the question (Due to limited time, analysts should start first with sources likely to provide the best answers.) As discussed later in Chapter 10, an analyst wants to appear as knowledgable as possible about a company's strategy and competitive advantage when meeting management in order to take the discussion to its highest level. There are certain questions that should be avoided because they show lack of preparation, such as those that could be answered by reading a basic company presentation or regulatory filing, or aren't likely to be answered by management. (See the blank boxes in Exhibit 8.2 in the column titled Appropriate to Ask Executives at Meeting.) The exception to the "be prepared" rule is when an analyst is asked to take a meeting with company management (usually a small company) at the last minute, which occassionally happens; sell-side salespeople have been known to contact buy-side analysts at the last minute to offer up a company management meeting if a spot opens up during a road show or at a sell-side sponsored conference.

Exhibit 8.2 Best Practice (Knowledge): Questions to Investigate before or during Interviews with Management

Questions to be investigated	Company documents, data, and website	Market data & news provider	Industry trade journal or website	Economic data	Company investor relations contact	Sell-side report or model (for buy-side analysts)	Customer of or supplier to the company	Information from forecasting service	Consultant, expert, or company retiree	Sell-side analyst (for the buy-side)	Appropriate to ask executives at meeting
STRATEGY											
How does the company create value for its customers and shareholders?	•				•		•		•	•	
What is the company's competitive advantage?	•				•		•		•	•	•
What are the risks to the company maintaining its competitive advantage/returns?	•				•		•		•	•	•
How does the company's strategy differ from its competitors?	•				•		•		•	•	•
Which lines of business are the most and least valuable?	•				•	•			•	•	
Which lines of business are seasonal, cyclical, defensive, or growth?	•			•	•	•	•		•	•	
Which lines of the business are going through transition?	•	•			•	•	•	•	•	•	•
Where are the best areas of investment outside of the company's core business?	•	•			•						
Is management a good capital allocator (does the company earn its COC over a cycle)?	•	•			•	•	•		•	•	•
What are the biggest mistakes being made by the competition?	•	•	•			•			•	•	
Are there any material regulatory or legal risks that could impact margins or growth rates?	•	•	•		•				•	•	
FINANCIAL											
Why have key financial metrics changed materially over the recent past (e.g., 2–3 years)?*	•	•			•						
What are the key assumptions for the company to achieve consensus expectations?	•				•	•				•	•
Has the company made, or intend to make, any changes to its accounting policies?	•				•	•				•	•
How will the company finance future capital needs?	•				•	•				•	•

*Such as growth rates of EPS, FCF, and revenue as well as material changes in margins, ROIC, and ROE

(Continued)

Questions to be investigated	Company documents, data, and website	Market data & news provider	Industry trade journal or website	Economic data	Company investor relations contact	Sell-side report or model (for buy-side analysts)	Customer of or supplier to the company	Information from forecasting service	Consultant, expert, or company retiree	Sell-side analyst (for the buy-side)	Appropriate to ask executives at meeting
REVENUE											
Does the company or its competitors have pricing power?	•				•	•	•		•	•	•
How does the company set pricing?					•	•	•		•	•	•
Have there been any major customer wins or losses recently?			•		•	•	•		•	•	•
Which factors are most likely to cause a material change in demand?		•			•	•	•		•	•	•
Where will growth come from (economic, market share gains or new markets)?			•		•	•	•	•		•	•
How is the company positioned in the highest and lowest margin market segments?			•		•	•	•	•	•	•	•
COSTS											
Are there likely to be any changes to the company's cost structure beyond typical inflation?	•				•	•			•	•	•
Are there any major productivity initiatives? For publicly-stated targets, are they net of inflation?	•				•					•	•
Where is the company making its major investments?	•				•	•	•	•	•	•	•
How is management compensated and is it likely to change?	•				•	•				•	•
MGMT											
How does the quality of this mangement team compare to its competition?		•			•		•		•	•	
VALUATION											
How does the company's valuation differ from the past and currently from its peers?					•	•				•	
Is there anything misunderstood by the market that is distorting the company's valuation?					•	•	•		•	•	•
Are there any catalysts likely to impact valuation over a typical investment time horizon?					•	•	•		•	•	•

Start with this source to investigate before meeting management

Copyright McGraw-Hill and AnalystSolutions

Exhibit 8.3 includes a list of the documents that are most helpful when collecting information for a meeting with management, ranked in order of importance.

Exhibit 8.3   Best Practice (Knowledge): Documents to Review before Interviewing Management

Document	Purpose
Analyst's critical factors and catalysts list.	Ensure focus of preparation is on topics that pertain to critical factors and their catalysts.
Most recent annual regulatory filing (e.g., 10-K) and past two quarterly filings.	Understand MD&A and any discussion of risks. Good to know management bios. Use services that show changes since prior filing such as Blackline, 10-K Wizard, and Bloomberg).
Earnings model with a minimum of five years of historical data and two years forward projections. Current year should include quarterly data.	Focus on the forecast, especially where it differs from the historical trends.
Full list of sell-side earnings estimate projections, ranked from highest to lowest (EPS or FCF).	Understand the reason for the range of estimates and how the analyst's own estimate differs from consensus.
Transcript of the two most recent quarterly company presentations.	Develop insights about critical factors and catalysts.
Personal or colleague's notes or reports generated from prior meetings or calls with management (preferably within the past two years).	Reviewing in reverse chronological order, look for insights about critical factors and their catalysts.
Buy-side only: sell-side reports highlighting ratings changes or think pieces over the past year.	Identify the critical factors and catalysts surrounding investment controversies.
Company presentations from conferences over the past six months.	Develop insights about critical factors and catalysts.
Analyst's (or third party's) historical valuation analysis.	Determine where the company's stock trades now relative to its past, its peers, and the overall market.
Analyst's (or third party's) historical capacity and demand analysis.	Identify historical changes in market share.
Information on corporate restructurings or M&A.	Understand any major restructurings or M&A.
List of the top 20 shareholders.	Identify the style of the current holders.
Information from the company's "investor" portion of its website that isn't in any of the documents above.	Ensure no important piece of information is overlooked.

Monitor Critical Factors

The short list of two to four critical factors per stock and their catalysts become the foundation for all proprietary work in an effort to forecast the direction of stock prices better than the market. The next step in this process is to set up a network for monitoring the critical factors to develop a better forecast (e.g., creating a financial forecast and identifying catalysts) than the broader market. This network should go well beyond the market participants mentioned above because *identifying* a factor that moved a stock in the past requires a different skill than providing information to help *forecast* the future movement of a stock (e.g., the investor relations manager who helped explain why a company's stock underperformed during the past isn't likely to be as helpful in forecasting its future performance). See Exhibit 9.1 for details about the types of information sources to use for this next step in the process.

Approach your information sources with a strategy, namely seeking out insights rather than waiting for them to surprise you in the form of an unexpected announcement from one of your companies. The strategy employed by Bill Greene, a Morgan Stanley analyst with more than 12 years of sell-side experience, is to "find something where you disagree with consensus and explore to see if it could make a difference in the stock." One of the most gratifying experiences as an equity analyst is watching a stock react to a catalyst you forecast, well in advance of the market. Investigate the critical factors in order to refine your upside, downside, and base case scenarios (a process discussed later in Chapter 18).

To ensure that you're contacting your information sources in a timely manner on the topics that are likely to move your stocks, create a matrix of critical factors, issues to explore, potential catalysts, contact sources, and frequency of discussion. Review the list regularly to ensure that you're staying ahead of the competition on the critical factors likely to drive your stocks. Here is an example:

Critical Factor	Issue to Explore	Potential Catalysts	Contact Source	Frequency
Price of western coal	Supply and demand	Publicized discussions from upcoming industry conference	Bill Smith, industry consultant	Monthly
Salary and wage expenses	Inflation level for upcoming labor contract	Outcome from upcoming union negotiations	Ann Thompson, union officer	Monthly
Size of fall grain harvest	Impact from weather conditions during growing season	Release of monthly government crop condition reports	Dawn Johnson, agriculture consultant	Weekly, from early June to early September
Financial community sentiment about a potential change in management	Is it priced into the stock that the CEO will leave soon?	Upcoming sell-side hosted dinner with CEO	Ken Lee, sell-side analyst	Monthly

There's an art to conducting the interview, which is discussed in Chapter 10.

Be on the Lookout for New Critical Factors

"The only constant in life is change."* An analyst's job would be much easier if the initial list of critical factors never changed, but that's unrealistic. In fact, once an analyst has identified two to four critical factors per company along with sources of insights to forecast these factors, the next significant part of the job is to identify new critical factors.

---

* This quote is attributed to the philosopher Heraclitus (535–475 BCE).

For most analysts, almost every day will include a new piece of information that could lead to an additional critical factor. To remain on task and efficient with time, an analyst should use the flow chart in Exhibit 8.4 to determine if a new critical factor has emerged:

1. Determine if new information is more likely to be an opportunity or risk.
2. Briefly surmise the potential impact on the stock from this factor:
   a. Likely to occur within investment time horizon?
   b. Material (e.g., move financials more than 5 percent)?
   c. Will be triggered by a catalyst that can be forecast?
3. If the factor meets the criteria above, determine if it's not yet in the stock in terms of consensus expectations or the valuation multiple.
4. If it meets all of the criteria above, it likely warrants further research to determine if it's a critical factor.

For illustrative purposes, let's say you're picking up Canadian National, a major railroad operating in Canada and the United States. After reviewing all of the relevant company information and news stories, and speaking to industry and company experts, you've created your list of two to four critical factors. But then, as part of your ongoing monitoring of information, you come across these potential opportunities and risks:

1. As you read about the stronger Canadian dollar, you wonder if it may slow exports the company hauls to the United States because the products are essentially becoming more expensive for Americans.
2. An internal colleague tells you that one of his industry sources believes the Canadian government may attempt to re-regulate the sector.
3. While reading a trade journal, you discover the company has sole access to a new container port being constructed on the Canadian west coast.
4. You read a story on the news wire stating this fall's Canadian grain harvest, which the company hauls, will be down to 5 percent.

Exhibit 8.4   Best Practice (Skills): Flow Chart of Ongoing Activity for
Identifying a Critical Factor

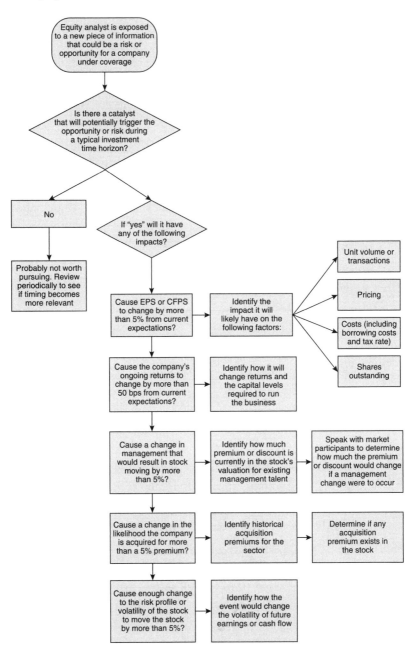

Should all of these points be added as new critical factors? By following the steps in Exhibit 8.4, you determine the following scenarios aren't critical for the following reasons:

1. Your research reveals the company's debt is denominated in U.S. dollars and your firm will own the stock in U.S. dollars, which both *benefit* from a stronger Canadian dollar. In addition, a stronger Canadian dollar historically stimulates more U.S. exports to Canada which are hauled by the company. Based on a historical analysis, these factors almost fully mitigate the impact of potentially slower exports to the United State.

2. Your research reveals that it will take at least three years before the government gets serious about re-regulation, which is well outside of your investment time horizon.

3. Your research reveals the container port will add only 1 percent of new revenue when it opens in 18 months, which is too small and far out in time to have a major impact on the stock during your investment time horizon.

4. Your research reveals the Canadian grain harvest, while important, is less than 10 percent of the company's revenue, and so even if it's down 5 percent, it's not likely to cause a collapse in the stock.

Dispelling these factors as not critical takes time, but once they're taken off the list, an analyst can ignore most of the noise surrounding the non-factors, thus freeing up time to focus on the real factors likely to move the stock. This isn't to say never look at any of these factors again, but only if something changes their importance. Periodically challenge yourself to ensure you haven't become complacent. Similarly, as you're periodically reviewing your list of critical factors, make sure to remove those that have played out as expected or no longer meet the criteria discussed above.

While all analysts should avoid being distracted by factors that have been ruled out as critical, sell-side analysts may need to keep some on their front burner due to client interest. For example, even though demand for ethanol was increasing in the late 1990s and early 2000s, I knew it wouldn't amount to more than 2-3% of the railroad industry's revenue during the next 3-5 years. Eventually I had to write about the topic to illustrate to clients why it wasn't a critical factor. Sell-side analysts shouldn't confuse this effort of *marketing to clients* with conducting research for stock picking.

It's worth noting that this best practice is focused on *identifying* and *monitoring* critical factors, which is only part of the process towards identifying insights and making stock recommendations. Critical factors are important elements of best practices discussed later in the book:

- Chapter 9. Create Sustainable Proprietary Sources of Insight
- Chapter 10. Get the Most from Interviewing for Insights
- Chapter 13. Conduct Surveys to Acquire Unique Insights
- Chapter 18. Forecast Scenarios for the Most Important Critical Factors

In closing, here are some considerations I picked up from other research analysts and portfolio managers in terms of seeking out critical factors:

- You're not looking for data points but rather changes in trends.
- Don't "go underground" when conducting research; get out there and learn by having conversations. Inexperienced analysts hide in their spreadsheets, which fails to get them out into the debate.
- You can't do this on your own, especially when you're new. You'll need to ask for help from:
  - Colleagues in your firm
  - Investor relations
  - Sell-side (if on the buy-side)
  - Industry contacts
- "The market often over-simplifies the investment thesis, which offers us an opportunity."

Exhibit 8.5   Best Practice (Skills): Identify and Monitor a Stock's Critical Factors

1. Instead of approaching traditional company analysis with the intention of learning everything about a company, concentrate the effort just on the critical factors likely to move a company's stock. This allows the analyst to better allocate time and be a better stock picker.
2. For a factor to be *critical* it will likely meet these criteria:
   a. Occur during the investor's typical investment time horizon.
   b. Have an associated catalyst that, when triggered, will cause the factor to become a greater opportunity or risk in the view of market participants. In most instances, this factor causes one or more of the following:
      (1) Material changes in earnings or cash flow growth.
      (2) Material changes in returns.
      (3) Material changes in the probability:
         (a) The company makes an acquisition.
         (b) The company is purchased by another entity.
         (c) There is a change in senior management.
   c Material change in the volatility profile of the stock.
3. Dedicate a place in your notes to compile the critical factors (and their catalysts) for each company and sector. It's important to have this information in one easy-to-reference place.
4. Following similar steps as the *sector* analysis conducted in Chapter 7, but this time at the *company* level, identify and understand the historical (10 years or more) cause of anomalies or fluctuations to each company's:
   a. Financial metrics in absolute terms and relative to its peers.
   b. Valuation levels relative to its peers and the market.
5. Record the events that caused these historical anomalies as factors (on a company or sector level) as well as the catalyst that triggered the event (e.g., stronger customer pricing is the *factor*, while the *catalyst* is an upside surprise at the company's upcoming quarterly earnings release).
6. Review current valuations to identify what's in the stock, in terms of current expectations. Record the factors that drive key assumptions necessary for each company to achieve consensus expectations.
7. For analysts who have the time and resources, meet with company management to understand if it's aware of the analyst's critical factors and determine if there's a plan to exploit or mitigate them. Ask appropriate questions during the meeting as highlighted in Exhibit 8.2, and prepare in advance by reviewing the documents discussed in Exhibit 8.3. Use the meeting as an opportunity to prioritize critical factors.

8. Of all the factors recorded, rank them in terms of impact on earnings and cash flow over a reasonable investment time horizon (e.g., 6 to 12 months). Those that are most likely to move consensus EPS or CFPS by 5 percent or more are generally among the better candidates for critical factors.

9. Identify potential catalysts for the more significant critical factors. Those with catalysts that can be identified and forecast through detailed research are usually the best critical factors for the purpose of stock picking (e.g., it's much more difficult to forecast the next recession than assess a company's likely success or failure with a new product launch).

10. Aggressively monitor your network of information sources to forecast the catalysts for two to four critical factors (for each company) better than the broader market.

11. Over time, add new critical factors to the list and remove old ones, based on their probability to move EPS or CFPS by your threshold. To remain on-task and efficient with time, an analyst should follow the subsequent process to determine if a new critical factor has emerged:

    a. Determine if new information is more likely to be an opportunity or risk.

    b. Briefly surmise the potential impact on the stock from this factor:

       (1) Likely to occur within investment time horizon?

       (2) Material (e.g., move financials more than 5 percent)?

       (3) Will be triggered by a catalyst that can be forecast?

    c. If the factor meets the criteria above, determine if it's not yet in the stock in terms of consensus expectations or the valuation multiple.

12. If it meets all of the criteria above, it likely warrants further research to determine if it's a critical factor.

Chapter 9

Create Sustainable Proprietary Sources of Insight

The toughest part of being a successful analyst is finding good industry sources.

—Sell-side analyst who was top ranked for over 10 years

M any equity analysts believe that managers within the companies they're researching are the best sources of information because they're so close to the action. While there are some good inside sources, the problem is that they're inside. In countries with the most developed financial markets, this means that they can't speak about some of the most crucial information, and if they do, the information is often biased to meet the company's needs.

It's for this reason that you should always have good industry sources—individuals who are not employed by the companies you're following. They're usually candid with their answers and willing to help at no cost if you provide information or recognition in return. As my career progressed I found that I spoke less to company management and more to my unique sources. On one phone call I made to an investor relations (IR) contact, I heard, "I haven't talked to you in a while," which made me pause. Was I not doing my job? After the call I reflected a bit on that question; considering the objective data used to evaluate my performance, I was doing as well as if not better than when I had more frequent discussions with the company. Granted, I had the benefit of a talented research associate who would periodically call the company for the routine topics, but I still didn't feel the need to speak frequently with management, partly because the time was better spent with independent information sources and partly because companies often led me astray. One of my most colorful buy-side clients put it well when he said, "The more I speak with companies, the stupider I get."

Seeking proprietary insights is sometimes referred to as *channel checking*, a phrase I've slowly come to adopt. Although I don't have a problem with channel checking per se, I do question the way this phrase came into wide use on Wall Street. Prior to the tech bubble, those of us who did day-to-day research were discovering proprietary information about our companies, including insights from the channels we checked, as part of a daily routine. The bull market of the late 1990s brought with it a number of newly minted terms, including "channel checking", suggesting a new way of conducting research. My assertion that this phrase was more hype than reality (especially among the tech analysts) became validated when we saw the market implode in 2000, a disaster that presumably could have been avoided (or mitigated) had the channels been checked better. We now have this coined phrase that identifies with the current generation of analysts and so I'll use it throughout my thoughts, but understand it's an activity the best equity analysts have been conducting for decades.

There are two primary forms of channel checking: (1) informal, open-ended discussions with your industry sources; and (2) surveys conducted either one-on-one or in an automated manner. I'll discuss the first of these in this best practice and leave the survey process until Chapter 13.

You might think that only a limited number of sectors lend themselves to channel checking, but it's actually quite broad. Granted, for sectors where macro factors drive most of the price movement, such as oil prices for the energy sector and interest rates for the banking sector, discovering an industry source that leads to a major differentiating factor may be tougher than for other sectors. Some analysts initially think that the retail sector, with its stores open for analysts to visit, is one of the few appropriate for channel checking, but I found that even sectors as industrial as railroads and trucking had industry sources who provided an edge to make great stock calls. On the topic of suitability, it can also be more difficult to channel check small companies than large companies, simply because there are fewer people who know the company.

Background research, such as reading industry journals or looking at historical relationships between data series, is critical for understanding the basics and developing a holistic perspective, but you'll need to speak to information sources to develop an edge. Kenneth A. Posner, chief of research and analysis, North American Financial Holdings, Inc. and former sell-side analyst, makes this point, "Just because you have a detailed model doesn't mean it's accurate – confirming assumptions with outside sources is critical to success." This is further reiterated by a senior buy-side analyst, who believes analysts should "get out of the office to make new contacts to think the way the business people are thinking." Below is a list of contact types that are most likely to help assess changes to critical factors, and who don't work for the company being researched. These are highlighted further in Exhibit 9.1:

- Fellow analysts within your firm who cover sectors that have influence over the critical factors impacting your sector(s).
- Large customers and suppliers of companies you're following (suppliers can include union leaders who represent labor, which is often a large cost component to companies).

John Quackenbush, CFA, senior investment analyst at UBS Global Asset Management, reinforces this point: "Some of my best insights come from meeting with a company's suppliers, competitors, customers and regulators."

- Management of competitors to the company being researched, especially those working for privately held companies (because they're not held back by Regulation Fair Disclosure [Reg FD]).
- Consultants specializing in your sector.
- Retirees from companies you'll be following.
- Experienced industry journalists or bloggers.
- Trade association employees and members.
- Those who have a cross-sectional view of the sector such as employees who record applications or process transactions for your sector.
- Government officials or staffers who are close to your sector.
- Sell-side analysts (for buy-side analysts) and buy-side analysts (for sell-side analysts).

When you come across potential new contacts that don't fit one of the categories above, there's a good chance they're not going to provide an investment-significant insight for critical factors of your company. The contact could still be of help in getting you up to speed on sector basics, but assess the relationship for what it is. As your knowledge of the sector progresses, you're less likely to find the contact valuable to the investment process.

While I enjoyed finding and interviewing my industry contacts, Chad Bruso, who worked in my team from 2000 to 2006, excelled at this. I could tell him that I needed an answer to a question about parcel sector pricing and by the end of the day he'd come back with anecdotes from 5 to 10 major shippers. Chad was excellent at searching for good contacts early in the process, but I think his secret weapon was that he knew exactly how much each contact could *add to the investment debate*. He might have 100 potential parcel shippers on his contact list, but only 20 had enough insight about UPS and FedEx's dimensional pricing, or whatever was the topic du jour. It's this understanding of a contact's capabilities that is so critical to the fact-finding process. There are limitless industry contacts, but only a handful who can answer any single question. For this reason, it's important to have plenty of contacts to choose from and to size up the contact early in the process. Don't forgo the getting to know you process, because it's critical to get information (as discussed in Chapter 4), but once it's established, determine how this contact can be of help.

It's also important to understand a contact's biases as quickly as possible. Does the contact have a reason to hope the company you're discussing does well or poorly? Without this understanding it's tough to assess the objectivity of the information.

As with most efforts, the process of finding unique proprietary sources has two important constraints that must be appreciated: *time* and *money*. Some analysts have budgets for expert networks, which helps the process, but all analysts need to have a strategy for this overall effort to be effective in helping pick stocks. There are dozens of expert networks, although Integrity Research estimates that Gerson Lehrman Group (GLG) has at least two-thirds market share, making it the dominant market provider. In Exhibit 9.1 I list the typical sources of information based on cost and time commitment.

So how do you develop a list of proprietary contacts? I'll share my personal experience as well as insights from J. P. Mark, founder of Farmhouse Equity Research, a firm specializing in channel checking. In looking for information sources, it's critical to join or develop networks that are target rich for potential industry sources. These networks can be established formally, such as LinkedIn and alumni groups, or informally, such as making new contacts at trade shows or other sector events hosted by trade associations. I always made a point of recording the names of individuals who were quoted in trade journals, because I knew they were willing to speak about the topic (they were quoted in the press after all) and likely knew something about

Exhibit 9.1. Best Practice (Knowledge): Time and Cost for Information Sources (ranked from lowest to highest based on typical cost)

Source for Information	Pros	Cons	Typical Cost	Time Commitment
Company documents/website	Free. May be only source for certain information.	Tends to be biased positively.	LOW: Usually this data is free.	LOW to MEDIUM: Depends on the complexity of data analysis.
Financial press	Low cost. Somewhat objective.	May not fully understand implications for company or stock.	LOW: Most services low cost.	LOW to MEDIUM: Depends on how many stories are written about the sector each day.
Industry trade journal, website, or blog	Low cost. Somewhat objective. Understands complex issues.	May be biased in the sector's favor. May not fully understand implications for company or stock.	LOW: Most services are low cost.	LOW to MEDIUM: Depends on how many stories are written about the sector each day.
Economic data	Reliable and objective.	Past trends don't forecast the future.	LOW: Usually this data is low cost unless reformatted by third party in a unique manner.	LOW to MEDIUM: Depends on the complexity of data analysis.
Buy-side analyst or portfolio manager (as source for buy-side or sell-side)	Best place to gauge investor expectations.	May not be representative of the larger investor base.	LOW: The buy-side will not charge for their thoughts. Often will only offer their view if approached by trusted colleague.	LOW to MEDIUM: Probably need to speak to at least five buy-side analysts/PMs to draw a defendable conclusion regarding investor psychology.
Trader of stock (buy-side or sell-side)	Usually familiar with short-term psychology of stock.	May not fully understand company or long-term issues.	LOW: No cost if in-house.	LOW: Conversations tend to be short, focused on one or two issues.
Company's competitor	Knows the sector and the competitive dynamics.	May not be familiar with other company's factors to speak with authority. May try to bash the competition.	LOW: Most companies will gladly speak about their competitors (privately) especially if the person doing the interview provides reciprocal information.	MEDIUM: Requires some preparation to create relevant questions. Also requires verification afterward because information is likely to be biased.

· 124 ·

Exhibit 9.1. Best Practice (Knowledge): Time and Cost for Information Sources (ranked from lowest to highest based on typical cost) *(Continued)*

Source for Information	Pros	Cons	Typical Cost	Time Commitment
Company investor relations contact	Usually forthcoming about opportunistic factors.	Usually downplay or ignore potentially negative factors.	LOW: Companies will not charge for their time, but it may be limited.	MEDIUM to HIGH: Requires high degree of preparation because time with management is usually limited.
Company executives	Usually forthcoming about opportunistic factors.	Usually downplay or ignore potentially negative factors.	LOW: Companies will not charge for their time, but it may be limited.	MEDIUM to HIGH: Requires preparation because time with contact is usually limited.
Sell-side report (for buy-side analysts)	Easy to access and search (if client).	May be biased by analyst's rating.	LOW to MEDIUM: Available to clients of almost any size.	LOW: Ability to search by key word makes it a fast process.
Sell-side salesperson	Close to many buy-side investors.	Generalist salespeople may not have full understanding of any single stock.	LOW to MEDIUM: Salespeople will generally speak with any analyst of a fee-paying client.	LOW: Salespeople are usually available for follow-up if necessary and so intense preparation is not required.
Customer of or supplier to the company	First-hand knowledge of the company's value proposition.	Sample may not be representative of the larger customer base.	LOW to MEDIUM: Can be free to mildly expensive, depending on where you find the sources.	MEDIUM: Requires preparation even if using expert networks. Could be "HIGH" when finding experts on your own.
Government officials or staffers	Often the closest to regulatory or legislative changes.	Often won't speak on the topic. If so, may not provide accurate forecast.	LOW to MEDIUM: Depends on the level of the individuals and the method of contact.	MEDIUM to HIGH: Requires high degree of preparation because time with officials is usually limited.
Information from forecasting service	Often the best at forecasting trends for the factor.	Not always provided in a timely manner. Can be expensive. Not proprietary.	LOW to HIGH: Can be free or very expensive, depending on the forecast provider.	LOW: Data is usually in user-friendly format.
Consultant, expert, or company retiree	Very close to the issue.	Can be difficult to find.	LOW to HIGH: Can be free or very expensive, depending on where you find the source.	MEDIUM: Requires preparation even if using expert networks. Could be "HIGH" if need to find an expert on your own.

(Continued)

Exhibit 9.1. Best Practice (Knowledge): Time and Cost for Information Sources (ranked from lowest to highest based on typical cost) *(Continued)*

Source for Information	Pros	Cons	Typical Cost	Time Commitment
Sell-side analyst (for the buy-side)	May be the only place to gauge consensus thinking and to obtain proprietary research.	Subjectivity or low-quality work can result in incorrect output.	MEDIUM to HIGH: Many sell-side firms require a minimum client commission charge before providing access to the analyst.	LOW: Substantial preparation is not always required, especially if you're a large client who has unlimited access to the analyst. Often need to call more than one analyst to get a good perspective.
Proprietary survey	Output is proprietary.	Expensive and can take a lot of time.	MEDIUM to HIGH: To conduct a thorough survey requires substantial resources (either in-house or outsourced).	HIGH: A proper survey can take weeks or months to conduct.

Copyright McGraw-Hill and AnalystSolutions

the topic. Always carry business cards with you, even if you're on vacation, because you never know when you'll bump into a potential good contact. As J. P. Mark highlights, one of your objectives should be to find industry contacts who would never be motivated to be part of an expert network, because this will offer you exclusivity of information.

I became a member of a few industry trade associations that gave me access to their membership directories. If I was going to attend a trade show, I'd try to get a list of the attendees who were registered so I could set up meetings in advance. In the event that I had been asked to speak at the conference, I would only do so contingent on being given a list of attendees at least a week beforehand so that I could set up one-on-one meetings with participants. If you receive their e-mail addresses, survey the attendees on the investment debates currently taking place in your sector(s).

Analysts who take the time to build networks are those who make a big difference over time. While building a vast network of contacts who are experts in many topics won't occur overnight, don't assume it takes years to get started. When I began as a senior sell-side analyst in the early 1990s, I developed a reputation among my clients relatively quickly for seeking out unique industry experts. This effort ultimately led us to start an investor conference that focused on the critical factors rather than the standard company management format.

Just because you've identified these individuals doesn't mean that they'll speak with you. The critical question to ask comes from awareness of others' needs, which was discussed in Chapter 4, specifially, "What's in it for them (WIIFT)?" *You need to answer this before having your first discussion.* More often than not, they are also looking for information, and given your unique position as an equity research analyst, you can probably get them information that they wouldn't normally have access to. As such, your currency to pay them back is made up of insights you glean from other discussions. When we came back from a meeting at FedEx or UPS headquarters my associates and I would make a point of calling some of our best industry sources to tell them what we learned. It showed them that we valued their insights because we were repaying with our insights. If you're a sell-side analyst, always add new information contacts to your e-mail distribution list so they begin getting your written work. You may even want to get them online access to the rest of your firm's research so that they can explore other sectors for professional or personal reasons.

Some industry sources aren't looking for insights as much as they're looking for public recognition. They like to be known throughout the industry as the chief guru. You can reward these individuals by asking them to speak at a conference or referring a journalist to them for a quote, showing you think of them as the industry thought leader.

Another way I thanked my industry sources was by holding a dinner for them at industry events they were likely to attend. I would invite all of my contacts who were attending (usually 10 to 20 people) as well as 5 to 10 buy-side analysts to a nice restaurant for an engaging dinner where everyone discussed critical factors. If you reward your industry contacts, they will continually come back to you with new insights.

Finding good contacts and extracting value-added investment-significant insights is hard work. It's not uncommon for analysts to throw in the towel or compromise the process due to a lack of time, money, or focus. Here are some of the most common mistakes analysts make when channel checking:

- They are ill prepared because:
  - They don't build a network of the right people.
  - They don't immerse themselves into the field to meet contacts or get closer to the ones they know.
  - They don't ask the right questions or understand the topic enough when questioning a good information source.

- They don't spend time wisely; specifically, they have discussions about factors:
  - The analyst already fully understands.
  - That aren't likely to impact a stock price.
- They draw conclusions based on channel checking with only one person, especially someone who may have a bias like a company CFO (this isn't channel checking, it's called interviewing management).

Exhibit 9.2   Best Practice (Skills): Assessing and Approaching Information Contacts

1. When seeking industry contacts, look for individuals who are *not* employed by your companies, because management is often biased and likely muzzled.
2. Identify the following types of individuals who are close to the critical factors that drive your assigned sector(s) and stocks:
   - Fellow analysts within your firm who cover sectors that have influence over the critical factors impacting your sector(s).
   - Large customers and suppliers of companies you're following (suppliers can include union leaders who represent labor, which is often a large cost component to companies).
   - Management of competitors to the company being researched, especially those working for privately held companies (because they're not held back by Reg FD).
   - Consultants from firms specializing in your sector.
   - Retirees from companies you'll be following.
   - Experienced industry journalists or bloggers.
   - Trade association employees and members.
   - People who have a cross-sectional view of the sector such as employees who record applications or process transactions for your sector.
   - Government officials or staffers who are close to your sector.
   - Sell-side analysts (for buy-side analysts) and buy-side analysts (for sell-side analysts).
3. As you're reading industry trade journals, blogs, or news stories specific to your industry, record the names of individuals who meet the criteria above. (I found that if someone was willing to be quoted in a news story and didn't work for a public company, the person was usually willing to speak to a financial analyst.)
4. Seek contacts in target rich locations. Preferably, find individuals who already have their own network such as journalists, bloggers, and consultants:
   - Trade associations.
   - Social networking groups such as LinkedIn.

(Continued)

- Industry journals (journalists and the experts who are quoted) or bloggers.
- Alumni networks.
- Industry conferences and trade shows (get an advanced list of attendees to set up meetings with before the event or survey them afterward).
- Industry task forces or committees.
- Contacts of other analysts in your firm (ask before calling them).

5. Look for contacts every chance you get because you never know when you might need someone's insights. (Have business cards wherever you go, even on vacation.)

6. Before approaching potential contacts, answer the critical question, "What's in it for them?" Potential ways to compensate your contacts (without money) include:
   - Answer their sector or company questions that you're qualified to answer, such as why a stock is priced where it is.
   - Access to your research (if you publish) or your firm's research.
   - Recognition such as asking the contact to speak at a conference, to your firm's investment committee (via conference call), or referring the press to the contact.
   - Access to other industry experts such as through a dinner or round table discussion (with or without other analysts in attendance).

7. Ensure that you've done enough preliminary research on the topic to be credible and have a worthwhile discussion. The best industry experts usually enjoy high-end discussions and tire quickly when explaining the sector basics.

8. Conduct research on contacts in advance of speaking with them (e.g., Google, LinkedIn, ZoomInfo, Bloomberg).

9. When you've made a personal connection with an industry contact, determine quickly how this individual's expertise can help forecast critical factors. If it becomes clear that the contact doesn't have expertise, see if he has connections to those who can help. If not, be polite by thanking the contact for his time and move on to the next contact.

10. When a contact responds to your request, immediately put her in your contact database; you'll be glad you did when you need her information in the future.

11. When you discover a significant piece of information, attempt to verify with at least one other proprietary source, especially if it's critical to your investment thesis.

Note: This Best Practice doesn't recommend relying heavily on company management as an information source, because it's usually not in a position to offer material, proprietary information, or unbiased insights. This may not hold true in some less developed financial markets, where management selectively disseminates information.

Keep Communication with Management Open

While analysts don't want to become too close to management because it can impair their objectivity toward the company's stock, they also don't want to be an unknown or become such an annoyance that management goes out of its way to ignore them. In an effort to strike the right balance, I encourage analysts to follow the best practices found in Exhibit 9.3.

Exhibit 9.3   Best Practice (Skills): Keeping the Right Distance with Company Management

1. Don't directly call senior executives of publicly traded companies unless you have explicit permission from senior management (such as the CEO). If you call executives directly without permission, they will likely feel awkward, possibly requiring a call to their general counsel due to Reg FD concerns. Separately, the IR contact will take this as an insult because it undercuts his or her authority. Many IR contacts may not be sitting in the same meetings as CEOs and CFOs, but to ignore or disrespect them is to guarantee that you're put on the bottom of the list for something you'll need in the future.

2. Don't insult executives, especially in public; they have feelings and egos too. Rather than ask, "What were you thinking when you made this bad acquisition?" the question could be reworded as, "It appears the acquisition hasn't met all of your original expectations. Can you please help us understand management's thought process when the acquisition was made?" If you feel the need to take management to task, do it in private, either over the phone or in person.

3. When meeting with management, share insights senior executives may find helpful, which shows respect and can lead to reciprocation. It can range from the market psychology about their stock to tidbits you picked up at a meeting with their competitors.

4. Tell management when it's doing something worth commending. "The cost cutting effort is going better than the Street anticipated." Being a corporate executive, responsible for cranking out quarterly growth in perpetuity while fighting fiercely with the competition, can be a very difficult job. They don't get accolades very often and so if you see something good, let them know.

(Continued)

5. When possible, attend the most important elements of a company's institutional investor events (if it has them). If you can't attend, send an e-mail to the company explaining that you have a conflict; management will appreciate knowing that you wanted to come. If you do attend, don't feel compelled to participate in elements that aren't likely to help assess critical factors, such as a plant tour.

6. If you attend a management presentation at a conference, go up and introduce yourself afterward (or go up to say hello if you already know them). Taking that extra little step may come in handy the next time the company is on a road show in your town trying to allocate one-on-one meetings.

7. For the buy-side, if management is coming to your town and asks for a one-on-one, try to take it or at least explain that you have a conflict. Don't take unnecessary meetings but also understand that corporate executives will feel more committed to get you information in the future if you invite them into your office.

8. For the sell-side:

   a. If you're about to downgrade a stock, call management after the market close the night before the ratings change to explain why. Speak with the IR contact. If possible, leave a voicemail for the CFO (call after hours so you get voicemail) to show that you understand the executive is an important part of the process.

   b. Put all interviewees (management and industry contacts) on your research e-mail distribution list. Most will appreciate reading about the sector from your perspective.

   c. Try to set up at least one non-deal road show with each of your companies every 24 months. It will get you some research time with management and show the clout you have with clients.

Your Best Information Source May Be Sitting Next to You

This may sound like a no brainer, but you'd be surprised how often equity analysts don't speak with their in-house colleagues about critical factors that spill across more than one sector. This can often be a great source of proprietary content. I'd suggest that this is one of the top five best practices on the *benefit-relative-to-effort* scale.

Go back to your food chain analysis, discussed in Chapter 7, to determine which companies supply to your sector—either raw materials or any important part of delivering the final good or service to customers. Add to this companies that are customers of your sector. If you have colleagues outside the United States, make sure to include relevant companies in those regions as well. Now go through this list of companies and identify if you have in-house analysts who cover any of these names. If so, identify specifically what you need from those individuals; this will be your wish list. For example, if you're the auto analyst, you probably want to know if there are likely to be any changes to input costs, such as steel and plastics, as well as transportation costs for these inputs.

Before you go to the next step of laying down a wish list on your colleague, think about some of the unintended consequences. The best financial analysts are cynical by nature and as such, if you aren't clear that your motive is to simply stay on top of your companies' fundamentals, your colleague may become concerned that you're empire building, attempting to eventually take away his sector. At a minimum, if not positioned correctly, your co-worker may simply think you're wasting his time. So approach him in a non-threatening way, preferably at a time when it's clear that you both can benefit from collaboration. For example, if you're covering transportation stocks and discover Union Pacific Railroad is raising Ford's transportation costs 10 percent next year, you could stop by to discuss this with your auto analyst and bring up the possibility of collaborating on a number of issues. If it's clear that your intentions are genuine, this is the point when you provide the colleague with your wish list, a list of information you need to know to analyze your sectors. Unfortunately, if you don't spell this out, the colleague may not think of you when it comes up during research. Ask him or her to reciprocate by letting you know exactly what is needed from your sector. Unfortunately, it's not always a two-way street. As a tech analyst, you may want to know if Best Buy is going to start selling the newest computer produced by your company, but the Best Buy analyst probably isn't that concerned about knowing if your company's newest computer will be one of the ten thousand items sold in Best Buy stores. When your colleague has little to gain by sending you information, you have to work all that much harder at staying on his mind.

After your initial meeting, make a point of forwarding insights to your colleagues on anything that may help her in her analysis, even if it's relatively minor. You're attempting to model behavior of another individual, which can take years, and so the more you do to reinforce the concept, the more likely it will eventually take hold. Always respond to an e-mail with, "Thanks for the information," even if it's meaningless; you want Pavlov's dog to keep salivating when the bell rings. It only takes one e-mail back like, "Thanks but this doesn't pertain to my company" before you'll see a slowdown in information flow.

If another sector is critical to yours, make a point of speaking with your colleague on a regular basis—possibly holding 30-minute calls or meetings once a week or once a month. This will help reinforce the importance of the topic in her mind. If you get invited to an event that might have applicability to your co-worker, make sure to get her an invitation too. Showing your respect for her will increase the likelihood that you'll get information in return.

You may also want to set up an e-mail group or shared file site to help facilitate collaboration. Whenever I would come across an issue that benefited our global air freight analysts, I would forward it to "globalairfreight" which was an e-mail group of 15 internal colleagues with an interest in the topic. You'll probably need to make an effort to get everyone added because once again, your colleagues may not see the initial benefit. The North American airline analyst at one of my former firms kept a global supply spreadsheet on a shared server that could be updated and accessed by counterparts in Europe and Asia. I can't stress enough that *these efforts won't magically begin on their own*; you'll likely have to spend much more effort than benefit in the initial stage, but once your co-workers begin to see the benefits, they'll be more receptive to volunteering their time to help the effort.

The biggest challenge in fostering these types of relationships are the cross-border, cross-cultural problems. At one of my former firms, I watched the Korean container shipping analyst *downgrade* a stock because he thought global industry pricing was about to drop, only to be followed a week later by the Japanese container shipping analyst *upgrading* a stock because he thought global prices were on the rise. In general, people find it more difficult to collaborate with individuals who are from other countries and located in other time zones. But understand that this is an inherent challenge for *everyone*, including your competitors. If you can overcome the challenge, you'll be at a significant competitive advantage. There's no magic potion to bring international associates closer together, but here are a few steps I found helpful:

- Know your counterparts' names and how to pronounce them. If you're not sure, ask your local manager for the name of his or her local manager who can set up an introduction.

- Approach your colleague in a non-threatening manner, making your intentions clear.

- Nothing builds trust faster than meeting face-to-face. Meeting when you're both attending a global industry conference is the most cost-effective method. For sell-side analysts, meet your counterparts when marketing in their region, treating them with as much importance as a client in that region.

- Be mindful of time zone issues, as they can be the greatest point of contention. If you send an e-mail from New York City at 8 a.m. to your Hong Kong colleague, don't reply back at 5 p.m. asking why they haven't responded because they were probably sleeping most of that time. I've seen this occur more than once. If you're going to schedule a call, attempt to set a time that's convenient for everyone involved (4 p.m. New York time might be good for you, but it's 9 p.m. in London and 4 a.m. in Asia-Pacific).

If the efforts of your colleague ultimately result in a good stock call, make sure to give him or her some of the credit. It's difficult for most equity analysts to see the benefit of helping their co-workers. As good behavior gets reinforced you'll see it occur more regularly.

Exhibit 9.4   Best Practice (Skills): Network within Your Firm

Steps to the Process:

1. With your food chain analysis and list of critical factors at hand, list all of the sectors or companies you don't cover that have an impact on your companies, including your company's customers and suppliers if publicly traded. Include international companies if your firm has international research personnel.
2. Determine which in-house colleagues cover these other sectors and companies.
3. If your colleagues work in a different location than you, consider asking your manager to help set up an introduction via their manager.
4. In your initial discussion with your co-workers, make your intentions clear. You are attempting to understand your companies, not take away their coverage or waste their time.
5. Provide your colleagues with a list of things you'd like to know when they occur in their sector(s) (e.g., whenever their companies discuss transportation costs or service).
6. Ask these colleagues for a wish list of things they want to know from you, if applicable. When a colleague has little to gain by sending you information, you have to work all that much harder at staying on his or her mind.
7. After your initial meeting, make a point of forwarding your colleagues insights about anything that may help them in their analysis, even if it's relatively minor.
8. If another sector is critical to yours, make a point of:
   a. Speaking with your colleague on a regular basis—possibly holding 30-minute calls or meetings once a week or once a month.
   b. Setting up a shared e-mail group.
   c. Setting up a shared file location.
9. When attempting to facilitate global collaboration, ensure the time you choose for calls is appropriate for everyone involved.
10. Make sure to thank your colleagues for their help, and recognize their efforts when they help you with a stock call, such as in year-end reviews.

Chapter 10

Get the Most from Interviewing for Insights

Ask questions that will help to understand how management thinks rather than just get the answer. Rather than asking the margin for a new contract, ask how pricing is set to ensure there is enough margin—is it cost plus or market based pricing?

—Buy-side analyst with over 10 years of experience

Introduction

The most valuable, unique insights gained during my career came from interviewing industry contacts and company management. This isn't just my view; in broker votes, the buy-side often places as much value on the management access provided by the sell-side as the sell-side research itself. Mike Manelli, an analyst with sell-side and buy-side experience, remarked on this topic, "A lot of research is just making the calls to check the facts."

Given its importance to the research process, great efforts should be taken to ensure that you get the most from your interviews. In discussing this best practice, it's important to appreciate that good interviewing skills are impossible to acquire without good *listening* and *influencing* skills, which were discussed in Chapter 4.

To ensure that they get the most from interviewing for insights, analysts should have a strategy for each of the following elements in the process:

- Thoughtful preparation
- Lead an interview to obtain insight
- Read body language to detect deception
- Triangulate to derive unique insights
- Document the meeting for future reference

Thoughtful Preparation

Routinely, I would witness sell-side competitors showing up ill-prepared for meetings with management, as evidenced by the lack of thoughtful questions. If you're going to the trouble of setting up an interview, possibly requiring a plane flight, dedicate some time to prepare. Obviously, your experience level with the company or information topic will dictate the amount of preparation required, but in general expect to spend at least 30 minutes of preparation for every hour of formal interview time. (If it's your first time meeting company management and you're doing most of the questioning, expect to spend two to three times this ratio.) The more you know going into the interview, the higher the level of discussion, which results in higher-level answers. Never use an interview with a C-level executive to get basic questions answered, such as, "What lines of business are you in?" "Where do you operate?" or "What are your margins?" unless it's a very obscure company or he or she asked for the meeting (see Exhibit 8.2 for a list of questions to explore before and during a meeting with management). Such questions damage your credibility and waste everyone's time.

Try to cultivate a relationship with your interviewee well before the interview because it will make the interviewing process easier. (Refer to Exhibit 9.3 to see how to keep the right distance with company management.) In cultivating the relationship, don't compromise your objectivity or be disingenuous, but the more you work to have a *respectful* relationship with your interviewee (notice that I didn't say *favorable*), the more productive your interviews will be.

In addition to knowing the key issues about the company or sector to be discussed (see Exhibit 8.2 for a list of questions), conduct basic research on the people you're going to interview. (Good places to start include the company's website, Bloomberg, Capital IQ, ZoomInfo, LinkedIn, and Google.) When meeting with company managers who have changed companies in the past two years, ask about their former employer, because it's unlikely they've severed all ties. Make sure to understand in advance the interviewee's likely biases, as it will impact your questions; if you're interviewing the chief lobbyist for your sector, don't expect a critical review of the sector's problems.

In advance of the meeting or conference call with company management or an information source, create a list of interview questions, following the guidelines in Exhibit 10.1.

Exhibit 10.1 Best Practice (Skills): Create Interview Questions That Will Get Answers

1. Create a list of questions well in advance of any meeting or conference call where you will be leading the line of questioning.

2. Ensure that you've done preliminary work on the critical factors so as to ask questions that will yield new insights and haven't already been answered in the past (see Exhibit 8.2 for the questions that should be answered before an interview with company management, and Exhibit 8.3 for documents to review before interviewing management). Don't ask questions on factors that won't drive a stock price unless you have exhausted all questions on the critical factors.

3. Preferably, have at least one question covering a critical factor for every three minutes of meeting time (e.g., have 20 good critical factor questions for a 60-minute meeting).

4. Build a mosaic by approaching critical factors with basic questions that can add up to a complex answer. You may not get all of the answers during your meeting or call, but if you get two or three pieces of the puzzle, it will help you gain an edge on the competition. Expecting management to help build the entire mosaic in one meeting or call is unrealistic.

5. Ask questions that will help you understand how management thinks, rather than just getting straight answers.

(Continued)

6. Approach critical factors from multiple angles by asking each of the managers about his or her individual perspective.

7. Appreciate that influencing skills are critical to success, namely the manner and order in which questions are asked often impact the quality of the interviewee's responses. Here are some psychological considerations for preparing questions, especially if meeting with management or an unknown information source:

   a. Unless you're paying the contact for his or her time, don't go right in for the kill (the information you want) but instead get to know the person by breaking the ice. Spending a few minutes learning about one another is key to developing trust and will go a long way to helping get information in the future.

   b. Somewhere early in the interview, ask a question that demonstrates you hold sector or company insights your interviewee doesn't have or hasn't made public; it doesn't need to be a material piece of information. This prevents interviewees from later exaggerating or embellishing, because they know that you understand the sector. With this approach, I've found that interviewees would be more forthcoming because I was "worthy" of a more detailed answer.

   c. Start with more simple questions first and then move on to more difficult ones; it will help the interviewee build confidence and feel less defensive, which is critical for getting insightful answers to some of the more sensitive topics.

   d. There are two primary types of questions: open and closed. Both open and closed questions should be used in the process of influencing (Dent & Brent, 2006: 35). Open questions allow respondents to give any type of answer they wish, which allows them the feeling of more control than does a closed question that requires a specific answer.

8. If you're meeting with management and have a question that may cause Regulation Fair Disclosure (Reg FD) concerns, ask a leading or double-direct question, which offers a specific assertion in your question. This will allow management an opportunity to respond to your *assertion* rather than answer a direct question that could violate Reg FD. For example, rather than ask a very direct question such as, "Do you think your California employees are going to unionize?" include an implied assertion by asking, "Will your costs increase if the unions are successful in unionizing your California operation by December?" Note, you're not asking management if the employees are going to unionize, because management won't answer that. With the elephant in the room now clearly defined, most management will take a swing at it as long as it's not responding directly to a sensitive question. In these situations I would often get enough feedback from the way management answered the question to better gauge the probability and timing of the issue. Remember that you're trying to build the mosaic, not a one-shot photograph.

9. Don't ask questions beyond the scope of the interviewee's expertise. If the manager is responsible for the Northeast region, don't ask about the West Coast unless you're prepared to accept that the person's response is probably not accurate.

If you're meeting with information sources, appreciate that they may not understand your ultimate goal of forecasting earnings or cash flow if they aren't close to the financial side of the business. For example, a John Deere dealership owner isn't likely to have a full understanding of the company's quarterly earnings or even its quarterly production, but it's plausible that you can get a feel for local product pricing or quality.

Lead an Interview to Obtain Insights

Once it's time to have the interview, make sure to follow the best practice found in Exhibit 10.2.

Exhibit 10.2   Best Practice (Skills): Lead an Interview to Obtain Insights

1. Regularly cultivate relationships with your intended information sources, not just when you need something from them.
2. For company management meetings and conference calls, especially for those where you'll be leading the discussion, conduct at least 30 minutes of preparation for every hour of interview time. Make sure to create an insightful list of questions (see Exhibit 10.1), and research the individuals you'll be interviewing to make sure you fully understand their current and prior roles.
3. If you're on the sell-side:
   a. For company visits, try to bring clients (the more assets the client controls the better); this can result in more senior management in the lineup and better responses to your questions.
   b. Make your question list available to buy-side clients just before the meeting or call begins (not any earlier because the list could make its way into the hands of management, which will allow them to rehearse answers and potentially cause their responses to be less transparent). Sell-side analysts should make the questions available in the future to buy-side clients who are interviewing management.
4. For in-person meetings, choose a good location. Normally you won't have much choice, but if you do, avoid these options:
   a. Noisy restaurants. If you've been offered a lunch or dinner spot, find a restaurant that has a private room or quiet corner. When possible, get a table that has at least 20 percent more room than the size of your party so that you have room for your notebook.
   b. Meeting outdoors. The weather is unpredictable and you're more likely to be disturbed by noise.

(Continued)

    c. Activities where you can't take notes. Playing a round of golf with a C-suite executive is a great way to build rapport, but you may not come away with any details beyond what you can write on your scorecard using a three-inch pencil.

    d. Large hotel meeting rooms. If you've been given a one-on-one with management during a sell-side conference, ask for a small room so that your interview will feel more personable. If you're given the Grand Ballroom, try to get a private room through the hotel or find a quiet coffee shop.

5. For conference calls, ensure that everyone has the dial-in number and pass code well in advance. Preferably, send out an Outlook invitation that includes the details in the event so that it's on everyone's calendars in their time zones and available on mobile devices. Use a speakerphone in a quiet room or wear a headset so as to have your hands free to take notes.

6. Be aware of time. If it takes 15 to 30 seconds to ask a question and three to four minutes for a response, you'll probably only get to seven to nine thematic questions every 30 minutes. (They may include many more brief responses, but you're not likely to tackle more than seven major themes in 30 minutes.) So make sure to ask questions that are well constructed and pertinent to the critical factors likely to drive a stock. (See recommendations in Exhibit 10.1.)

7. Run the interview.

    a. Begin the interview by showing respect to your interviewee by:

        (1) Thanking the person for his or her time.

        (2) Complimenting a quality that identifies the person as the expert you sought out to speak with (e.g., 10 years as a CFO or 25 years in the sector).

        (3) Reciprocating the favor by offering to provide the interviewee insights where your expertise can help.

    b. Some managers will drag out answers so they don't need to get to more questions. If it's clear management doesn't want to answer a question, move on unless you detect deception, in which case continue asking related questions to see if you're getting further signs of deception.

    c. Pose the question in a manner that will be answered (Dent & Brent, 2006: 35):

        (1) Phrase questions positively; if you're too forceful or negative, it will exert control over the interviewee, who will likely attempt to gain back control by being restrictive with the response.

        (2) Use language the interviewee is likely comfortable with.

        (3) Focus on one topic at a time.

    d. Use a professional and pleasant tone of questioning. If the question is asked in the wrong tone, it could illicit a negative emotion and a truncated response.

  e. Ask follow-up questions when the response: (1) isn't clear, (2) creates more questions, or (3) has signs of deception. Note that if someone appears to be using too much jargon, the person may be hiding insecurity because he or she doesn't know the subject well. If you've heard a few acronyms or jargon you don't understand, stop the speaker and ask for an explanation. Don't continue until you're comfortable with the answer.

  f. Be a good listener and show respect by (Dent & Brent, 2006: 33):

   (1) Being open-minded; don't start the interview convinced that you already know the answers.

   (2) Not interrupting.

   (3) Showing interest in the subject and avoiding distractions (e.g., not looking at your BlackBerry every two minutes).

   (4) Occasionally checking for understanding.

 8. Take notes with as much detail as possible without losing insights from what is being said. Don't be so focused on your notes that you lose an opportunity to ask a great follow-up question.

 9. If there's an on-site tour, observe the intangibles:

  a. Are the executive offices:

   (1) Opulent or run-down?

   (2) Near the operations or very distant?

  b. Do employees take pride in their workspace (desk or factory floor) and show respect for one another?

  c. Is the warehouse empty or over-filled?

  d. Are the comments from management during your interview consistent with its public presentations and regulatory filings?

10. After the interview, review your notes to: (1) highlight and tag key points; (2) create follow-up reminders regarding information you heard, such as telling firm colleagues about things you learned that may impact their companies; and (3) include details such as interviewee name, date, and location so that the notes will be easy to reference in the future.

Read Body Language to Detect Deception

Among those who research the topic of body language, there's debate about how much can be concluded when attempting to detect deception. We'd all like to know when the person on the other side of the conversation is being untruthful or at least sending us down the wrong path, especially executives of stocks we're researching. As one highly ranked sell-side analyst put it, "One of the most important jobs of an analyst is to assess the quality of management." The primary lesson from training I received in this area, which is reinforced in law enforcement books on interrogating suspects, is that there is significant subjectivity involved and much practice is required to master the skill. As you'll see in the best practice on this topic, for every cue there is a qualifier that says you can't rely on it 100 percent of the time. Further complicating matters, very often the cue must be identified within a second of introducing the stimulus (e.g., asking the person a question), which leaves opportunity for error.

With these caveats in mind, it's still useful to be aware of methods to detect deception. A best practice on this topic can be found in Exhibit 10.3 that includes elements of research conducted by the psychology and law enforcement fields, as well as lessons learned during the 300-plus face-to-face interviews I've had with company managements, all in an effort to help detect deception conveyed through body language. This is an area, probably more than any other best practice, that likely requires additional training to master.

Joe Navarro and Marvin Karlins highlight in their book *What Every Body Is Saying* that when observing body language to detect deception, most people start with a person's face and work their way down, although the face is the area that allows for concealment, unlike more revealing parts, such as the feet and legs. In their words, "Truthfulness decreases as we move from the feet to the head" (Navarro & Karlins, 2008: 55).

If you begin to see cues that you're being deceived, continue to ask questions in the topic area to see what kinds of responses you receive, but do so gently and not in an accusatory manner. If your interviewee begins to assume that you've picked up on the deception, the subject may change altogether or the interview may end. Remember that you are either onto something or you have misread the body language. During my training in this area, I was encouraged to watch television interviews like the Sunday morning political talk shows to fine-tune the skills because practice is critical to successful detection.

Given that you want to read the person's body language as well as develop rapport, when entering a room for a meeting with management, attempt to get the closest seat to the person who will be interviewed. Somewhat related, if you have the chance to choose which manager to sit next to, make a point of getting to the person who influences or understands the critical factors the best. Don't leave your seating to chance. It's critical to get information as well as build a relationship with the managers who you think are likely to move up in the organization.

Exhibit 10.3 Best Practice (Knowledge): Observing Body Language to Detect Deception

- Body gestures: One of the best indicators to watch is the interviewee's demeanor during a meeting. Does he or she appear happy you're there, or aggravated and on the defensive? If your line of questioning is accusatory (which should be avoided), you might be the cause of the reaction rather than the person's intent to deceive.
  - The interviewee not aligning with you can be a sign of deception, such as leaning away from you, stretched legs toward you, or abnormal distance given the circumstances (Navarro & Karlins, 2008: 211; Gordon & Fleisher, 2006: 64).
  - Blocking moves such as crossed arms and legs (Gordon & Fleisher, 2006: 65).
  - Placing obstacles between you, such as a glass of water or a book (Navarro & Karlins, 2008: 213).
  - Conducting diversionary activities, such as playing with an object, clearing off desk, or fixing hair while talking (Nance, 2000: 190; Javers, 2010). (An insecure CEO I interviewed watched TV for part of the interview.)
  - A complete lack of normal body movement during the interview, such as no typical gestures to show emphasis (Navarro & Karlins, 2008: 226).
- Manipulation: Some people are masters of deception and may use techniques to influence you to overlook their deception:
  - Touching you briefly on the shoulder or arm, which is used by restaurant waitstaff seeking a bigger tip (Goman, 2008: 132).
  - Mimicking your body movements, such as crossing arms after you do so (Pease & Pease, 2006: 260).

(Continued)

- Mouth:
  - A dry mouth can be sign of deception, which can manifest itself in the form of a person licking lips, clearing throat, making hard swallows, or a cracking voice (Navarro & Karlins, 2008: 194, 217; Gordon & Fleisher, 2006: 69).
  - If a smile is held too long, appears tight, doesn't include eyebrow movement, or the expression looks forced, it could be a sign of deception (Navarro & Karlins, 2008: 169; Gordon & Fleisher, 2006: 67).
  - When lips appear tight in response to a question, there could be deception, especially if this hasn't been characteristic of the person during other parts of the interview (Navarro & Karlins, 2008: 189).

- Face:
  - When interviewees cover the mouth, touch the nose, or look down, it may indicate lack of belief in what the speaker is saying (at least for Americans), but it could also be a stress-reliever, which is simply a sign that the person is uncomfortable and doesn't have to be linked to deception (Navarro & Karlins, 2008: 222; Gordon & Fleisher, 2006: 63).
  - If the head is nodding up and down (a typical gesture for *yes*) and the person is saying *no* to the question (or vice versa), there could be deception. I've seen this first hand more than once.

- Eyes:
  - When the eye pupils are dilated or there is inappropriate closing of the eyes or squinting, it can indicate deception (Gordon & Fleisher, 2006: 69). If you know you're about to ask a controversial question that could lead to deception, stay focused on the eyes to see if pupils dilate or the interviewee squints (Navarro & Karlins, 2008: 173).
  - If the person won't look you in the eyes, you should be on guard for possible deception (Nance, 2000: 185), but some experts say it only indicates the speaker is having a problem (Navarro & Karlins, 2008: 216) (e.g., trying to form a thought more clearly without distraction).
  - Increased eye blinking can also be a sign that a person is troubled, but once again, not necessarily because of deception (Navarro & Karlins, 2008: 183).
  - Prolonged eye contact may be a trick to convince you of the speaker's sincerity (Gordon & Fleisher, 2006: 67) or an attempt to dominate you (Navarro & Karlins, 2008: 183).

- In situations where management has been accused of wrongdoing, if the interviewee personally attacks the accuser, it can be a sign of a cover-up; a highly personal attack may indicate a high level of defensiveness from management, which should start to raise yellow flags.

Triangulate to Derive Unique Insights

Some might call it mosaic theory, while others call it triangulating. The logic is that you piece together a conclusion from elements of the puzzle, without being given the direct answer. For management to give you a critical piece of information without disclosing it to the public would be in violation of Reg FD. As such, if you want insightful information, you'll likely need to ask about the pieces of the puzzle and build up a reasonable conclusion, which may give you a proprietary edge in picking stocks.

This concept is probably best understood by highlighting an example. During a Shanghai facility tour, a fictitious global parcel company tells you the following: (1) the facility processes 50,000 import/export packages per day, and (2) Shanghai is the largest facility in China, making up over 50 percent of China's volume. From a prior discussion you know Asia-Pacific packages generate about $60 per piece. Based on this information, you can compute China generates roughly $1.4 billion of annual revenue, which turns out to be 3 percent of the company's overall revenue (geographic segmentation the company doesn't disclose).

To get to this answer, you need to make a few estimates, such as the percent Shanghai makes up of all China. If management said it makes up "more than 50 percent" of China revenue, I would use 55 to 60 percent; if it was a much higher number, management probably would have said it makes up "more than two-thirds" of China's revenues. (To avoid computational errors, when converting from small numbers, like shipments per day, to big numbers, like annual revenue, I find it best to avoid truncating numbers to millions until all the math is done.) Here's the math:

Packages per day in Shanghai	50,000
Revenue per package	$60
Shanghai daily revenue	$3,000,000
Working days per year	250
Annual revenue from Shanghai	$750,000,000
Shanghai as a percent of China	55%
Revenue from the rest of China	$613,636,364
Total China revenue	$1,363,636,364
Company's annual global revenue	$42,000,000,000
China as a percent of total revenue	3.2%

Why is this information important? The company has never disclosed the size of China, but it regularly eludes to the fact that China is growing at "high double-digits" each quarter. Now you can back out China to determine how much the company is growing from the rest of its international markets. If it turns out the company's entire international division grew revenue $700 million last year (as reported in the company's financial filings), you can see that almost all of it came from China. Here's the logic: If "high double-digits" growth (per management) resulted in $1.4 billion of revenue from China (estimated above), this implies that $560 million to $645 million of growth over the past 12 months came from China. If the company's total global growth was only $700 million last year, you can quickly conclude that it's all coming from China, which should raise some questions about the slow growth in the other regions.

Assumed "High Double-Digit" Growth Rate for China	Implied Prior Year Revenue from China (MM)	Implied Annual Revenue Growth from China (MM)
70%	$802	$561
80%	$758	$606
90%	$718	$646

In another example, during a company visit, when speaking with the chief marketing officer early in the day, he boasts that the company just took pricing up 20 percent on a customer's contract renewal. You check with him to make sure the contract wasn't unusual in terms of size or its previous pricing level. Later in the day you ask the CFO, "What percentage of contracts are likely to be renewed this year?" to which she replies "25 percent." You check to make sure this is normal by asking, "Is it normal for about 25 percent of your business to roll over each year?" And verify that almost all of the company's revenue is under contract by asking, "Do you generate more than 10 percent of your revenue from spot business?" to which she replies, "No, it's a small amount." From these data points, you can begin to conclude overall pricing will go up 5 percent this year (25 percent × 20 percent), *and each of the next three years,* barring any change in market dynamics. This example comes from a real experience that led to my secular call on railroad pricing in 2005. I'm not sure management realized that it were giving me all of the pieces to the puzzle, but it wasn't difficult to get excited when my earnings estimates were 10 to 20 percent above consensus due to these large, unexpected price increases that were almost certain to take place given that they were being rolled into multiyear contracts.

Many analysts don't reach these types of conclusions for two reason. First, they don't ask questions in a manner to quantify critical factors. Instead, they ask open-ended questions that let management meander down the "happy lane" by describing everything management wants to showcase in the interview. Or they ask a question so directly that the manager can't answer it over concern of violating Reg FD. The second biggest problem is that they don't take detailed notes when speaking with management (missing out on having the information to refer to later) or they don't organize their notes in a manner that lets them easily refer back to the mosaic tiles.

It's also important that when you're asking questions of management, not to be perceived as trying to catch a manager in a logic trap. One of my sell-side competitors would relish in getting management to trip up in a meeting or a conference call, which management eventually caught on to. Over time management just stopped answering his questions or would provided him a non-answer answer. (I think the competitor suffered from the "I want everyone to know I'm smarter than management" syndrome, which hurt his ability to get good information.) Instead, be the humble person who politely smiles after getting a response, as though all is good in the world. There will be time for celebrating newfound insights later.

Also, before making a big call with triangulated information, it's best to go back to senior management with your assertion and let it try to tear it down. (Assertion does not mean discussing your stock recommendation; have the discussion around the factor that's likely to lead to the change.) A manager likely won't confirm your view because that may violate Reg FD, but if he or she doesn't dissuade you from your newfound view, you can be fairly certain you're on to something. Also, for sell-side analysts, be careful how you publish your view. By writing, "After a recent meeting with management, it's clear pricing is increasing 5 percent for the next four years," you'll likely raise red flags with regulators, your compliance department, and the company's law department, something no analyst should ever want. Since you truly pieced this together, it should be conveyed as, "Our work finds that pricing is likely to increase much faster than consensus expectations, a view the company did not refute during our recent meeting."

Triangulation doesn't have to be just with management information. It can be the result of information learned from multiple sources. In fact, in the customer pricing example above, I went to a number of large customers of the companies I followed to ask if they were experiencing 20 percent increases on their contracts. When I learned a number of them were (some said they were experiencing 100 percent rate increases), I knew there would likely be a big upside surprise. This may sound like common sense, but always be looking for different angles from which to quantify and assess your critical factors. I had a large *privately held* company tell me how much its new fuel-efficient diesel trucks were hurting fleet utilization due to higher maintenance costs, which I then applied to a *publicly traded* company that had just purchased a large number of the trucks. When I spoke to the publicly traded company, it said it "couldn't quantify" the negative impact yet, which may have been an honest statement, but I didn't want to wait for the answer to be released to the entire financial community before taking action on the stock.

Document the Meeting for Future Reference

Most of us were required to take notes during college and, as such, we assume we're good notetakers. That might be the case, but I've been surprised by how often analysts aren't taking notes during an important meeting. (Refer to Exhibit 5.2 in Chapter 5 for the pros and cons of each type of notetaking system.) If you have perfect recall of everything you hear, notetaking isn't necessary, but for the rest of us, here are thoughts that should help to capture important insights:

- Appreciate that as experience and knowledge grows, the level of notetaking can decline. But this doesn't mean someone who's become an expert doesn't need to take any notes. The volume of notetaking will depend upon:
  - Your prior knowledge of the topic
  - The value of the source
- If it's a new topic that could cover critical factors for your stocks, and you're taking less than one page of notes every 10 to 20 minutes, you're probably losing good information (I would usually take 10 to 20 pages of notes in a half-day meeting with management).
- If you're so focused on notetaking that you can't ask relevant questions, you may be writing down too much detail.
- While there's no written rule, digitally recording interviews for notetaking is frowned upon. However, if you're interviewing an industry source who has no connection with a publicly traded company, you're more likely to be allowed to record.
- When in person, avoid taking notes on a computer (laptop, notebook, netbook, etc.) unless the interviewee is from an industry where it's common practice. Having a laptop between you and an executive, while the keyboard is clicking and you're looking at the screen, sends a message that you don't have much interest in his or her view, especially if the interviewee is of the baby boomer generation and didn't grow up in a world of laptop-based interviews. It also sends the message that everything said is going to be published for the world to read.

- As mentioned in Chapter 5, if you conduct many telephone interviews and intend to type your notes, use a quiet or silent keyboard (one that doesn't click, like most laptops—a number of vendors sell them).* When the person on the other end hears the keyboard clicking every time that person speaks, he or she will be less forthcoming because every word is being documented.

- To make the notes more valuable for future use, make sure the following are at the beginning of each interview:
  - Name of interviewee
  - Date
  - Location (e.g., person's office, hotel conference room)

- Try to number every page, if not during the meeting, then afterward.

- After the interview, (e.g., downtime sitting at the airport or on the flight), read through the notes, highlighting key points (I would put a star in the left margin). Enter the key points into an electronic format that can be searched and retrieved in the future, such as the tools discussed in Chapter 5.

---

* The IT department at my firm considered me a headache because I was always testing new technology to see if it would help make me or my team more productive. Unfortunately, I didn't find many winners. With that said, I'm a big fan of Lenovo's laptop-style keyboard that can be used with a desktop PC. The keys are quiet, which is important during telephone interviews, and the built-in mouse incorporated into the keyboard speeds up navigation. I also like the digital pen that integrates with OneNote, made by Capturx, because it speeds up transferring hand-written notes to a digital format for storing, retrieving, and indexing. At the time of this writing, it was the only digital pen that integrated with OneNote without the need for additional accessories.

PART 3

GENERATING QUANTITATIVE INSIGHTS

In the prior section I explored identifying and speaking with industry sources to isolate the critical factors likely to drive a stock. In this section, I discuss the use of the quantitative elements of financial analysis to convert information learned from those sources into earnings and cash flow forecasts. I also explore tools that help to identify or quantify critical factors such as forensic accounting, statistical analysis, and Microsoft Excel. These tools, more than any others in the book, are best mastered through formal training.

While these quantitative tools can be very useful, the ultimate goal is to pick stocks, not to show others you've conducted a complex survey or created a detailed spreadsheet. All of the quantitative efforts should be focused on forecasting critical factors, which will be combined in the next section with valuation in order to derive price targets. It's too easy to find yourself sitting at your desk until 10 p.m. reviewing 300 rows of a spreadsheet, only to later conclude that the time wasn't spent in an area likely to move a stock. For most analysts, there's an innate temptation to focus on the numbers, but just make sure it's leading down a path that could result in a stock idea.

Research by its very nature will result in dead ends, but knowing when to cut your losses and move on to the next project is a skill developed over time.

This section begins by raising an analyst's skepticism about data, because often there are deceptive games played with numbers. I then explore the most applicable elements of statistics, because although it can be a powerful tool, it's also one that leads a user unknowingly to the wrong answer if not utilized correctly. Before conducting any analysis of data, it's imperative to ensure that the analyst understands how it's computed and if any adjustments have been made. Once an analyst is comfortable that the data is comparable, there are many Excel statistical tools that can help improve financial modeling.

I then explore surveys, one of the most proprietary forms of research. Depending on their size, surveys can become a major undertaking and should only be considered if the benefits far outweigh the costs of both time and money

The next chapter uses the basic principles of forensic accounting to identify the yellow flags that could indicate management deception. I'm not expecting analysts to be forensic accountants, but you shouldn't just ignore a company's accounting. There are a number of basic steps that can be taken to identify companies that are under pressure to manipulate their results as well as methods to spot anomalies.

Given that Excel is such a critical element of a financial analyst's job, an application that can leverage intelligence, insight, and time, it's imperative to master more than just the basics. It's unrealistic to cover every relevant Excel feature in the limited space of a chapter, which is why the best practice focuses on helping analysts self-assess their knowledge of Excel's 43 most applicable features for equity research. I then highlight the best practices used for building workbooks for financial analysis in an effort to avoid creating files that are unruly or difficult for others to follow.

The section concludes with the best practices for generating a company earnings and cash flow forecast, including the possibility of acquiring the model as well as building it from the ground up. All of the efforts above culminate in creating an accurate financial forecast or range of forecasts. I advocate starting by quantifying the two to four critical factors for each company under base, upside, and downside scenarios and then putting them into the financial model to create three forward earnings or cash flow forecasts. These forecasts will be the key input to the valuation discussion in the next section.

Chapter 11

Detect Deceptive Numbers

Be skeptical of any data you receive from others. Just because a chart looks good in a company's presentation doesn't mean it's conveying the information in a form you need for making investment decisions. Most importantly, start by assessing the biases of those providing the numbers; they will almost always have them. Even the press has an agenda—getting more viewers or readers, which is why they often inflate the importance of new information. Taking a line from the Watergate scandal, "follow the money" to see who is paying for this particular data series to be collected and distributed. If it's funded by anyone other than analysts similar to you, there's a good chance it has biases that must be understood before using it to make an investment decision.

Exhibit 11.1 has my top 10 most common factors to consider in order to avoid deception with numbers, followed by specific discussions of charts, ratios, and statistics.

Exhibit 11.1 Best Practice (Knowledge): Spotting the Top 10 Deceptions When Presented with Data

1. Complexity offers opportunity for deception. If it's too difficult to understand (or the other person to explain), ask for a breakdown of the components. Even something as complicated as landing a 747 jumbo jet can be broken down into simple-to-understand components.

(Continued)

2. Be leery of sources that extrapolate future trends at the same rate as the past. If Microsoft had continued its 1980s growth rate into the 1990s and beyond, it would have become the entire U.S. GDP. "Trees don't grow to the sky" is a good adage to keep in mind when someone fails to have a slowdown in his or her future trends.

3. Don't let someone else choose the time period for your analysis. Companies are notorious for providing information back to when things troughed so that management can look fantastic at running the business. If a company says it has had five quarters of double-digit growth, it should beg the question, "What happened six quarters ago?" In general, companies focus on time periods that accentuate the positives and hide the negatives.

4. Be mindful of survivorship biases that are prevalent in the investment community. Struggling companies are often dropped from popular stock indexes even though the stock is still held in portfolios, which causes the pain to be felt twice (stock does poorly before it's dropped; then when it's removed from the index, the benchmark index is immune while the portfolio is not).

5. Be skeptical of survey data unless you're comfortable that the publisher has minimal biases. There are many tricks that can be played to get the desired answer, such as how the questions are asked or how the survey population is selected. For example, asking 30 high-school-aged adolescents, "Would you prefer to chew this brand of gum or increase your chances of getting cavities?" would likely yield results that could lead the company to say, "80 percent of respondents said they prefer to chew our gum." If survey data is critical to your analysis, do your best to see the questionnaire and identify how the population was selected.

6. When a company releases earnings, read its release but look at the numbers in *your* format. Companies have an incentive to spin the numbers in the most positive light possible. My general rule is to immediately compare the company's pretax income with my forecast and then work up the income statement to find the variance. For some industries, cash flow is the more transparent data point.

7. At a minimum, a company's revenue and earnings should grow from inflation each year. As such, be skeptical when a company says it "achieved record revenue" in the quarter or "has grown EPS for the past five years." What you really want to know is how much have earnings grown beyond general economic inflation or compared with the company's peers.

8. The fewer facts and numbers used by an expert, the more skeptical you should be. Try it yourself by watching a few guests respond to questions on

CNBC and see how many facts or numbers are used. Information sources who use data for their analysis should have the most important ones in memory, whereas those who aren't fact-based repeatedly say they'll have to "get back to you."

9. If you're given facts or data that appear too far from reality, you have every reason to ask for the back-up supporting data. Too often the "rookie mistake" is not asking follow-up questions over concern of looking like a rookie.

10. Reputable data is usually sourced. If a data series is important to your investment conclusion, then make sure you know the source.

Detecting Deceptions in Charts

Charts can be misleading. Be leery when:

1. The left and right scales are for different information but the scales are not proportionate to one another (e.g., the left axis scale goes from 100 to 200, which is a 100 percent increase, whereas the right axis goes from 50 to 150 which is a 200 percent increase). Ideally, if two data series are being compared, they are both on one relative scale (starting at 0, 1, or 100).

2. The range of the vertical scale is either so wide that the data looks like it hardly moves from one data point to the next, or the range is so narrow that wild fluctuations appear from one to the next. If the vertical scale doesn't start at zero, make sure you appreciate why; there could be a good reason, but it could also be deception.

3. The most current data is on the left and the oldest data is on the right. In the modern financial markets, data is usually displayed with the oldest data on the left and the most current data on the right. You should question the motive of the data's presenter if it's in reverse order.

4. Time series:
   a. One data series that includes inflation is being compared with another that doesn't.
   b. A log scale is not used where it should be, or is used where it shouldn't be. In a log scale, the distance between two points will represent the same percent change anywhere in the graph. It's most frequent valid use is to display inflation-impacted data over long periods of time, such as a stock price movement or economic trends over a 20- to 30-year period. If a log scale is not being used for this type of data, you should try to convert it to get a better visual perspective.

Detecting Deceptions in Ratios

1. If you're being given data as a ratio, make sure you fully appreciate the numerator and denominator. If a company says it operates in half the country, is it a geographic half or population half (or something else)?
2. Appreciate the difference between a percent change and a point change. If GDP is 4 percent compared with 2 percent last quarter, it shouldn't be characterized as "doubling" (although the press regularly makes this incorrect mathematical leap). In this instance, the proper way to describe the change is a 200 basis point (bps) or two full points increase from one period to the next.
3. When discussing market share, companies will often define it very narrowly when discussing their current share but widely when discussing growth opportunities. I saw this with an express parcel company in terms of its exposure to China. When discussing how well it was doing relative to the competition, it would define the addressable market very narrowly, as only the percent of *small packages imported to or exported from China*, but when the topic of growth opportunities came up, it would

remind everyone that China has four times as many people as the United States. The rub here is that the domestic Chinese package market is so competitive that Western companies would struggle to make a profit if they approached it like they do the U.S. market; so to imply it could offer four times the revenue or profit of the U.S. market is misleading.

4. When a company says there has been X percent improvement in its product or its efficiency in producing a product, ask, "Off of what?" For example, if the company had one defect every 1,000 units sold and now has one defect every 2,000 units sold, it could say that "quality has doubled," which is misleading because the focus is on the defects rather than the non-defective products.

Statistical Misconceptions

1. Correlation does not automatically mean causation. Umbrella sales are highly correlated with precipitation levels, but they don't cause the rain. If there is a strong correlation, additional work should be done to determine if there is causation.

2. All averages are not created equal. If it's an important number, make sure you know if it's the mean, median, or mode. For example, the "average" price of a house in a given market may be $200,000 using the mean but only $150,000 using the median. This occurs because a few very highly priced homes distort the market. If you have access to the data, put it on a scatter plot to see if there is a normal distribution. If not, the three types of averages will vary.

As a financial analyst, you'll come across thousands of numbers every day and won't have the time to scrutinize every one. But the numbers that surround the critical factors of your highest-profile companies, especially those that are the basis for your investment thesis, should be reviewed carefully.

Chapter 12

Leverage Statistics
for Insights

S tatistics can help financial analysts identify trends and create more accurate forecasts. You're an equity research analyst, not a statistician; so don't be embarrassed if you haven't learned some of the more mysterious statistical terms, like Spearman's rank coefficient. But it's relatively easy to learn some basic concepts to improve your analysis. To avoid getting lost in the complexity of the statistics field, this best practice is heavily focused on creating example solution sets for an analyst researching Burlington Northern Santa Fe (BNI became a privately held company in 2010). One can't expect to cover all elements of statistics in one chapter, which is why I've chosen to focus on a few statistical concepts that most analysts can use in their daily routines:

- Appreciating differences among data series
- Using *regression* analysis to improve forecasting
- Using *multivariate regression* analysis to help prioritize financial modeling

I would like to thank Chris Gowlland for his contribution to the best practices covering the area of statistics. Chris is a senior quantitative analyst at Delaware Investments. Any material discussed here does not necessarily reflect the opinions, methods, or views of his firm.

Before delving into these topics I begin with a word of caution. There are more ways to use statistics incorrectly than correctly, even unintentionally. So beware that just because you know how to get output from an Excel statistical function doesn't mean that you're going to draw the right conclusion. Lesson here: Statistical tools can be dangerous if not fully understood.

Appreciating Differences among Data Series

In working with new research associates and junior analysts during my career, it was common to come across flawed analyses because they failed to understand that all data is not created equally. Make sure if you're comparing two data series, computing a rate of change, or appending a historical data series with new data, that you're really comparing apples with apples. Here are some important considerations that are explained more fully in Exhibit 12.1:

- Adjustments for seasonality
- Annualizing a monthly or quarterly run rate
- Adjustments for inflation
- Moving averages
- Data revisions

Using Regression Analysis to Improve Forecasting

It's fairly safe to say stock price movements are significantly impacted by changes in expected earnings or cash flows. As I discuss later in Chapter 20, these certainly aren't the only influences on stock prices, but they are definitely one of the main areas of attention. Consequently, a model to help forecast the future is an important tool. There are at least two areas where an analyst can use statistics to improve forecasting:

- Identifying macro factors that can help predict company-specific factors.

Exhibit 12.1 Best Practice (Knowledge): Considerations When Comparing Data Series

Concept	Mechanics	Why Should You Care?	Solution
Adjustments for seasonality: There is seasonality in almost all economic data series because our economy doesn't run at the same rate 52 weeks of the year. Shopping peaks in December for the holidays, while Florida rental home pricing peaks in April for spring break.	Computations are made using historical data to determine the average activity in each month or quarter as a percent of the entire year. This *seasonal adjustment factor* is then applied to the raw data to derive a seasonally adjusted figure.	If you're trying to use macro data to better understand the drivers of quarterly corporate results, which aren't seasonally adjusted, you'll probably need to use non–seasonally adjusted data for comparative purposes. Also, the seasonal adjustment factor will usually change over time, which (1) will make comparing a current period with one in the distant past less meaningful, or (2) could cause your historical data to become stale as adjustment factors change.	• Do not compare one data series that is seasonally adjusted to another that isn't unless you're sure it has no seasonality. An easy way to eliminate this problem is to analyze the change on a year-over-year basis (e.g., March this year versus March last year). • Make sure to download the entire historical data series every time a new analysis is conducted in order to ensure it's using the most current adjustment factors for all of the data. • Some seasonality can't be easily adjusted because it changes every year, such as the timing of Thanksgiving, Easter, and the Chinese New Year.

(Continued)

Exhibit 12.1 Best Practice (Knowledge): Considerations When Comparing Data Series *(Continued)*

Concept	Mechanics	Why Should You Care?	Solution
Annualizing a monthly or quarterly run rate: Somewhat related to seasonality adjustments, some monthly and quarterly data is reported on an annualized run rate, such as auto sales.	The raw data for the period (which also may have been seasonally adjusted) is multiplied by 12 if monthly and by 4 if quarterly.	The biggest challenge here is making sure you're not comparing monthly data with annualized data. If you're deriving the number of new monthly auto loans from monthly auto sales, you'll need to use the monthly auto sales figure rather than the annualized run rate.	• Ensure that the two data series are covering the same time period for each data point, or make adjustments to ensure that you're comparing like with like.
Adjustments for inflation: Almost every data series conveyed in a currency (such as the dollar value of retail sales) will have an inflation component, whereas most non-currency data does not have this element.	The *nominal* number that is reported is the actual dollar amount spent, whereas the *real* number backs out the impact of inflation.	If a portfolio manager asked for the long-term growth rate of *demand* for your sector, would you use revenue or units? They will likely yield very different answers. Your response should be, "Which would you like?" or provide both.	• When comparing a currency-based data series with one that isn't, inflation may need to be removed to make the comparison meaningful. • Always know if your data series has been adjusted for inflation.

Exhibit 12.1 Best Practice (Knowledge): Considerations When Comparing Data Series *(Continued)*

Concept	Mechanics	Why Should You Care?	Solution
Moving averages: Some data is too volatile to glean insights on a daily, weekly, or even monthly basis and is thus converted to a moving average, which has a smoothing effect.	The most recent data point is expressed as part of an average, which is computed over a date range such as the past 10 days or past 6 months.	New data points can begin to move in a new direction before the overall moving average makes a pronounced change. Those watching the individual points may have a competitive advantage over those just looking at the average.	• Understand how the moving average is computed. • If it's an important data series, look at each new raw data point added in addition to the moving average.
Data revisions: Data series that rely on sample populations are often revised later. Separately, as seasonal adjustment factors change over time, it can cause all of the historical data in the series to be revised.	When new, more accurate information is made available, the *preliminary* data is revised to *final*. Or, in the case of seasonality, as new adjustment factors are computed, historical data may be restated.	If you're given a spreadsheet of historical data, don't assume it's accurate. It may have been when that person downloaded it, but revisions have made the data obsolete.	• When possible, get a fresh new data series to ensure that all adjustments are made (unless you're interested in looking at the accuracy of the preliminary data).
Comparability of time periods: If the data is presented as a *percent change* from one period to the next, it needs to cover the same time period if being used for comparison with another data series.	A "5 percent change in quarterly sales" can be year-over-year or quarter-over-quarter. If the latter, the data may or may not have been seasonally adjusted.	A common mistake is when the change in quarterly GDP (which is often expressed as a quarter-over-quarter figure) is compared with the change in a company's quarterly earnings per share (EPS), which is usually expressed on a year-over-year basis.	• When using a percent change data series, make sure to know if it is computed year-over-year or sequentially. • Ideally, get the underlying data (that the percent change data is derived from) to avoid comparison problems.

- Identifying the elements of a company's financial forecast that require unique insights versus those elements that move with other factors in the forecast.

The next section provides examples of how to accomplish both of these.

Professional statisticians can use powerful stand-alone software for their analysis, but most financial analysts won't need anything beyond Microsoft Excel for their work. Of course, if you do have more advanced knowledge of statistics, or if you're working with particularly large or intractable data sets, then you may want to use more sophisticated software. Many academic statisticians use the R application, which is free to download and reasonably user-friendly once a few hours have been invested in understanding its idiosyncrasies. But I'm going to use Excel exclusively in this chapter. If you're using Excel, you'll want to ensure that the *Analysis ToolPak* or *Data Analysis* is available in the toolbar (depending on your version of Excel, this may already be installed).

If you have a general understanding of statistical regression, you may be tempted to start working on that immediately. But there's a recognized body of knowledge in statistics known as *exploratory data analysis,* which is helpful for understanding the characteristics of your data. In particular, plotting the data on various types of charts can help reveal patterns that may not be immediately obvious when expressed in tabular form. One valuable first step is to use a scatterplot in order to identify potential relationships between two variables. It's conventional to put the explanatory variable on the horizontal x axis, and the response variable on the vertical y axis.

The scatterplot may reveal a non-random pattern that indicates how the explanatory and response variables are linked. In collecting data for an analysis, it's usually best to go back as far as possible, ensuring you capture at least two economic cycles and use time intervals that are as short as available (e.g., quarterly company data for at least the last 10 years).

Exhibit 12.2   Scatterplot with No Association

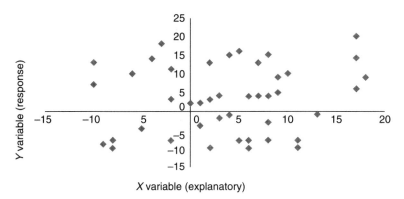

Exhibit 12.2 is an example of a scatterplot that suggests that any relationship between the explanatory and response variables is fairly weak, or perhaps non-existent. Judging from the graph, different values of x between -10 and $+15$ can lead to almost any value of y between -10 and $+20$. The graph does show that when x is between $+15$ and $+20$, all the observed values of y are positive, but it's difficult to be confident that this is a strong relationship, since there are only four observations. In general, this scatterplot suggests that statistical analysis may not be fruitful.

The graphs in Exhibit 12.3 show some of the most common patterns we see in a scatterplot when there is a relationship between x and y:*

After determining whether the scatterplot reveals an association, the analyst should examine the direction, shape, and variation around the

---

*There are multiple other possibilities too. If the relationship between two variables has shifted over time, then you may be able to see a step change in your scatterplot. In some circumstances, you might see curves with multiple inflection points—quadratics, cubics, and other odd shapes. There are statistical models for coping with all these situations, but they're well beyond the scope of this discussion. If you encounter such patterns, don't blindly rely on linear methods for your analysis, as your results will probably be unreliable. Find someone who knows enough about statistics to be able to advise you on how to proceed.

Exhibit 12.3   Scatterplots Where Association Exists

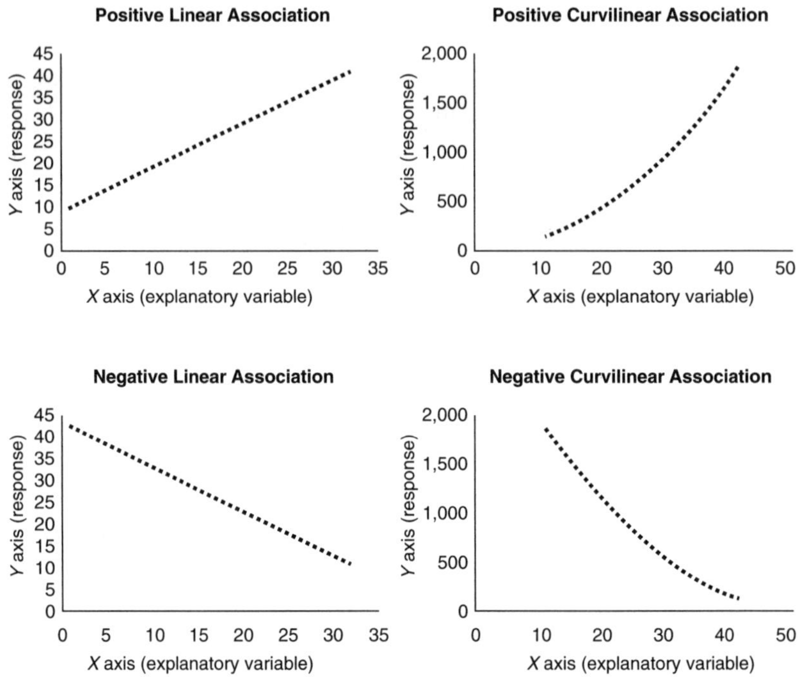

Copyright McGraw-Hill and AnalystSolutions

pattern. Do the x and y variables increase in the same direction or opposite directions? Does the pattern resemble a curve or a line? And, finally, are there few or many data points that seem to be scattered far from the main pattern—what statisticians refer to as *outliers* (Stine & Foster, 2010)?

Very often, you will be using data that has been generated through time, for instance, quarterly revenues or monthly production statistics. In such cases, you may want to plot the series through time in order to see the longer-term trends, or if there is evidence of seasonality.

The most commonly taught statistical procedure for examining the relationship between two variables is *linear regression*, sometimes known as *ordinary least squares* (OLS). As the term suggests, a linear regression assumes that the relationship between x and y approximates a straight line, like the scatterplots in the left panels of Exhibit 12.3. If the scatterplots show some curvature, like the ones in the right panels, then it may be appropriate to transform one or both series so that the relationship is brought toward approximate linearity (Mills, 1991). If you make such a transformation, then regression methods may provide sufficiently detailed analysis for forecasting purposes.

Example Problem: Predicting Intermodal Revenue

An analyst is trying to forecast the intermodal revenue for Burlington Northern (BNI), which is basically the revenue from hauling truck trailers and international containers on railroad cars. The first step is to look at the intermodal revenue series itself, which is shown in Exhibit 12.4.

The graph shows that intermodal revenue grew quite steadily from 1996 to 2003, then much more rapidly from 2004 to 2007, before crashing in late 2008. Of course, a financial analyst at the beginning of 2004 would only have had access to the data from 1996 to 2003, and thus would not have been able to use the historical series to predict the

Exhibit 12.4 Quarterly Intermodal Revenue

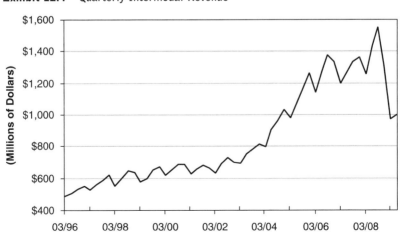

acceleration from 2004 onward. Similarly, a financial analyst in early 2008 would only have seen the series from 1996 to 2007, and would not have been able to use that information to predict the abrupt decline in the fourth quarter of 2008 and first quarter of 2009.

When building and testing statistical models, it's often valuable to try "pseudo-out-of-sample" approaches—for instance, taking only the information known up to the end of 2003 in order to see how well the model would have performed in 2004, or taking only the information known up to the end of 2004 to see how the model would have performed in 2005. In general, statistical models tend to perform poorly when trends change abruptly, and it's important to be aware of their limitations.

The graph in Exhibit 12.4 shows that the intermodal revenues have a sawtooth pattern that may indicate seasonal influences on the data. Intermodal revenues peak in the second half of each year, and then drop significantly in the first quarter. A statistician building a time-series model might decide to incorporate that seasonality into the analysis in an explicit fashion, but this may not be necessary for your purposes.

Suppose that you want to test whether macroeconomic factors can help you predict BNI's quarterly intermodal revenues. You would expect that intermodal revenues are linked to industrial production, so you might decide to look at two components of the U.S. industrial production statistics published by each month, namely durable manufacturing and total motor vehicle assemblies. A scatterplot can help you determine which of these two variables may be appropriate in a regression model to predict BNI intermodal revenue.

As seen in the Exhibit 12.5 scatterplots below, the manufacturing index appears to have a better association with BNI's intermodal revenue than motor assemblies. The data points in the first scatterplot are grouped tightly together, which suggests a relationship. In contrast, motor assemblies show a weak association with BNI's intermodal revenue, as is seen

Exhibit 12.5   Examples of Scatterplots

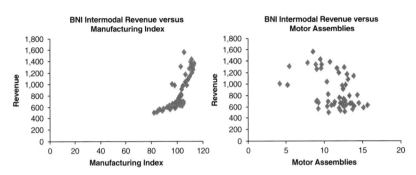

by large amounts of scatter. This intuitively makes sense because inter-modal consists of a wide range of consumer goods and other durables, and not just auto parts.

There are a couple of other noteworthy features in the first scatterplot. In terms of the patterns described earlier in the chapter, there appears to be a positive curvilinear association. Moreover, though there are a few outliers, the relationship appears to be reasonably tight. But given the characteristics of the scatterplot, it seems reasonable to test how well linear regression can explain the relationship between these two variables.

A quick way to examine the performance of a linear regression is to use Excel's regression line option on the scatterplot already created. As expected, this doesn't fit the curved relationship very well (see Exhibit 12.6): the points which are lowest and highest on the vertical axis tend to fall on the left of the line, while those in the middle of the distribution fall on the right. Actually, the regression line doesn't do a terrible job here; in some statistical contexts, an R-squared of 0.62 would be considered acceptably high. But since you already suspect that there may be a nonlinear relationship between intermodal revenue and the durable manufacturing index, you want to try adjusting for that nonlinearity directly.

Exhibit 12.6 Scatterplot and Regression Line for Intermodal Revenue and Manufacturing Index

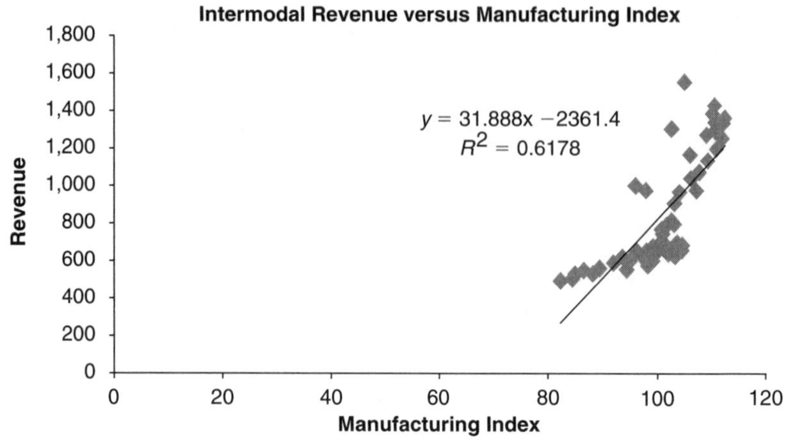

Intermodal Revenue versus Manufacturing Index

$$y = 31.888x - 2361.4$$
$$R^2 = 0.6178$$

These results suggest that it may be desirable to transform the variables so that the relationship between them will be linear. An easy way to accomplish this is by applying a logarithmic transformation to both the explanatory and response variables. The relevant command in Excel is $LOG(x, n)$ where x is your number and n is the logarithm base; if you omit n, then it will default to base 10, which is fine for the work here.* Taking logarithms will change how the regression coefficients are interpreted. If you take the logs of y only, you interpret the relationship this way: a unit change in x is associated with a percentage change in y. By contrast, if you take the logs of both y and x, then the slope can be interpreted as *elasticity* in economic terms; in other words, the slope provides an estimate of how a percentage change in x will produce a percentage change in y. Logarithms can also be useful when you're dealing with data whose values cover wide ranges such as four companies with market caps of $100 million, $500 million, $1 billion, and $50 billion.

---

* Taking logarithms in base 10 also provides an easy reality check for your results. If you take numbers in millions of dollars and apply the LOG command, then a logarithm with a 2-handle should indicate hundreds of millions, one with a 3-handle should indicate billions, and one with a 4-handle should indicate tens of billions.

Exhibit 12.7 Regression Output for Log of Durable Manufacturing and the Log of Intermodal Revenues

Regression Statistics	
Multiple R	0.81
R-squared	0.66
Adjusted R-squared	0.65
Standard Error	0.09
Observations	54.00

ANOVA

	Df	SS	MS	F	Significance F
Regression	1.00	0.74	0.74	100.63	0.00
Residual	52.00	0.38	0.01		
Total	53.00	1.12			

	Coefficients	Standard Error	t Stat	P-value	Lower 95%	Upper 95%	Lower 95%	Upper 95%
Intercept	−4.26	0.71	−5.96	0.00	−5.69	−2.82	−5.69	−2.82
log (manufacturing index)	3.58	0.36	10.03	0.00	2.86	4.29	2.86	4.29

Using Excel's regression tool, the relationship between the log of durable manufacturing and the log of intermodal revenues is shown in Exhibit 12.7.

Interpret the output in graphical form, which can be found in Exhibit 12.8. Notice how the scatterplot of log of intermodal revenue versus log of manufacturing index now appears more linear compared with the original scatterplot.

As discussed above, because both intermodal revenue and the durable manufacturing index have been transformed into logarithms, the slope of 3.58 can be interpreted in terms of elasticity. In other words, a 1 percent rise in the U.S. durable manufacturing index will generally be associated with a 3.6 percent increase in BNI's intermodal revenue.

Exhibit 12.8 Scatterplot and Regression Line for Log Intermodal Revenue and Log Manufacturing Index

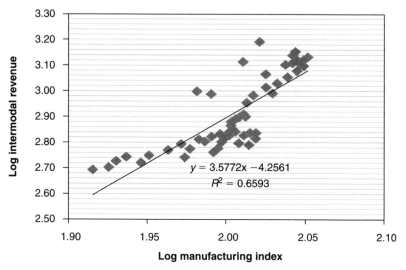

Copyright McGraw-Hill and AnalystSolutions

You may remember the term "R-squared" from a statistics course; it is one way of measuring the extent to which the model can explain variation in the response variable. Excel reports that the regression in Exhibit 12.7 has an R-squared of 0.66, which indicates that changes in the durable manufacturing index have a reasonably good ability to explain changes in BNI's intermodal revenue.* An R-squared of 1 would imply that changes in the explanatory variable can perfectly predict changes in the response variable, which doesn't seem likely in this context, and the R-squared of 0.66 suggests that there are other influences on intermodal revenue. The standard error of 0.09 informs you that if you use regression in Exhibit 12.7 to predict BNI's intermodal

---

* R-squared is a useful, quick indication of a model's explanatory power in statistical terms. In different contexts, widely varying levels of R-squared may be considered acceptable. In engineering or physics, models will often achieve R-squared above 0.98. In academic research in finance or accounting, many articles have been published even though their reported R-squared is below 0.10.

revenue growth, then the growth figures can be off by as much as 9 percent.*, †

Before concluding that the durable manufacturing index and BNI's intermodal revenue are strongly associated, you need to investigate whether *autocorrelation* exists. Regression models that employ historical macroeconomic and financial data, such as manufacturing index, sales, or GDP, often give rise to autocorrelation. This can lead to less precise estimates of slopes, intercepts, and standard errors, and thus reduce the predictive ability of the regression results.

One way to detect autocorrelation is to look at the residuals from the regression—in other words, the gap between the actual values and those that were predicted by the model. Excel can automatically generate the residuals of the regression, and these can then be plotted against time to look for patterns. If the residuals cluster together, or appear to go up and down in a regular fashion, this may indicate autocorrelation. The residuals from the regression in Exhibit 12.7 suggest that there may be autocorrelation problems in this model (see Exhibit 12.9).

---

* As already noted, the regression discussed here is using the entire known data series. In order to test the model's forecasting power in a more rigorous way, you might want to apply "pseudo-out-of-sample" testing. For instance, you could take only the information available in June 2002, and predict the intermodal revenues in September 2002; and then you could take only the information available in September 2002, and predict the intermodal revenues in December 2002; and so on. This approach would provide a more nuanced view of the model's ability to predict intermodal revenues over time. The model might have better explanatory and predictive power during the period up to 2003 than subsequently, for instance. Remember also that the standard error of 0.09 refers to the logarithm of revenue, not the revenue itself.

† Some of the standard regression diagnostics used by statisticians also look quite reassuring. The t-statistic for the estimated coefficient of the log of the manufacturing index is 10, which suggests that the relationship is strong from a statistical perspective. The associated p-value for that coefficient is 0.00, which also suggests that there is very little likelihood that this estimated coefficient could have occurred purely by chance.

Exhibit 12.9   Residuals from Regression

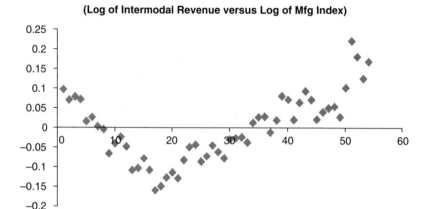

(Log of Intermodal Revenue versus Log of Mfg Index)

One way to deal with autocorrelation is to take lagged values of the response variable and/or the explanatory variable. In this context, you will use lags of the response variable and the explanatory variable; this essentially means that a financial analyst would be using the figures from the prior period for both variables in order to predict the current value of the response variable.* *Lagging* a variable in Excel can be accomplished by shifting the data one period away from its original position, so that the response variable for the second quarter of 2002 is associated with the explanatory variables for the first quarter of 2002, for instance.

According to Excel's regression tool, the relationship for the new model, which includes lagged values of the log of durable manufacturing and the log of intermodal revenues, is shown in Exhibit 12.9.

---

* This is also a more realistic way to think about forecasting. The regression in Exhibit 12.6 implicitly assumes that the financial analyst already knows the quarterly value of the durable manufacturing index, and then can use that number to predict the same quarter's intermodal revenues. Using lagged values is much closer to how financial analysts actually make their forecasts.

Exhibit 12.10 Regression Output for Lagged Values of the Log of Durable Manufacturing and the Log of Intermodal Revenues

Regression Statistics	
Multiple R	0.97
R-squared	0.94
Adjusted R-square	0.94
Standard Error	0.03
Observations	53.00

ANOVA

	Df	SS	MS	F	Significance F
Regression	2.00	1.01	0.51	413	0.00
Residual	50.00	0.06	0.00		
Total	52.00	1.07			

	Coefficients	Standard Error	t Stat	P-value	Lower 95%	Upper 95%	Lower 95%	Upper 95%
Intercept	−0.55	0.39	−1.40	0.17	−1.33	0.24	−1.33	0.24
lag1 (log of BNI intermodal revenue)	0.86	0.06	14.63	0.00	0.74	0.98	0.74	0.98
lag1 (log of manufacturing index)	0.48	0.26	1.83	0.07	−0.05	1.00	−0.05	1.00

Exhibit 12.11 Residuals from Regression

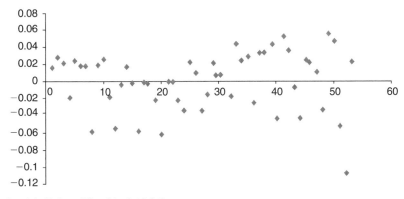

Residuals
(Log of Intermodal Revenue versus Log of Mfg Index)

The second regression, found in Exhibit 12.10, has a higher R-squared (0.94) and lower standard error (0.03) compared with the first regression shown in Exhibit 12.7. Further, since the residual plot from the second regression does not show any pattern, the autocorrelation problem has been addressed.

The estimated coefficient for the log of the manufacturing index in the second regression is much lower than in the first regression, and its t-statistic is also lower while its p-value is higher. This isn't surprising, because it's perfectly reasonable that the last quarter's intermodal revenue is a reasonably good predictor of this quarter's intermodal revenue. And because the lagged value of revenue has high explanatory power, there's less room for the log of the manufacturing index to show that it's influential from a statistical point of view.

The p-value on the log of manufacturing activity is 0.07, which is a bit above the normal hurdle of 0.05. However, the model seems to make intuitive sense, and its overall explanatory power is better than the first regression. So from the perspective of a financial analyst, this model is probably good enough for forecasting work.

Using Multivariate Regression Analysis to Help Prioritize Financial Modeling

Financial analysts' models can be very complex, sometimes involving 30 or more inputs each quarter. (I've seen some with as many as 100.) Using statistical analysis can help identify which assumptions require the most attention. Rather than spending equal time on each variable within an earnings model, you can use statistics to distinguish the variables that require a more thorough analysis from those that move in tandem with other variables. A *multivariate regression* helps determine which variables really matter, as it estimates how each explanatory (x) variable independently affects the response variable (Stine & Foster, 2010).

Suppose that the analyst wants to test statistically which expense line items are variable and which are fixed; in other words, which ones seem to vary with revenue and which ones appear to grow independently. In the example from Excel for a major railroad shown in Exhibit 12.12, the analyst has quarterly figures for compensation and benefits, fuel, equipment rents, purchased services, and materials and other from March 1996 through June 2009.

One way to determine which expense line items should be considered as variable costs is to use a multivariate regression, where y is the revenue and x are the various expense line items. To determine which expense line items are statistically associated with freight revenue, look at the sign of the estimated coefficient and the p-value associated with that coefficient.

Exhibit 12.12   Output for Freight Revenue versus Expense Line Items

Regression Statistics					
Multiple R	1.00				
R-squared	0.99				
Adjusted R-squared	0.99				
Standard Error	82.81				
Observations	54.00				

ANOVA					
	Df	SS	MS	F	Significance F
Regression	5	33300197	6660039	971	0.00
Residual	48	329138	6857		
Total	53	33629336			

	Coefficients	Standard Error	t Stat	P-value	Lower 95%	Upper 95%
Intercept	153.24	208.81	0.73	0.47	−266.59	573.08
Compensation and Benefits	1.47	0.49	2.99	0.00	0.48	2.46
Fuel	1.38	0.10	14.23	0.00	1.18	1.57
Equipment Rents	2.83	1.08	2.62	0.01	0.66	5.00
Purchased Services	1.69	0.45	3.77	0.00	0.79	2.59
Materials and Other	−0.98	0.71	−1.38	0.17	−2.42	0.45

Based on the regression results in Exhibit 12.12, we would conclude that compensation and benefits, fuel, equipment rents, and purchased services expenses are all positively and significantly associated with freight revenue. The estimated coefficients for these expense line items are positive, which means they move in the same direction as revenue, and their p-values are below 0.05, which indicates that there is less than a 5 percent probability that each of these estimated relationships could have occurred purely by chance.

Conversely, the estimated coefficient on materials and other is negative. Purely on logical grounds, you might be skeptical about a negative estimated coefficient; this would imply that spending on materials would actually decline when revenues rise. An alternative interpretation is that spending on materials is a fixed cost rather than a variable cost, which seems more plausible. The p-value of the estimated coefficient for materials and other is 0.17, which also indicates that there is not a statistically significant linkage between this expense line item and revenue.

At this point an analyst can consider linking the growth rates of each expense item, other than materials, with the revenue growth forecast. There may be reasons not to have a link (such as fuel, which is better forecast by using the spot price of oil), but it's a good starting point to consider making this linkage, especially for the smaller expense items, because it reduces the amount of assumptions the analyst is required to make each time the model is reviewed.

Reality Check

The last area to explore here is less about statistics and more about making sure a bottom-up forecast can be reconciled with a top-down forecast. Analysts, especially sell-side analysts, have a tendency to be too optimistic (which is also discussed in Chapter 21). To help conduct a reality check, periodically look at how your future projections compare with the past. This may seem like a no-brainer, but when you're buried in line 75 of your model for a given quarter, you may not be thinking about the long-term. Set up a tab in your workbook that graphs the historical figures for key metrics (e.g., absolute margin levels and growth rates for revenue, earnings per share) and your forecast for as far out as your valuation time horizon.

If there appears to be a "hockey-stick" inflection point in your forecast, there had better be a sound reason for it. You might have a great stock call due to your view about this inflection point, but make sure you've done the work and it's not just a positive bias creeping in. I recall when I modeled that the margins for FedEx's Express division would increase to 10 percent; they looked a bit suspect on a chart showing that they had bounced between 6 percemt and 6.5 percent for 9 of the prior 11 years. That was a warning to me that I had to do extra work to justify my view, but it paid off because the company broke out of that historical range and the stock hit all-time highs.

Before leaving this best practice, I must reiterate the earlier point that there can be significant insights gained and time saved by properly using statistical tools. But if you're doing anything beyond some of the basic tasks mentioned here, seek help from professionals who do this full-time, because there are a staggeringly broad number of ways that statistics can be used incorrectly, knowingly or unknowingly.

Exhibit 12.13   Best Practice (Skills): Use Regression Analysis to Improve Forecasting

1. Use regression analysis to determine if one time series can help forecast another.
2. In obtaining the data series, attempt to get as many periods as possible covering at least two economic cycles.
3. Ensure that the data is comparable. If expressed as a percentage, are they both comparable (year-over-year or quarter-over-quarter)? If one data series is seasonally adjusted, is the other as well? If so, has all the historical data been updated to reflect the most recent seasonal-adjustment factor? Is it necessary to remove inflation from currency-based data such as retail sales?
4. Examine your data in several different ways to make sure its characteristics are understood. Look at time series plots to identify seasonality, step changes, or other features that may require special treatment.

(Continued)

5. If you think a regression model may offer insights, create a scatterplot of the two data series to observe if a relationship appears to exist. If not, stop here.

6. If a curvilinear association appears to exist, consider converting the data using logarithms or some other suitable transformation. Examine the transformed data scatterplot to see if it looks more linear than before. If in doubt, find someone with statistical experience to help interpret the revised scatterplot.

7. Create a regression using the two data series. Look at the output to check the R-squared. In general, for financial modeling purposes, if the R-squared is above 80 percent, a strong relationship potentially exists. If the R-squared is much lower, other statistical methods may be necessary.

8. Create a scatterplot of the residuals to identify autocorrelation. If a pattern exists, try lagging one of the data series and then running another regression, to see if this procedure can eliminate the residual pattern.

9. If autocorrelation has been eliminated, check to see if the p-value on the estimated coefficient is below your confidence threshold, which is often set to 5 percent (or equivalently, 0.05). A p-value below that level indicates that there is at least a 95 percent probability that the association between the explanatory variable and response variable is not purely due to chance.

10. Convert the regression to a formula that can be used for forecasting purposes. Be aware that the regression estimates may not deliver good predictions during inflection periods.

11. When building financial forecasts, try using a multivariate regression to identify line items that are highly linked with key factors, such as revenue or volumes. Where a strong relationship exists, set up the model to link those variables, rather than attempting to forecast independently each quarter.

12. Create a tab in the financial forecast workbook that graphically illustrates *your forecast* for key factors, such as revenue, EPS, and free cash flow compared with the *historical data* (going back as far as possible), all in an effort to determine if the forecast is well above or below trend.

13. If you're not sure about a statistical tool being used, seek help from a trained expert, because mistakes are easy to make and can cause you to be inappropriately confident about your forecasts and insights.

Chapter 13

Conduct Surveys to Acquire Unique Insights

Introduction

Generating alpha requires possessing a unique insight. One of the best ways to achieve this is through a survey of industry experts or market participants. Unfortunately, it's also one of the most costly in terms of time and budget; conducting surveys should be approached with caution. The level of resources necessary for a survey is often dependent on how formal the survey is. It can be as simple as asking five buy-side colleagues, "Do you think the market expects this company to beat earnings this quarter?" or as complex as a 50-question online survey distributed to 20,000 industry experts. (But as discussed below, there should never be 50 questions long.)

Best Practices for Conducting Surveys

Based on a career that involved regularly conducting surveys, as well as input from others interviewed on this subject, here are the best practices I developed for formal surveys:

- A survey can be a lot of work. As such, make sure it's being conducted to answer questions surrounding a stock's critical factors, and can only be answered by polling multiple experts. If an analyst is trying to assess the likelihood of new legislation being passed that impacts a sector, the best answer can probably be obtained by speaking with two or three Washington experts, rather than conducting a survey.

- Decide who will manage the survey process; someone must take responsibility to ensure that it keeps moving along. The size and complexity of the survey will likely dictate which of these options is best:
  - The in-house equity research analyst responsible for the sector or company being researched.
  - An in-house resource dedicated to supporting analysts.
  - A statistician with expertise managing surveys including question construction and analyzing results. (This person can be hired through a college or network such as LinkedIn's Statistical Consultants group.)
  - A project manager from a full-service survey firm who can conduct the entire survey, from question creation to analyzing the results (try to find one that has expertise in *analyzing* results, as some are primarily software or online site designers with minimal statistics knowledge).

- Based on the decision made in the step above, budget time for all of the steps where involvement is required. The survey won't reach completion if it's treated as an afterthought. If conducting the survey on your own, ensure that time is scheduled in advance to analyze the output. We conducted two major surveys semiannually in my team for about seven years, and if we didn't block out two to three days (in advance) to compile and analyze the responses, we found ourselves pushing the publishing of the results out by a week or two later than we planned, which meant the survey wasn't as fresh.

- Determine where and how to find the potential sample respondents. Does a defined population of qualified respondents who could help answer these questions even exist? If so, is it likely a list of contact details for this population exits? And what is the cost per contact? Ensure that the potential sample of respondents is in a position to know the answer.

- Obtain survey participants. Throughout my career, I aligned with two major industry publications as well as collected contact details during industry travels. The list ultimately exceeded 30,000 contacts. Here are some of the ways to obtain survey participant lists:

  ○ Join "communities of practice" on the Internet, such as LinkedIn's professional groups, that will have the types of individuals who are qualified to answer the survey. Depending on the group, it may be possible to post a survey or get permission to do so from the group's owner or manager.

  ○ Partner with a trade association, trade journal, magazine, or blogger. This was my preferred and most fruitful method. It took time, but after a few conversations with the editors of two large trade journals, they agreed to send my online survey link to their subscribers in exchange for the insights I gleaned from the survey, which they used as content in their journals. It was a win–win for us both because we were each looking for information on critical factors. And since their subscribers didn't overlap much with my client base, we weren't competing with one another. Over time, I added the members of two large trade associations to the participant list, in exchange for giving the results back to the association's members.

  ○ Purchase a list. There are list services that sell this information, such as ZoomInfo and LinkedIn. In addition, some expert network firms compile lists of model participants for their clients.

- ○ Collect names during interactions with others at trade shows, on field trips, and from experts discovered during the research process.
- ○ Sell-side analysts attempting to gauge buy-side sentiment can send surveys to their clients.
- • Determine how many individuals need to respond for the survey to be reliable.
- • Construct questions with these points in mind:
  - ○ Pose as few questions as critically necessary. Unless the respondent is being paid, more than 10 is too much. Remember that there is a cost for every extra question asked because it increases the drop rate. If the question doesn't provide an answer about a critical factor or verify the respondent is qualified to answer the question, it's likely detracting from your efforts.
  - ○ To get an extra few questions from respondents, create two stages: (1) the *must-answer* questions, and (2) the *would-be-nice-to-know* questions. In the survey, give the respondent the option to proceed to the expert questions in part two of the survey; I found that over 80 percent would answer these questions in my online surveys.
  - ○ Avoid asking leading questions, such as, "How much do you believe your input costs will increase next year?" (They could decrease.)
  - ○ Ask questions in a manner such that quantifiable data is collected (e.g., a rating on a scale or an actual number). Avoid asking questions that won't provide numerical data, because they offer less to analyze and can't be used with future surveys for time-series analysis. For example, rather than ask customers of a company, "Do you think prices will increase next year?" the question should be, "How much do you expect prices to increase or decrease next year?" The responses from the first question would simply be a bunch

of yes and no answers, whereas responses to the second question can be quantified into a mean, median, or mode, which will be helpful for modeling purposes and for comparing with future versions of the survey.

- ○ Analyze a mock set of answers from the first draft of the survey to see if the questions were asked in a way that generates data helpful in quantifying issues surrounding a critical factor. If not, go back and revise the questions.

- For online surveys:
  - ○ Select a vendor. There are good do-it-yourself programs like SurveyMonkey.com, but I chose to use a company that would manage the entire online process for me from cradle to grave. The advantage was that I could ask complex branching questions, but there was a cost ($5,000 per survey design), and it took a few extra days to edit the survey form because I needed to speak with the vendor for every change. Some expert network firms can help construct the survey and provide a list of participants (Gerson Lehrman Group conducts over 2,000 surveys each year for its clients).
  - ○ Here are some considerations for online surveys:
    - – According to Vovici, a major survey software and analysis company, "Once someone clicks on the invitation, you have less than eight seconds to make a good first impression." As such, include a brief cover page, as seen in Exhibit 13.1, that explains:
      - ▪ The intention of the survey
      - ▪ What's in it for them
      - ▪ How the data and the person's identity will be used and not used
    - – Try to have one question per web page, so that when a respondent clicks to the next page, each of his or her responses is automatically recorded; if there are five questions on the page and, for whatever reason, a

respondent doesn't get to question number five, the responses to questions one through four will not be recorded.

- – Have a progress gauge on each page, showing how far along the respondent is in the survey.
- – Only allow one survey response to come from any given computer. If someone tries to take the survey a second time on the same computer, to presumably skew the results, her or she won't succeed.

- At the end of the survey, ask the respondent, "Do you want to be in our expert network?" allowing the person to provide a name, phone number, and e-mail address. In my team's semiannual survey, we would receive about 400 responses and of that, about 40 percent were willing to be experts. This meant we had over 150 industry contacts to call to discuss service and pricing issues with the companies we covered.

- For a larger survey, pretest on a small population to ensure that there aren't any confusing or ambiguous questions. This also ensures that the technology for the online survey is working correctly.

- There are a number of methods that can be used to analyze the results:
  - ○ If the data is very straightforward, Excel can often be sufficient.
  - ○ For more complicated surveys, where connections are trying to be made between responses from multiple questions, more horsepower will be needed, such as hiring a college statistics professor (or graduate student) or using a resource within a survey company. They'll likely use more powerful statistical software than Excel.

- Don't draw conclusions if they don't exist. This was always a temptation in my team when we conducted our semiannual surveys, because the work involved was immense. But for some of the surveys, there wasn't an actionable call to be made.

- Document questions that should have been asked but weren't, so that they can be included in a future survey.
- If a stock call or trade is going to be made on the basis of the survey, do it as quickly as possible before the insight becomes known by the broader market.
- Sell-side analysts who write about the survey should focus on the investment conclusions surrounding the critical factors and avoid the common mistake of writing about conducting a survey.
- After the call or trade has been made, distribute the results to everyone who took the survey, and if possible, avoid distributing to those who were asked but didn't take the survey. If respondents find the outcome insightful, they're more likely to participate in the future.
- Follow up with one-on-one discussions with any of the respondents who agreed to join your expert network and may offer new insights not captured in the survey.
- For surveys conducted routinely, try to conduct them about the same time each period so that respondents learn to expect them and can prepare to participate.

Exhibit 13.1   Example Cover Page for Online Survey

[Analyst's firm name and if applicable, partner organization helping to co-author the survey] are conducting a survey to [purpose of survey—make it interesting so they'll want to get the results]. The survey should take no more than [put time here, and try to keep it under 10 minutes] of your time and we will send the aggregated results of the survey to those individuals who complete it. As a token of appreciation for conducting the survey, at the end of the survey we offer you the opportunity to [register to receive something—could be as little as a $5 gift card. Sell-side analysts should offer to put the respondent on their research distribution list if not a firm client]. To better understand our objective, we have provided examples of research generated from our prior surveys [post this if it helps the participant build trust with your effort].

(Continued)

As research analysts and a widely read trade journal, we are conducting this survey to gain a better understanding of the marketplace. Please be assured we are not trying to sell you anything, nor are we trying to get you to change the products or services you currently use. As you can see in our prior published work below, we keep all individual identities strictly confidential. We are not compensated by any company mentioned in this survey. We do not sell the individual responses, nor do we pass them along to third parties. Please contact us at the phone number or e-mail address below if you should have any questions.

In the event you are not [describe the role or task that would characterize the respondent being sought, such as a purchasing manager or familiar with deep sea oil drilling], this survey is likely not for you.

Please complete the survey no later than [insert a date that is no more than 10 days away; most respondents will reply in the first 48 hours].

We thank you in advance for your participation.

[Name, e-mail address, and phone numbers of the most senior person involved from each organization—it adds tremendous credibility, which is needed to get the respondent to take the survey and it's rare that any will call or e-mail. Adding logos of the firms under each person's name will also make it look more credible.]

Exhibit 13.2 Best Practice (Skills): Conduct Surveys to Acquire Unique Insights

Steps to the Process:
1. Determine if there are critical factors associated with the assigned universe of stocks that can only be forecast with insights from more than just a few industry experts or financial market participants.
2. Determine if accurate insights can be obtained by surveying a few respondents via a telephone interview or if it requires a more extensive broad-based written survey.
3. Identify the manager of the survey project. It will likely be one of the following:
   a. Analyst responsible for the sector or company being researched.
   b. An in-house resource dedicated to supporting analysts.
   c. A statistician with expertise managing surveys.
   d. A full-service survey firm that can conduct the entire survey.
4. The analyst should budget time in advance to conduct the survey *and* analyze the results, even if outsourced because the analyst's expertise will be needed all along the way.

5. Obtain a qualified list of potential respondents. These lists can come from:
   a. Professional online communities of practice, such as those found on LinkedIn.
   b. Partner with a trade association, trade journal, magazine, or blogger.
   c. Purchase a list from a list vendor or established expert network.
   d. Contact details collected during industry events, such as conferences and conventions.
6. Create survey questions with this in mind:
   a. Have as few questions as critically necessary.
   b. To get an extra few questions from respondents, create two stages, with the second labeled as an optional expert section.
   c. Avoid asking leading questions.
   d. Ask questions in a manner such that quantifiable data is collected (e.g., a rating on a scale or an actual number).
   e. Analyze a mock set of answers from the first draft of the survey to see if the questions were asked in a way that generates data helpful in quantifying issues surrounding a critical factor.
7. For online surveys:
   a. Select a vendor, which can range from a do-it-yourself interface to a full-service provider.
   b. Build the survey with these considerations:
      (1) Have a clear cover page that explains the survey intent, how the respondent will benefit, and how the data and the respondent's identity will be used.
      (2) Have one question per page.
      (3) Have a progress gauge on each page.
      (4) Allow only one response to come from a computer.
8. At the end of the survey, ask respondent if he or she can be contacted for follow-up.
9. Pretest surveys on a small sample when feasible.
10. Analyze the results. If complex, hire an expert.
11. Don't draw conclusions if they don't exist.
12. Document questions that should have been asked but weren't, so that they can be included in a future survey.
13. If a stock call or trade is going to be made, do it quickly.
14. Sell-side analysts who write about the survey should focus on the investment conclusions surrounding the critical factors and avoid the common mistake of writing about conducting a survey.
15. After any call or trade is made, distribute the responses to the respondents; avoid sending them to those who were asked but didn't respond.

(Continued)

16. For surveys conducted routinely, try to conduct them at about the same time each period so that respondents learn to expect them and can plan to participate.
17. Follow up with one-on-one discussions with any of the respondents who agreed to join your expert network and may offer new insights not captured in the survey.

Chapter 14

Identify Yellow Flags through Forensic Accounting

Introduction

In a perfect world, equity analysts would be omnisciently aware of every aspect of a company's inner workings, including the level of conservatism or aggressiveness in its treatment of accounting issues. As much as the general media expects us to see through walls and use our clairvoyance to read management's minds, this is beyond the ability of most equity analysts. Very often, when financial fraud occurs, the company has fooled even its own auditors, but this gets lost on the press, which point the blame at Wall Street analysts for missing the problem.

This isn't to say that analysts should just ignore accounting, but rather they should set expectations for what it is: an opportunity to see early warning signs that problems are developing; I like to call them *yellow flags*. I had a low-profile find when I published a report questioning the accounting behind an abnormally low tax rate for one of my companies, suggesting that it was unlikely to be sustainable. (A few years later, the company took a substantial charge because it deemed the tax rate had been set artificially too low.)

This chapter was coauthored with Dr. Barbara Lougee, assistant professor of accounting, University of San Diego.

Discovering these problems can require plenty of time and in some cases, specialized resources. At Morgan Stanley, we had a Global Valuation and Accounting Team (GVAT) that had a staff of former and existing university professors and a few other senior team members who specialized in finding these accounting problems. If you don't have in-house resources dedicated to helping spot accounting anomalies, there are a few other options:

- Develop a discipline in your financial analysis to spot yellow flags.
- Hire a firm that specializes in spotting accounting problems.
- Accept the fact that you're not likely to spot these.

I don't advocate the last option, but sadly it's the course many analysts take.

Spotting yellow flags requires that the analyst understand the underlying economic transactions that generate each important financial statement item. If you don't know how a particular item is generated and measured, find out. Understanding how values are measured using the applicable accounting rules will enable you to identify items where management can take advantage of flexibility in accounting rules to achieve its financial reporting objectives. Ask questions and be relentless. Do not give up until you understand enough to determine the likelihood that the item is materially misstated. Adjust any materially misstated values before using them for analysis. This step is critical to avoid inaccurate valuations and incorrect inferences. Beyond the best practices discussed here, one of the best resources on this topic is the book *Financial Shenanigans* by Howard Schilit and Jeremy Perler, now in its third edition. Furthermore, market data service providers have tools that can speed up the assessment of a company's financial data (StarMine Professional provides an "earnings quality" rank for most companies including over a dozen financial metrics in this area).

Assess the Pressure for Financial Statement Manipulation

Companies that are under excessive pressure to make their numbers look good are more likely to push the limits of accounting rules. The more analysts learn about accounting the more they appreciate that it's as much an art as a science. There are thousands of pages of accounting rules, but in the end, the management team often has tremendous leeway in interpreting these rules. Here are some of the most obvious circumstances that put pressure on management to be aggressive with its accounting:

End to High Growth

Is the firm under pressure to maintain high growth rates in earnings or revenues? Almost every company has pressure in this area, but if the stock has an abnormally high valuation multiple it's likely due to lofty expectations for growth. In these instances, management may resort to misrepresenting results in its financial statements in order to maintain the multiple.

Pending Management Stock Sale

If management has a large amount of stock vesting soon, a common occurrence after an initial public offering (IPO), it has an incentive to hide any bad news until after the shares are sold. Put yourself in the shoes of senior management, where most of their colleagues, many of whom started the business with them, are pinning their future dreams on cashing in from the IPO proceeds. Are they going to rain on the parade by suddenly taking a conservative stance on an accounting issue? In the case of an IPO, identify when the selling restriction (often called the *lock-up*) expires and then look carefully for accounting irregularities as the date draws nearer. If the lock-up expired well into the past, it's also a valuable exercise to go back to see if anything in the company's accounting policies changed around that time, because it says something about how management behaves in these circumstances.

Excessive Stock-Based Compensation

While the concern mentioned above pertains to a one-time stock sale, this issue covers a company that is regularly using large amounts of stock to attract and retain its talent. Executives who receive a large portion (or large dollar amount) of their total compensation in the form of stock or stock options have strong incentives to keep the firm's stock price rising. If the senior executive team is receiving more than 50 percent of its compensation in stock, this is a good reason to keep an eye on this topic. The proxy statement includes detailed information regarding the compensation of the firm's five most highly paid executives.* Capital IQ's ExecuComp database contains annual executive compensation data for publicly traded firms.

Debt Covenant Violation

Is the firm likely to violate debt covenants? To obtain information about debt covenants, look in the long-term debt note in the firm's 10-K. Common debt covenants specify minimum levels of working capital, net worth, current ratio, or earnings before interest, taxes, depreciation, and amortization (EBITDA) and preclude certain transactions, such as issuing new debt. A firm close to violating its debt covenants might resort to financial statement manipulation in order to avoid defaulting on debt.

Need for Capital to Survive or Maintain Aggressive Growth

For those companies that don't have debt or debt covenants, look to see if the company is burning cash to the point that external financing is required for survival or, in the case of high-flying growth stocks, the company needs capital to maintain its aggressive growth strategy. Studies show that in instances where a company needs to raise capital, there is often earnings management (and a drop in operating performance

---

* The proxy statement (form DEF 14A) is filed with the Securities and Exchange
  Commission prior to a firm's annual shareholders' meeting

afterward) (Cohen & Zarowin, 2010). A quick inspection of a firm's cash flow statement should reveal whether it generates enough cash to finance growth and other discretionary spending internally.* To keep its cost of capital at the lowest level possible for an impending capital raise, the company may engage in financial statement manipulation.

Delisting

A firm struggling to survive might misrepresent results in its financial statements to keep its stock price and market cap from falling below the minimum and avoid being delisted. Similarly, a firm that is included in an index might misrepresent results to prevent being dropped from the index because its market cap fell below the minimum required, which is approximately $5 billion for the S&P 500. The minimum values vary by exchange and by index and are occasionally relaxed during bear markets (see http://www.sec.gov/answers/listing.htm for specifics).

Looking for Yellow Flags in the Income Statement

Many equity analysts have a misperception that a thorough review of a company's accounting starts by digging into the footnotes. While this is an important step in the process, it's best to step back and develop a big picture view by creating common-size financial statements to identify irregularities, including anomalies in trends, discontinuities, and outliers.† Each break from the norm warrants further investigation to determine the cause. To look for these anomalies, create a common-size

---

* If a firm's net cash provided from operating activities in a given period exceeds its cash outlays for dividend payments, debt principal repayments, and maintenance capital expenditures, then the firm has cash left that it can spend on growth.

† Examining financial data across different periods of time is called vertical analysis. Common-size financial statements also facilitate comparison of financial data across different firms at the same point in time. For more information, see *Financial Accounting,* 3rd edition, by Dyckman, Magee, and Pfeiffer.

income statement by expressing each line item as a percentage of net sales revenue and include at least 5 years or 12 quarters of historical data (this may be automated through your market data vendor).

Plotting these items on a graph will facilitate identifying trends and irregularities. When they appear, investigate the cause by reviewing the company's regulatory filing. If that doesn't yield an answer, speak with the company. Common business activities, including mergers and acquisitions, spin-offs, borrowing, issuing stock, discontinued operations, and restructuring, cause discontinuities in financial statements. However, fraudulent transactions or aggressive accounting practices can also lead to discontinuities. If the company hasn't provided a thorough answer, get the help of a forensic accountant.

At the risk of over-simplifying this process, there are two elements that need to be identified when management is manipulating the income statement: *timing* and the *value* of the line item. In terms of *timing*, management usually is attempting to boost current period earnings at the expense of future earnings. However, occasionally this will occur the other way, when management has an exceedingly good period and wants to store away some of the earnings for a rainy day. In thinking about an approach to this analysis, the four broad income statement line items to watch are revenues, expenses, gains, and losses.

Starting at the "30,000-foot view" look at the difference between the growth rates of revenues and earnings. When there is a large increase in earnings concurrent with flat or shrinking revenues, it should cause concern because it indicates earnings growth is likely from reducing expenses or from non-operating income. This also touches on the concept of earnings quality; namely, the highest quality earnings come from growth in revenue (units and pricing), because it's more likely to be sustainable than earnings growth from cost cutting or asset sales. (Most companies can't grow earnings into perpetuity solely by cutting costs or selling assets.)

It's also important to look at how much revenue is coming from changes in volume versus average selling price (ASP). ASP can increase due to the company extracting more economics from the customer, which should drop to the bottom line. Although, it can also be from other factors that won't necessarily benefit earnings, at least not over the long-term. Information about these factors can often be found in the MD&A section of the 10-K filing or through discussions with company management. *Unsustainable* increases in ASP can come from:

- Currency gains: If ASP rises during a certain period from currency benefits, it will likely reverse at some point when exchange rates revert. Also, if currency is inflating revenue growth, it tends to have the same impact on costs incurred in those local markets, potentially having a net neutral, or even negative effect on margins; the lesson here is in not assuming that higher ASP from currency is automatically positive for earnings.

- Special assessments to cover higher expenses, such as a fuel surcharge, or to cover new government taxes: These types of boosts to ASP are usually offset by higher costs, thus resulting in no net benefit to margins.

- Change in mix: When companies proudly state their ASP is up due to a greater percentage of higher-end product sales (more high-end laptop sales than low-end netbooks), make sure to understand the margins for each of these product lines. In the railroad sector, moving automobiles has historically yielded one of the highest ASPs of any freight type but also one of the lowest margins.

- Change in revenue recognition: Accounting changes can impact ASP, but they're usually one-time in nature and therefore don't have a long-term benefit.

The next major "30,000-foot view" step is to look at the relationship between the income statement and cash flow. Specifically, compute the ratio of net income to cash flows from operating activities over multiple time periods. If the ratio is not close to 1.0, it could be due to a new accounting rule (which generally affects net income but not cash flow) or recurring transactions (such as recording depreciation or amortization, which reduces net income but does not consume cash), or it could be a yellow flag. A ratio above 1.5 means that more than half of the firm's earnings are from non-cash or non-operating items and may be a sign of inflated earnings. A ratio below 0.5 could be caused by a non-cash or non-operating loss in the current period, which might be legitimate or might be a maneuver used to create a reserve of earnings for a future period. A negative value for net income to cash flows from operating activities is also a yellow flag, because it reveals a discrepancy between net income and cash flows from operating activities; specifically, either the firm reports a net loss when its operating activities are generating cash, or the firm reports a net profit when its operating activities are consuming cash.

Moving closer to the details, look for these yellow flags in the income statement:

- Overstated revenue: Pulling future revenue back to the current period has the effect of inflating current period earnings and reducing future period earnings. Read the financial statement footnotes to understand how a company recognizes revenue and compare it with its peers as well as practices of the past (e.g., Has the company changed its practice recently?). The most common areas are:
  - Prematurely reporting revenue (such as when the customer's order is received rather than when the product is shipped).
  - Reporting too high of an estimate when revenue is estimated (such as long-term contracts that are based on estimates of the percent of work completed).
- Understated expenses: Pushing current expenses into future periods, such as delaying or understating an expense, has the effect of overstating current period earnings. Here are some of the more common areas where this is found:
  - Cost of goods sold (COGS) may be understated if:

- – Switching from LIFO (last in, first out) to FIFO (first in, first out) when prices are rising.
- – Depleting inventory when using LIFO (as more inventory is used, the average cost per unit declines).

○ Capitalizing costs that should be expensed or spreading cost recognition over an unrealistically longer time period reduces its near-term impact by understating expenses, and thus inflates current earnings. The latter abuse can include any type of depreciation or amortization expense, because management often has discretion estimating the useful life and salvage values. WorldCom's accounting problems were in this area. Specifically, WorldCom capitalized line costs too aggressively, and understated its expenses and overstated earnings by billions of dollars. AOL capitalized subscriber acquisition costs in the mid 1990s (which, as marketing expenses, should have been expensed), and later had to write them off. To detect capitalizing too aggressively: (1) Compare a firm's practice to that of other firms in the same sector; if a firm is the only one in its sector capitalizing a certain cost, the cost should probably be expensed. (2) If there is enough detail provided by the company, which often isn't the case, look for an increase year-to-year in the proportion of a particular cost a firm is capitalizing (instead of expensing).

○ Pension expense can be manipulated by changing certain assumptions. Analyze changes in the pension assumptions over time to ensure that they are consistent with market trends and that none of the company's assumptions are substantially different than its competitors. Key assumptions that can be manipulated include the following:

- – Raising the *discount rate* causes pension expense to decrease.
- – Raising the *estimated return on plan assets* lowers pension expense.

– Notice in the table below, in 2005, at the time of the
analysis, FedEx had among the highest discount rate and
expected return on plan assets. As an analyst following
the stock, I wasn't concerned about any manipulation by
management, but rather that as the company made
adjustments to move toward the norm, it would have a
drag on earnings.

Company	Discount Rate 2005	Expected Return on Plan Assets
Arkansas Best	5.5%	8.3%
Burlington Northern Santa Fe	6.3%	8.3%
Canadian National	6.0%	8.0%
Canadian Pacific Railway	6.0%	8.0%
CNF Inc.	6.3%	8.5%
CSX Corporation	5.8%	8.5%
Norfolk Southern	5.8%	9.0%
YRC Worldwide Inc.	5.8%	8.8%
Union Pacific	6.0%	8.0%
Average	5.9%	8.4%
S&P Average		8.5%
FedEx Corp.	6.3%	9.1%

• Special charges should be scrutinized because management
often has discretion, which facilitates earnings management.
Overestimating some current charges can reduce future
expenses, and thus artificially inflate future earnings. Special
charges can come in the form of:
  ○ Restructuring (due to change in company strategy).
  ○ Mergers and acquisitions (due to one-time costs associated
  with these activities).
  ○ Impairment (due to a shortened life of an asset or realizing
  less benefit from the asset than expected).
  ○ Tax valuation allowance: Increasing the tax valuation
  allowance entails a one-time increase in income tax
  expense. If the firm overstates the allowance, it can later

reduce the value, which in turn reduces income tax expense and provides a one-time boost to net income. Calculate the ratio of tax valuation allowance to gross deferred tax assets: Increases in this ratio warn that the firm thinks it will not generate enough profit to use its tax benefits before they expire, or it could be a sign that management is using the allowance as a reserve, which it can use later to boost earnings.

○ Inventory valuation allowance due to excess inventory: Inventory write-offs reduce a firm's earnings in one period and boost profit in a later period if the firm ends up selling the inventory. Cisco wrote off $2.25 billion of inventory in the third quarter of 2001, and later sold some of the written-off inventory for a $290 million *gain*.

○ Allowance for doubtful accounts is similar to concerns raised above, but in this instance, it's an unusually large bad debt expense charge (or increase in the allowance-for-doubtful-accounts-to-gross-accounts-receivable ratio) that could be due to management underreporting the quarterly allowance in the past or attempting to build an excess reserve to use for boosting earnings in the future. This type of charge should be scrutinized, unless it's due to one of the company's large customers suddenly going bankrupt.

• Non-operating income such as an asset sale: Interestingly enough, it's the small asset sales that can have the most benefit to a company, because they often don't get identified by analysts as a special item. When they are large enough to significantly distort earnings, management usually makes a point of highlighting the sale, which then gets removed by most sell-side and buy-side analysts as non-recurring. Identify the line item where companies bury their gains on sales and routinely watch for that line item to fluctuate.

• When a company suddenly has a materially lower tax rate or consistently has a tax rate well below its sector peers, you should investigate to ensure that your forward-looking tax rate isn't unsustainably low. In 2000, management from one of the companies I was following told me to expect its tax rate to be 20 percent for the year (down from 35 percent in 1999), which eventually jumped back to the high 30s in 2003 and beyond.

Looking for Yellow Flags on the Balance Sheet

Similar to the income statement above, the first step in analyzing the balance sheet is to create a common-size balance sheet. This is done by expressing at least five years or 12 quarters of each line item as a percentage of total assets. Look for items that are experiencing significant change over time.

When analyzing individual line items within the balance sheet, the objective is to detect weak liquidity or excessive leverage and to identify *assets that are overstated* or *liabilities that are understated*. Here are some specific areas to watch:

- Assets not likely to generate value: If either of the items below is more than 10 percent of a firm's total assets, it raises a yellow flag:
  - Goodwill: Goodwill is a write-off waiting to happen. Many firms do not realize enough value from acquisitions to justify the purchase premium and later must impair or write-off goodwill.
  - Deferred tax assets: Often these expire before a firm can use them. Look for information in the tax note. The tax valuation allowance is a reserve that represents the portion of the deferred tax asset (future tax benefits) that the firm expects not to use before it expires.
- Assets likely to generate less value:
  - Accounts receivable: Look for evidence that a firm is collecting from customers more slowly—decreasing accounts receivable turnover ratio or increasing days to

collect. This warns of a future write-off of receivables, because the longer receivables remains unpaid, the more likely they are to become uncollectible.

- ○ Inventory: Look for evidence that inventory is selling more slowly—decreasing inventory turnover ratio or increasing days to sell inventory. This may be a sign that inventory is accumulating in the warehouse, which warns of a future write-off or write-down of inventory.

- Assets and liabilities with uncertain values: For assets and liabilities with values based on fair-value accounting, question values based on level-three inputs much more than those with level-one inputs. As a reminder, level-one inputs include the least amount of uncertainty because the value is based on quoted prices in active markets, whereas level-two inputs are similar to those quoted in active markets. Level-three values contain the most uncertainty because inputs are unobservable; these assets and liabilities are not actively traded and no similar items are actively traded. Level-three inputs are generated by the firm, not an independent source, and therefore are easy to manipulate. Analysts can ask the company if there is an independent source verifying or helping with the level-three asset and liability valuations.

- Off-balance-sheet liabilities: If these were brought on the balance sheet, they would increase the company's leverage.

- ○ Operating leases: Operating leases enable a firm to lease assets and hide the liability. Although operating leases are contractual obligations with certain cash payments, they do not create a liability (or asset) on the balance sheet. Use information in the notes to the financial statements to estimate the value of the liability by calculating the present value of future cash payments associated with operating leases.

- ○ Equity method investments: Firms can use these investments to hide debt, because accounting rules require a one-line consolidation. The only impact of these investments on the owner's balance sheet is creation of an asset.

- ○ Special purpose entities (or variable interest entities): In the pre-Enron world, firms used these vehicles to hide debt. Accounting changes since Enron make this more difficult to do, but read the fine print and learn as much as possible about these entities.
- Weak liquidity:
  - ○ Unless the firm has a negative cash cycle, values for the current ratio below 0.95 mean the firm's current resources are not sufficiently large to pay its current liabilities. If the firm's operating activities are consuming cash or its operating efficiency is deteriorating (asset turnover ratios are decreasing), this warns of a potential liquidity problem.
- Excess leverage:
  - ○ A debt-to-equity or debt-to-total-capital ratio much higher than sector peers is a sign of a company that may be unable to cover its debt obligations. Average values vary by sector, but generally a debt-to-equity ratio above 4.0 indicates high leverage and risk for a commercial or industrial firm. This rule of thumb does not apply to financial services firms, which are more highly leveraged.
  - ○ Times interest earned (earnings before interest and taxes/interest expense): Values below 2.0 warn that the firm may not generate sufficient profit to cover its interest costs.

Looking for Yellow Flags in the Cash Flow Statement

When analyzing the cash flow statement, cash flows from operating activities should be positive and growing. For a self-sustaining firm, they should be the primary source of cash and be large enough to fund growth and other discretionary spending. Unless a firm is a start-up, negative net cash flows from operating activities are a yellow flag because they occur when a firm's core business activities use more cash than they generate.

Look for evidence that cash flows from operating activities are inflated. Similar to earnings, firms have incentives to inflate cash flows from operating activities because analysts often use them as an alternative performance measure when earnings quality is low (or a measure of liquidity). Common ways that firms can inflate cash flows from operating activities include:

- Delay paying bills: Look for a reduction in the payables turnover ratio or an increase in days payable.
- Postpone inventory replenishment until next period: Look for a decrease in inventory/cost of goods sold.
- Securitize receivables: Selling receivables enables the firm to collect the cash sooner, but the firm collects less cash because they are sold at a discount. Look for a decrease in accounts receivable/sales.
- Sell trading securities: Firms can time sales of trading securities in order to boost cash flows from operating activities. Look for a decrease in marketable securities/total assets.

The level and year-over-year change in cash flows used for investing reveal if the firm is making the investment for future growth, which can be helpful in applying a valuation multiple. Net negative cash flows for investing, driven by acquisitions (external growth) and/or large (or unusual) increases in capital expenditures or "capex" (organic growth), are evidence of growth because these expenditures are intended to grow the firm's ability to generate revenues and future cash flows. To distinguish growth capex from maintenance capex (and the current revenue stream), track changes in capex over time. An unusually large increase in capex in one (or more) period(s) is usually indicative of growth spending. Also, divide capex by depreciation expense. Values in the 1.2 to 1.5 range are fairly common for many industries, indicating that the firm is spending for growth (spending more than it needs to maintain capacity). Values near or below 1.0 warn that the firm may not be spending enough to maintain current capacity. This approach assumes that depreciation expense is a reasonable estimate of the amount of property, plant, and equipment the firm must replace in order to maintain its current productive capacity. Companies in the banking, insurance, and mortgage sectors have limited depreciation which makes the computation of little use for this exercise. Be aware that for firms that use operating leases, capex is understated because the cash payments associated with operating leases are deducted from operating cash flows (but they also don't appear in depreciation).

Other Yellow Flags

After completing your tactical review of the financial statements, look for other warning signs that aren't in the financial statements:

- Change in auditors: When a firm disagrees with its auditors and cannot resolve the disagreement, the auditors resign or the firm fires the auditors. This situation can arise when a firm uses an aggressive accounting treatment, and its external auditors tell the firm to use a more conservative approach. When any unscheduled event that is important to shareholders occurs, including a change in auditors, a firm is required by the SEC to file an 8-K.

- Negative audit opinions: Shareholders react negatively to a negative opinion from the firm's external auditors. A *going concern* opinion means the auditors doubt the firm will survive the next year. Material weaknesses in the firm's internal controls could enable employees to commit fraud and not be caught. Both are disclosed in the Report of Independent Public Accounting Firm in the 10-K.

- High turnover in top management team: If more than one of the company's key executives resigns (or is fired) during a short period of time, the company might have serious problems.
- Weak corporate governance: The board of directors should include enough outsiders to be independent of the firm's management team and act on behalf of shareholders (instead of simply rubber stamping management's decisions). If the majority of directors are insiders, the board is less likely to be independent. The outsiders should also have enough relevant expertise to think independently of management. Also, boards that are too small (fewer than 6 people) or too large (more than 15 people) tend to be ineffective because they are easy for management to control. On a large board, each director is dispensable and it is likely that no individual is powerful enough to contest management's decisions. Having the CEO also be the chairman of the board further reduces the ability of the board to be independent. Weak corporate governance is problematic because it will be difficult to stop management from making decisions that are not in the best interest of shareholders. Some of this information can often be discovered by reading the proxy statements.

Not-Quite-Yellow Flags

Much of the discussion to this point has been about helping to identify when a company is committing fraud or overtly attempting to deceive the public. Discovering these early can clearly make a huge difference in helping an analyst outperform a passive index. But there are also some not-quite-yellow flags that should be watched, which are often signs of management moving away from or avoiding transparency. Be cautious when a company does any of the following:

- Reduces the amount of information it discloses or discloses substantially less than its peers. Management will defend its decision by saying it's for competitive reasons, but the reality is that most industries have enough consultants and cross-hiring of employees that competitors know how well a company's various product lines or divisions are running. The primary reason to provide less information is to avoid being scrutinized by shareholders. Furthermore, if a company substantially changes the way it reports its results, make sure to dig deeply to understand why, because it's almost always to hide or downplay something.

- Fails to mention that it's benefiting from non-operating profits in good quarters but is quick to point out non-operating losses in bad quarters. This would occur all too often in my sectors, when I would be told by management that its quarterly results were actually better than reported because the same period one year earlier included a one-time benefit that the company failed to disclose back at the time.

- Takes special charges, write-offs, or restates earnings as though it's an ongoing part of the business. In most instances, these are acknowledgements by the accountants that the company has made poor assumptions or decisions in the past. If any are more than 5 percent of the quarterly results, management should make a point of discussing why the mistake occurred and steps that are being taken to ensure that it doesn't occur again.

- Routinely dismisses generally accepted accounting principles (GAAP) (or international financial reporting standards [IFRS]) earnings as irrelevant or meaningless. This can be heard when management criticizes a competitor for being too conservative with its accounting methods. There may occasionally be a reason why standard accounting rules distort the company's health, but not as a general course of business. In these instances, spend time with a senior member of the finance department to understand why this widely accepted set of rules doesn't apply to the company.

- Fails to discuss targets or hurdles for large investment projects. Great companies understand how and where to invest incremental capital, treating it as a core competency. If a company announces a major capital expenditure project and the CFO can't explain the expected return or at least the hurdle for new investments, the analyst should question the company's capital budgeting process.

- Fails to discuss complicated or counterintuitive issues, such as the thought process for a merger or acquisition (M&A) transaction or currency hedging. Great companies want to be transparent and will prepare to answer these tough questions as they get ready for analysts' calls and meetings.

- Changes the manner in which corporate overhead expenses are allocated among its divisions. This is a favorite shell game used by some management teams to suggest that a struggling division is being successfully turned around even though it's cosmetic because the costs are simply being shifted to the more healthy division.

- Reports results much later than the competitors. In an era of point-of-sale cash registers, bar-coded warehouse inventories, and globally integrated accounting systems, there's little reason for a company to report quarterly results much past 30 days after the quarter ends. While it could be a culture of perfectionism, it's also a sign of a management team not having control of its information. If it takes a company 40 days to determine what happened in the quarter that's already closed, what does it say about its ability to manage its business on a real-time basis?

Exhibit 14.1 Best Practice (Skills): Spotting Accounting Yellow Flags

1. Understand the underlying economic transactions that generate each important financial statement item. If something isn't clear, find an answer in the company's regulatory filings. If it's still unclear, speak with company management. If that doesn't provide clarity, get help from a forensic accountant.

2. Look for signs that a company is likely to be motivated to manipulate its financial results. More aggressive forms of accounting or outright artificial boosting of earnings is more likely to occur when:
   a. Companies have extremely high valuation multiples.
   b. There is a pending stock sale by management.
   c. The executive team is paid an excessive portion of its total compensation in stock.
   d. Companies are struggling to avoid violating debt covenants.
   e. Companies need to return to the markets to raise more capital.
   f. Companies' stock prices are nearing levels that would cause them to be delisted from major exchanges or removed from major indexes.

3. Analyze the income statement in the following areas:
   a. Look for changes in historical trends of common-size income statements by expressing each line item as a percentage of net sales revenue.
   b. Moving back to the raw numbers of the income statement, look to see if the earnings are growing approximately in pace with revenues. A large divergence should be investigated.
   c. Compute a *net-income-to-cash-flow ratio* over time. If it fluctuates well above or below 1.0, there is reason to investigate.
   d. Analyze changes in ASP to determine whether it's due to successful extraction of more value from customers or less valuable factors such as:
      (1) Currency gains.
      (2) Special assessments.
      (3) Change in mix.
      (4) Change in revenue recognition.
   e. Identify if the company has revenue recognition practices not followed by most of its peers.
   f. Look for companies understating expenses in these areas:
      (1) Capitalizing costs that should be expensed or spreading cost recognition over an unrealistically longer time period. This can be detected by comparing a firm's practice with that of other

firms in the same sector. Also watch for changes in useful lives or salvage values.

(2) For companies that provide pensions to a large number of their employees, look to see if the discount rate and estimated return on plan assets are relatively in line with other companies that have a similar workforce.

g. Scrutinize special charges because they are often a sign that management underreported expenses in the past or is creating a reserve to use for reducing future period expenses.

h. Scrutinize asset sales to ensure that they are not being misinterpreted as ongoing earnings.

i. Investigate when a company has a substantially lower tax rate than its peers over more than three to four quarters.

4. Analyze the balance sheet in the following areas:

a. Look for changes in historical trends of a common-size balance sheet by expressing each line item as a percentage of total assets.

b. Look at the company's inability to service its debt by computing a *times-interest-earned ratio*. A value below 2.0 should raise concerns.

c. To identify assets likely to be written off because they are less likely to generate value, look for decreases in receivables turnover or inventory turnover.

d. For assets and liabilities with values based on fair value accounting, question values based on level-three inputs much more than those with level-one inputs.

5. Analyze the cash flow statement in the following areas:

a. Look for a reduction in the payables-turnover ratio or an increase in days payable as a sign that a company is delaying paying its bills.

b. If a company is not generating positive cash from operations it's usually a sign of longer-term problems.

c. Compute a company's capital-expenditures-to-depreciation ratio over time to get an understanding of the level of growth capital being invested. A figure near or below 1.0 should raise questions, because it is a sign the firm may not be spending enough to maintain its current capacity.

6. Look for these other potential yellow flags that could be signs of internal problems:

a. Change in auditor.

b. Negative audit opinion.

c. High turnover in top management.

d. Weak corporate governance.

(Continued)

7. Look for these not-quite-yellow flags as signs that management is attempting to move away from or avoiding transparency. Be cautious when a company does any of the following:
   a. Reduces the amount of information it discloses or discloses substantially less than its peers.
   b. Takes special charges, write-offs, or restates earnings as though it's part of the business.
   c. Routinely dismisses GAAP (or IFRS) earnings as irrelevant or meaningless.
   d. Fails to discuss targets or hurdles for large investment projects.
   e. Fails to discuss complicated or counterintuitive issues, such as the thought process for an M&A transaction or currency hedging.
   f. Changes the manner in which corporate overhead expenses are allocated among its divisions.
   g. Reports results much later than competitors.

Further Resources

Mulford, Charles W., and Eugene E. Comiskey, *The Financial Numbers Gane: Detecting Creative Accounting Practices*, New York: Wiley, 2002.

Schilit, Howard Mark, and Jeremy Perler, *Financial Shenanigans*, Third Edition, New York: McGraw-Hill, 2010.

Chapter 15

Identify the Relevant Microsoft Excel Features for Equity Research Analysts

If left on a deserted island and asked to analyze stocks with only one computer application, most analysts would request Microsoft Excel. It's a critical element of every analyst's job and yet many don't get proper training in this area. If you're like most, you probably picked up some Excel in college and possibly more during on-the-job training. Just like learning a new language, it takes months or even years of using the application before an analyst can say that it's been mastered. *But don't fall into the common trap of assuming that just because you know the basics, you're proficient enough to succeed.* Given that Excel is such a critical element of the job, one that can leverage an analyst's intelligence, insight, and time, it's imperative to master more than just the basics. Excel has a massive number of capabilities, and therefore our discussion here focuses on the most relevant features an equity research analyst should learn.

I would like to thank Bob Jones of Murray Hill Associates for his contribution to the best practices that utilize Excel.

Many analysts believe that they only need to know basic Excel features, such as navigating, building formulas, and editing. There is a smaller population of analysts who understand the importance of knowing Excel's more advanced features. *Simply knowing a feature exists doesn't lead to mastery, especially for the more complex features.* Some features can be used in more than one manner, which can lead to a wrong answer if misapplied.

How much Excel should a proficient equity analyst know? The answer is somewhat dependent on the analyst's role. Some analysts will be just fine learning only the first category below, while others with more job responsibilities will need to learn all three:

- Building and using models: The process of building a financial model's structure, formulas, formats, etc., and adjusting the mechanics of how the model works.
- Analyzing and summarizing data to support model assumptions: The process of analyzing, compiling, summarizing, and testing data in order to produce the best input for the model.
- Reporting information from models: Using the output from a financial model to create a graph or table for use in another form such as a document or presentation.

For analysts to assess their Excel capabilities and potential training needs, they should ask themselves the following questions based on the list of the Excel features *relevant to their role* shown in Exhibit 15.1:

1. Can I accurately *explain* each feature's capabilities?
2. Can I consistently *implement* each feature in an error-free manner?
3. Can I *identify* the best feature to use in solving typical modeling challenges?

If the answer is generally yes to all of these questions for the 42 features listed in Exhibit 15.1, especially those categorized as "Critical for Success," then the analyst probably has amassed the necessary skills. But if there's a struggle to answer the questions for most of the features, the analyst should seek training.

When I interviewed Bob Jones, an Excel trainer of financial analysts, he remarked that an alarming number of new hires entering his classes are convinced they understand Excel features, but go on to discover from the classroom exercises that they don't. This is one of those areas where it's easy to become overly confident. Be open to help from others if necessary. At a minimum, have a good Excel reference book at your desk or an online resource available. I strongly recommend taking Excel model-building courses customized for financial analysts; most medium-to-large firms employing equity research analysts will either periodically offer in-house courses or reimburse analysts to attend private courses.

Exhibit 15.1 Best Practice (Knowledge): Relevant Excel Features for Equity Research Analysts

	Core Knowledge for Building and Using Models	Additional Knowledge for Analyzing and Summarizing Data	Additional Knowledge for Reporting Information
Critical for Success	File and folder management	Techniques for cleaning up downloaded data	Data tables and their rules
	Navigating regions, worksheets, and workbooks, including all navigation keyboard shortcuts	Data analysis functions (SUMIF, COUNTIF, and all DFunctions)	Creating charts Conditional formatting
	Basic formula composition (order of operations and the use of parentheses)	Text to column procedures	Using pictures of sheets in other sheets for reporting and checking
	Functions found in Exhibit 15.3, excluding text, date, and time functions	Text functions (see Exhibit 15.3)	
		Financial functions (see Exhibit 15.3)	
	Percentage formulas (projecting increases and deriving percent changes)	Pivot tables	

(Continued)

Exhibit 15.1   Best Practice (Knowledge): Relevant Excel Features for Equity Research Analysts *(Continued)*

	Core Knowledge for Building and Using Models	Additional Knowledge for Analyzing and Summarizing Data	Additional Knowledge for Reporting Information
Critical for Success	Multiple sheet formulas Edit (cut, copy, and paste), including all associated editing shortcuts Printing and solving print compression problems Formatting, copying formats Window controls (freezing panes, splitting windows, viewing multiple windows from the same book) Managing page breaks and repeating row and column information on printouts Error trapping, e.g., =IF(ISERROR(...)) Comments and text boxes for documenting and explaining Absolutes and partial absolutes Protecting cells and sheets Understanding the dangers of losing a password Find and replace (including formulas)	Vlookup, Hlookup, and match (including the difference between level matches and exact matches) Date and time functions (see Exhibit 15.3) Understanding and building array formulas	

(Continued)

Exhibit 15.1 Best Practice (Knowledge): Relevant Excel Features for Equity Research Analysts *(Continued)*

	Core Knowledge for Building and Using Models	Additional Knowledge for Analyzing and Summarizing Data	Additional Knowledge for Reporting Information
Important for Success	Tracing and auditing formulas		
	Names (range names) including using names for constants		
	Building and using templates		
	Custom number formats		
	All paste special features		
	Using GoTo Special		
	Concatenation		
	Understanding and controlling iterations		
	Group editing		
Helpful	Custom views including how they control printing		
	Managing toolbars (adding and removing tools, resetting toolbars). For 2007/10 versions, customizing Quick Access Toolbar and Status Bar		
	Group and Outline		
	Building and using styles		

Source: Murray Hill Associates

Useful Excel Tricks

Based on years of using Excel, here are some of the most useful under-used tips for equity research analysts:

- Spreadsheet picture: Take a picture of the current view, which can be viewed or printed in another location.
  - In Excel version 2003, install the camera tool and use it to create the linked picture.
  - In Excel 2007, copy the selected region and then on the Home tab, Clipboard group, Paste Pull-down, As Picture pull-down, use the Paste Picture Link feature.
- File location: The formula =cell("filename") provides the file's drive and path location as well as the name of the file and sheet where that formula resides, which is helpful in a printed report to identify where to find the digital version of the information. Alternatively, use the "Insert File Path" icon in Header or Footer to have the file name and path print in the header or footer.
- Quick projections: By selecting a time series of data and using the Autofill tool in the same direction, Excel will automatically provide forward regression projections based on the historical data selected. This won't help find inflection points, but it can be helpful in forecasting future numbers if the historical trend continues (such as GDP or S&P earnings during a stable segment of the economic cycle).
- Shortcuts: Exhibit 15.2 includes some of the more widely used shortcuts. Taking the time to learn them may be a bit frustrating at first, but the payback in time saved will be well worth it. Think of it as a mini time-savings dividend into perpetuity.

Exhibit 15.2 Best Practice (Knowledge): Useful Excel Keyboard Shortcuts

Ctrl *	Selects all cells in a contiguous region (**Ctrl A** can do it, but doesn't record variability in a macro).
Ctrl Space	Selects the current column.
Shift Space	Selects the current row.
Ctrl. (period)	Activates each corner of a selected region each time you press it—a good way to be sure that the entire region is really selected.
Hold **Ctrl** and drag a sheet's tab left or right	Makes a copy of a sheet, (great temporary backup).
Alt O C A	Get the best fit for a selection of cells without getting the best fit for the entire column.
Ctrl [	Traces precedents (selects cells that are feeding a formula). **F5 Enter** gets you back to the formula.
Ctrl + Ctrl −	Inserts the selection. Deletes the selection.
Ctrl `	Shows all formulas; use it a second time to toggle back to normal view.
F4 (the "do it again" key)	Repeats the last formatting or editing command that you used.
Alt =	Is equivalent to clicking the **Autosum** tool.
F2 F9	Evaluates a formula; select part of a formula and hit **F9** and you'll evaluate only that part.
Ctrl R	In a selection, it copies the first cell to all the selected cells to the right of it.
Ctrl D	In a selection, it copies the first cell to all the selected cells down under it.
Double Click on **Autofill** handle	Auto fills a formula or value to the bottom of a column (uses adjacent column to determine the length).
Group Sheets by selecting first and **Shift** selecting last or **Ctrl** while clicking individual sheets	Enables the user to make the same changes to all sheets at once. This includes formatting, adding labels, printer settings, etc.

Source: Murray Hill Associates

Exhibit 15.3 Best Practice (Knowledge): Most Relevant Excel Functions and Formulas for Equity Research Analysts

Essential basic calculations:
Sum, Average, Count, Counta, Min, Max

Rounding:
Round, Int, Mround,

Essential comparisons:
IF, And, Or, Not

Lookups:
Vlookup, Hlookup, Match, Index, Rank, Offset

Error checking:
Iserror, Isblank, Istext

Financial functions:
PMT, FV, RATE, NPER, NPV, PV, IRR, MIRR, EXP, SLN, DDB

Data analysis:
Sumif, Countif, Dsum, Dcount, Daverage, Subtotal, Sumproduct

Position and formula creation:
Indirect, Row, Column, Address

Text functions:
Len, Text, Value, Left, Mid, Right, Find, Concatenate (although the & operator is an easier way to concatenate), Text, Dollar, Fixed, Trim, Clean

Date and time functions:
Today, Now, Weekday, Date, Datevalue, Month, Year, Day, Weeknum

Source: Murray Hill Associates

Further Resources

Tjia, John, *Building Financial Models*, Second Edition, New York: McGraw-Hill, 2009.

Winston, Wayne L., *Microsoft Excel 2007: Data Analysis and Business Modeling*, Redmond, WA: Microsoft Press, 2004.

Chapter 16

Creating the Best Spreadsheet Architecture for Financial Analysis

Introduction

Financial models and other types of spreadsheets used for financial analysis are often passed on by their authors to successors, giving many files more than a 20-year useful life. No other files on Wall Street are used as heavily as those critical to the forecasting process. As such, creating a new spreadsheet that will be used routinely requires some thoughtful planning. Unfortunately, many analysts build their worksheets by adding each piece of information as needed. They often discover it becomes an unmanageable monstrosity, filled with broken links and errors, and ultimately difficult to follow. Unless you're working in total isolation from others or never look at the same company twice, it's critical to invest the time up front to build spreadsheet files correctly. I recommend following the best practices found in Exhibit 16.1 to make financial spreadsheets and workbooks easy to use and worthy of generating useful insights.

I would like to thank Bob Jones of Murray Hill Associates for his contribution to this best practice.

Exhibit 16.1 Best Practice (Skills): Creating the Best Spreadsheet Architecture for Financial Analysis

General

- If a forecasting or data file will be used by multiple people, indentify a single individual who will oversee and coordinate changes as well as communicate those changes to everyone using the file.
- Document all important information:
  - Create a cover page worksheet (not the legal disclaimer page found on some sell-side workbooks) for the following:
    - Explanation of how the workbook operates, including all of its component worksheets. Specific information should be provided to easily locate assumptions and important output.
    - Direction on how to use the file, highlighting which information can be changed and which should be left alone. If applicable, this includes a legend explaining color codes.
    - Explanation of complicated formulas or macros that will not be intuitively understood by anyone other than the file's author.
    - Sources of the information for the file, such as a company's 10-K, Bloomberg function DES, or a sector website.
    - Contact information, include phone numbers and e-mail address of those who author any elements of the file (including any experts who created the macros) or are responsible for updating the file.
    - List of any worksheets that are routinely hidden (unless they are for restricted use only).
  - Within individual worksheets:
    - Use text boxes for general explanations and notes. These can float on the surface and can be modified to not print.
    - Use the comments feature (shift F2) within cells to:
      - Explain the purpose and mechanics of complex formulas.
      - Document adjustments to formulas; paste the original formula into the comment if it will be referenced in the future.
- Avoid creating macros that attempt to run processes in the model. Macros may be useful for cleaning up or processing information that will be used in the model, but even then, avoid using macros unless the amount of time saved clearly offsets the risk of mistakes and complications for others.
- Avoid circular references as they can get complicated and difficult to manage, especially if others will be using the file. The one area of possible exception is calculating interest expense on the income statement based on the amount of cash on the balance sheet, but there are workarounds even for this. (See page 181 of John Tjia's *Building Financial Models*, Second Edition, for an explanation of options beyond the circular reference.)

- "Clean as you go" by fixing logical and cosmetic problems as soon as they are found; it's rare for an analyst to go back to fix these in the future. If neglected too long, the file will fall into disrepair and need a complete rebuild, which is time consuming.
- Create math checks when possible. For example, in a typical four-quarter income statement, add up the quarterly columns into a fifth column to compute the full year. Then, in the summary section for that fifth column, derive values, such as the revenue, expenses, and earnings before interest and taxes (EBIT), from the data above, as though an independent income statement is being built. The net income and earnings per share (EPS) from the vertical data should add up to the same as the four-quarter horizontal data; this is a good way to quickly audit the overall integrity of a financial model received from others.
- Ensure that everything is backed up on a daily basis. Preferably save the file in a place that is automatically backed up off-site. If this isn't possible, take steps to ensure that older versions of models can be restored if a file becomes corrupted.
- If building a model for someone else, know exactly what is expected of the model in terms of output, reports, and support analysis. Ask for clarification in writing if possible (e.g., an e-mail).
- As a general rule, use existing files as templates for new analysis in terms of column and row formatting, but do not attempt to use previous links for formulas unless they are very simple. (The risk of mistakes compounds as the file becomes more complex.)
- When possible, download data rather than creating or entering it manually. If information needs to be updated regularly, try to link it to the data source to avoid input error. Note that it's critical to be comfortable with the integrity and format of the vendor's data before using it.

Workbook and Worksheet Level
- Create a separate worksheet when the format of the data or its usage is distinct from other data (i.e., don't try to put everything into one worksheet). Examples of when dedicated worksheets should be created include:
  - Income statement.
  - Cash flow statement.
  - Balance sheet.
  - Operating division break-out of a complex company.
  - Assumption variables worksheets.
  - Company facts that may not be used in the financial forecast, (e.g., value of specific assets, employee count by country, names of largest customers).
  - Data analysis and calculations.

(Continued)

- Put all *assumption variables,* or cells that are changed by the user to influence the output, into worksheets that contain only assumptions (discussed in more detail later). To see the assumption variables and the cells they influence on one screen, create two windows of the same workbook as follows:
  - In version 2003, use Window, New Window, Window, Arrange, Horizontal.
  - In version 2007, use New Window in the Window group on the View tab; then the Arrange All choice from the same group.
  - In both versions, Ctrl F6 will switch from window to window.
- Keep all company-specific information in one workbook and all sector-specific information in another workbook; do not have multiple workbooks that pertain to one company or sector. This will make it easier to find information and streamline linking of information.
- Hide worksheets within a workbook if they are rarely used or would cause confusion for others who typically use the workbook.
- Keep formatting relatively simple; it can become a nightmare to manage when copied from one area to another.
- Color-code assumptions distinctly from researched data, while leaving formulas in black.
- Set the default font to be the same as the one used for firm-wide reports and documents. It saves time reformatting when elements of the file are put into a document or presentation.
- For all worksheets within a workbook, set up the columns as consistent time periods, so that if column G is the first quarter of 2013, it will be that same time period for all other worksheets in the workbook (group editing helps with this). If possible, do this for all company models within the assigned universe, which will make comparisons between companies much easier. (All of my models, even those created late in my career, started with 1Q89 in column C, so as to pick up the '90–'91 recession and allow for quick time-series analysis across companies.)

Cell Level

- When linking cells:
  - Avoid linking between files and instead, try to keep the links inside one file (i.e., link between worksheets).
  - If there must be links between files, create a cover page on the *source* file, documenting the name and path for any files that use the source file; a target file knows where the data is coming from, but a source file isn't responsible for telling the target file when its integrity, structure, or location has changed. Linking to a named cell, rather than a cell location, helps maintain integrity between linked files.

- Do not modify the contents of a formula for one time period without adjusting the corresponding formula for all other time periods. Tinkering inside one time period's formula, such as changing how the tax rate is computed for the upcoming quarter, will potentially be copied across to other time periods without a clear indication that a mistake has been made.
- Break down complicated formulas into multiple steps by displaying each step in a separate cell. This helps both as a math check and to make the computations easier to follow.

Training
- Ensure that the most relevant Excel features and functions for the job (such as those in Exhibits 15.1 and 15.3) are understood well enough to be consistently implemented in an error-free manner.
  ○ Have a good Excel reference book nearby or an online resource available.
  ○ Take Excel courses where deficiencies exist; most firms offer courses or will reimburse analysts who attend a course.
- Learn the keyboard shortcuts for the most frequently used Excel features (see Exhibit 15.2).

Unconventional Thoughts

Among the recommendations in Exhibit 16.1, there's one that's not necessarily a *common* practice, but it is a *best* practice. Typically, the most important elements of a financial forecast are the assumption inputs, because they are the "secret ingredients" provided by the analyst. The initial temptation is to put them immediately above or below to the variable they influence, which makes intuitive sense for a small spreadsheet that may be used only once or twice. But for a full-fledged company financial model that will have years of usage, these inputs, or assumption variables, should all be in their own worksheet(s) (ideally used for nothing but inputs) separate from the formulas they influence and the output. Because this appears so counterintuitive to many seasoned analysts, here is the rational for this best practice:

- It provides one easy-to-see place for changing and assessing forecast assumptions versus navigating through multiple spreadsheets to make changes.

- It allows the analyst to see forecast assumptions for previous periods, because they aren't overwritten as is typically done when the most recent period's forecast is pasted over with the actual results. This helps analysts see the strengths and weaknesses of their forecasting ability.
- It makes it easier to create structures that allow custom scenarios to be built (refer to Chapter 18 for further discussion).
- It reduces the likelihood of mistakes developing.

It may seem like more work to switch screens between the assumptions and the output they influence, but this can be quickly remedied by creating two windows of the same workbook on the screen:

- In version 2003, use Window, New Window, Window, Arrange, Horizontal.
- In version 2007, select New Window in the Window group of the View tab; then the Arrange All choice from the same group.
- In both versions, Ctrl F6 will toggle from window to window.

For displaying purposes, it's still possible to show the assumption variables in cells above or below the ones they influence, but it should be a link back to the assumption variable page rather than a cell that can be modified.

As a separate, unconventional thought, avoid macros. Excel macros are designed to automate a procedure that would otherwise be time consuming or complicated. These macros can range from highly complex, requiring skilled programmers, to relatively simple, only requiring an analyst who is willing to invest time. For example, if an analyst finds that routinely sourced data is formatted along columns that needs to be in rows, a macro may be the most efficient manner to automate the conversion. But unless an analyst has prior training in complex macro building, I recommend leaving the more difficult macros to trained professionals. IT department managers likely have someone on staff or an outside resource to help build these types of macros. Building macros can be time consuming, both up front and for continued maintenance. Furthermore, *problems often develop when worksheets are passed along to others who are not familiar with the macros.* As such, analysts should always look for alternatives before building macros. For example, if the data discussed in the earlier example comes from an in-house source, it may be possible for the team that creates the data to provide it in the required format.

Chapter 17

Develop Company Financial Models to Elicit Insights

In the previous chapter, I discussed some key Microsoft Excel features and best practices for setting up a workbook or worksheet. In this chapter, I go a step further by covering the basic elements required for setting up and building company financial models. While I attempt to lay a foundation, this is another area where analysts should consider taking formal training courses to fully master the skills needed for building effective models.

I've met many buy-side analysts who don't maintain any models for their companies and instead rely on consensus for valuation purposes. I have a tough time getting my head around this, because having a *unique financial forecast* is often the primary factor for differentiating an analyst's stock call. But as I discuss later, a good differentiated stock call can also be driven by a superior view on *valuation* or *market sentiment*. So for buy-side analysts who don't model, understand that it will be difficult to generate alpha by having a financial forecast that is superior to market consensus. With that said, during my research for this book, I met a number of successful practitioners who start with consensus and then tweak it based on their perception of where consensus is wrong. The remainder of this best practice assumes that the analyst builds company models in an effort to identify when the market is wrong about a stock.

While modeling is important, don't overdo it. Only dedicate the amount of time needed to help pick stocks. A buy-side analyst with over 10 years of experience believes, "When modeling a company, put in enough that matters but not too much to make it a burden to update." Detailed models can be a security blanket for many analysts, especially new ones; the more rows and columns a spreadsheet contains, the more secure the analyst feels. The problem is, the assumptions about the critical factors can only be validated by seeking insights from others—getting on the phone or out of the office to determine where the market is wrong.

Just as Goldilocks had to find the porridge that wasn't too hot or too cold, equity analysts should create financial forecasts that aren't too detailed or too simplistic. Drew Jones, a former Morgan Stanley analyst and manager of analysts, believes the essence of modeling should be to "spot future catalysts not recognized by the Street and frame the valuation debate." His philosophy is consistent with our model-building framework that focuses on the two to four critical factors discussed earlier. Analyzing historical and current trends in a company and its sector should help an analyst understand the pricing or growth of a key product or the inflation in a key cost input that *is likely to move the stock during the investment time horizon.* These factors deserve the most attention.

It's worth noting that sell-side analysts are expected to have detailed models for all of the companies they follow, which is a realistic request from clients, but much of a model's minutiae can usually be delegated to more junior members of the team. The senior sell-side analyst and most buy-side analysts should be focusing their financial modeling on the two to four critical factors in order to determine how much they can impact the stock. If the analysis shows that a factor is unlikely to move a stock, stop spending time on it. This is so difficult for analysts who try to model every aspect

Exhibit 17.1   Best Practice (Knowledge): Elements of a Good Company Model

A good model has all five of these characteristics (the A,E,I,O,U framework):

- **Accurate:** Is it technically sound? Do the columns add up properly, and are the financial statements properly integrated?
- **Efficient:** Is it easy to update and add columns and rows when necessary? Does it avoid complicated macros and circular references so that it's quick to make changes?
- **Illuminating:** Is it easy to see trends and anomalies in critical factors and key financial metrics, such as margins, earnings per share (EPS) growth rate, return on invested capital (ROIC), and spot accounting yellow flags?
- **Organized:** Is it well documented so that others can follow along? Are all of the assumptions in one place? Are there separate spreadsheets for each of the financial statements and the company's operating division breakdown?
- **Useful:** Does it allow for critical factor assumptions to be changed easily so that multiple scenarios can help the analyst think about the unexplored possibilities? Does the analyst look at it as a tool to help identify when consensus is wrong, rather than a useless but necessary step required before making a ratings change?

of a company, but they must cut their losses if a factor isn't likely to be material. I define the elements of a good company model in Exhibit 17.1.

Some analysts think of model building as one big process, but it's important to break it down into at least two distinct stages; one for building the *historical* model and another for building the *forward-looking* forecast. This distinction is critical, because the amount of time equity analysts spend on forward-looking aspects of their models should be five to ten times greater than they spend on the historical aspects; this can get overlooked by analysts focused on building historical models. History is important, but only because it helps to understand the future. If a historical model can be created by an assistant or outsourced, do so and spot check for accuracy.

Build or Buy? Company Models and Their Inputs

For most of my career, sell-side analysts built all of their models from the ground up, which was also the case for many of my buy-side clients. As part of the outsourcing trend, some of the lower-value elements of model building have been sent to lower-cost labor markets, such as Eastern Europe, India, and Costa Rica. Furthermore, market data providers have amassed entire model-building teams in order to provide this service to their clients. When determining which option is best, ask the following questions:

1. How concerned are you with the model:
   - Being 100% accurate?
   - Clearly identifying when the model's historical numbers deviate from the company's reported numbers?
   - Being in a format you prefer?
2. How much time do you have to build and maintain your model? Do you have a colleague to do this?
3. Do you have a budget to buy modeling services, or can model data be downloaded from an existing service used by your firm?
4. Do you need company and sector information that isn't likely to be in the company's regulatory filings, but is in the public domain?

If you want the model to be 100% accurate, and to include your preferred methodology for adjusting all one-time items, it can require 10 to 50 hours per model to build, depending on the required level of detail and years of history to be captured. If you're at the other extreme, being asked to closely cover more than 50 stocks, your only real option is to use somebody else's model—either a vendor or sell-side model (if on the buy-side). Exhibit 17.2 highlights the pros and cons for obtaining models using the most common options.

Exhibit 17.2   Sources for Company Financial Models

Option	Pros	Cons
Build your own from scratch	• Customize format to meet your needs. • Develop a personal understanding of how the model and company operates (which can be very valuable). • Best opportunity to identify and understand discrepancies between reported and adjusted results.	• Takes the most time among the three options.

Download from a model-building vendor or market data provider (e.g., Bloomberg, FactSet)	• Fast.
	• Depending on the vendor:
	  ○ May include uniform metrics across companies within a sector.
	  ○ May be easily updated via a web link.
		• Adjustments to reported numbers may have been made without an explanation.
		• Quality of data is only as good as the vendor's quality control process.
		• May have a cost, especially if company sells its model building as a service.

Inherit predecessor's model or for the buy-side, request from a sell-side analyst	• Fast.
	• No explicit cost.
	• Depending on the analyst:
	  ○ May include notes to explain adjustments to prior periods.
	  ○ May include company and sector information not found elsewhere.
	  ○ May include historical periods when the company reported results in a more transparent manner.
		• Adjustments to reported numbers may have been made without an explanation.
		• Among the three options, it's most likely to be in a format difficult to follow (analysts each have their own way of thinking).
		• The older a model gets, the more prone it is to having a mistake because of the multiple people working in it and lack of institutionalized quality control process.

There are a few additional factors to consider:

- It can be a great learning process to build a company's model, similar to building a model plane or car, in that you see how all of the components work with one another, but there's also a time commitment involved.
- If you're outsourcing your historical model building, don't assume that all vendors are created equal. Some have one or two separate quality control teams responsible for validating a model's accuracy, which work independently of the team creating the model.
- Outsourcing the creation of the *historical* elements of a model may be a time saver, but don't treat the *forward-looking* forecast in the same manner, because that's where an analyst adds value.

Layout and Detail

An analyst's financial model should be a tool to help pick stocks, whereas a company's 10-Q or 10-K is designed to meet its regulatory requirements. Sometimes these objectives are at odds, which means an analyst shouldn't automatically build models that only include information from a company's filings. To speed up the updating process during earnings season, it's wise to keep the *order* of the information in a similar manner as the company's financial details in its press release, but analysts should only add to their model where it helps generate new insights. Some analysts create a worksheet in their model where they dump the data from the company's quarterly earnings release, which is then linked to the parts of the model that use the data. While it speeds things up, extra care needs to be taken to ensure that the company's press release format hasn't changed (the introduction of eXtensible Business Reporting Language, XBRL, may help solve this as it becomes more widely adopted).

A helpful exercise is to rank the importance of each line item of a model on a scale of 1 to 10, with 1 as completely unimportant and 10 as mission critical. Those that are high on the scale should include more details where possible, either from company data or information collected from the analyst's other sources; those that are low on the scale should simply be entered as is or even collapsed within a broader set of numbers. There are certain modeling elements that are more likely to be important for value companies versus growth companies, which is highlighted in Exhibit 17.3. The line items that have historically been critical factors or could likely be a critical factor in the future, such as pricing or changes in volatile cost inputs, should be ranked at the higher end of the scale. A sell-side analyst noted for his modeling skills believes analysts shouldn't "fall prey to simple assumptions when the drivers are complex and critical to the model."

Here's a story to illustrate the point. When I began following CSX early in my career, I built a model that had an incredible amount of detail for all of its five divisions at the time, making the income statement portion of the model over 200 rows. As I became more experienced, I realized that the company's small barge division wasn't worthy of the 30 lines

Exhibit 17.3   Modeling Considerations Unique for Value versus Growth Companies

Value (or Cyclical)	Growth
• Identify factors that have helped forecast cycle inflection points of the past.	• Identify the ultimate size of the market (how big can it get).
• Capacity additions relative to demand.	• Sources of funding to grow.
• Post-retirement benefits.	• Dilution from stock options.
• Off-balance-sheet liabilities.	

Copyright McGraw-Hill and AnalystSolutions

I was giving it, whereas the area for the railroad's coal transportation pricing and labor costs needed more detail because they were the areas most likely to cause an earnings surprise. If I had taken some time early on to look at the factors that drove the stock over the prior years, I would have realized that the barge division simply needed four rows: revenue, margin, depreciation, and earnings before interest and taxes (EBIT). (Depreciation was necessary to reconcile with the consolidated cash flow statement.)

In another example, one of the firms I worked for required all analysts to identify the pension exposure for their companies, which was a very cumbersome process and involved an entire worksheet within each of our company models. But since the railroads only provide pensions for their white-collar workforce, this had very little impact on the financial statements and subsequent stock prices. *My stocks were never going to move substantially due to pension expense; so why spend time modeling it?* Ultimately, it was a waste of time for stock-picking purposes, but as a sell-side analyst, it may have provided value to clients evaluating this issue for all companies with pension exposure.

With this concept of prioritizing line items in mind, there are three primary stages when building a *historical* model:

1. Build a historical model to focus on those elements that:
   - Are currently critical factors, have been in the past, or are likely to become so in the future.
   - Are necessary to get the three financial statements to integrate.
2. Determine the factor that will drive the first variable in your model, such as volume or revenue. If a company tends to grow its volume two times gross domestic product (GDP), then start the model with GDP. As discussed in Exhibit 16.1, you will likely want to keep macro and sector data in a separate workbook that is linked to the individual company models, so you're not changing these assumptions, such as GDP, manually in all of the company models.

3. As highlighted in Chapter 12, use statistics to determine if there are relationships between revenue (or volume) and expenses as well as factors in the cash flow statement or balance sheet. When strong relationships exist, have one factor help forecast the others. For example, if personnel costs have an *R*-squared of 95 percent with revenue, have these costs be driven by revenue rather than by an independent computation.

When it comes to model building, complexity is your worst enemy. Some of my associates and colleagues have intricately complex financial models that bring them great pride. While they believe that complexity gives them a competitive advantage, I don't think they fully appreciate the countervailing downside. Specifically, the complexity means it takes longer to update, creates more opportunity for mistakes, and makes it almost impossible for someone else to use. This is especially problematic when it comes time to pass the model along to a successor or a colleague (or send to a client). As one buy-side client put it, "Simply having more inputs in a model does not necessarily lead to better investment conclusions." Before adding complex macros or links to a model, ask if there's an easier way to do it. Ultimately, the model is a tool to help create a financial forecast, one that's often required to be shared with others. Make sure it's easy for them to follow.

To strike the right balance in building or obtaining a company model, and ensuring it has useful insights, follow the best practices highlighted in Exhibit 17.4.

Exhibit 17.4 Best Practice (Skills): Develop Company Financial Models to Elicit Insights

1. As a general rule, spend more time confirming assumptions that drive a company's financial model than working in the model. Spending an entire career building a better Excel spreadsheet won't make it a better forecasting tool if the assumptions are wrong.
2. Be hesitant to assume historical trends will continue into the future, especially if they are critical to the investment thesis. When possible, use a top-down approach to confirm a bottom-up analysis (e.g., after building a bottom-up

(Continued)

three-year EPS forecast, look to see how it compares with historical growth rates and adjust for the broader economic and competitive outlook).

3. Ensure that the architecture of the company's financial model is constructed using the best practices found in Exhibit 16.1.
4. Before building a company's financial model from the ground up, explore obtaining it (or the data to build it) from one of the sources below:
   a. An experienced colleague within the firm who has a working model.
   b. Third-party firm, specializing in model building (often off-shore).
   c. Market data provider (e.g., Bloomberg, FactSet).
   d. If on the buy-side, request models from sell-side analysts who follow the stock, and use the model(s) that feels the most comfortable.
5. The only way to ensure that company financial data is accurate and has not been adjusted is to obtain it directly from the company's financial filings. This is usually the most time-consuming method, and should only be used if there is concern about adjustments made by others.
6. If models will be built by the analyst (or significantly modified before being used), the analyst should consider taking a one-to two-day course dedicated to model building.
7. In general, the detail or complexity of the model should be commensurate with the size of the company within the benchmark or assigned universe of stocks (or position in the portfolio if a big bet is being made). There will be exceptions to this recommendation, but avoid building the most complex models for the smallest companies, unless that's where most of the potential alpha is likely to be found.
8. Try to include important concepts that aren't available in the 10-K and 10-Q, as portfolio managers and clients will appreciate it much more than a standard model. (Most sell-side analysts only model the information found in the quarterly earnings releases.)
9. When creating a new company model, use the column date headings and possibly the row labels, but build new formulas. Trying to use an entire model as a template causes an increased risk of mistakes.
10. If it's a company with many different operating divisions, consider building a separate worksheet for each division, with all of the information rolled up into a consolidated worksheet.
11. In general, models should be more detailed in the following areas (sell-side analysts may have exceptions to this, namely more detail in areas of client interest, which may not always correspond with the criteria below):
    a. Current critical factors, as well as those that have been in the past, or are likely to become so in the future.
    b. Where there is a competitive advantage in spotting anomalies not understood by the market. (If the extra detail isn't likely to help make a stock call, then it's probably not worthwhile.)

(Continued)

12. When variables in the model move closely with others in the past, only one should be forecast (e.g., if personnel expense has a historical *R*-squared of 0.95 with revenue, it should be linked to revenue growth rather than forecast independently). See the discussion for Exhibit 12.12 for more details.
13. For analysts who create quarterly financial forecasts, start breaking out the quarters at least one year before the year begins (e.g., in late 2012, the analyst should be creating quarterly forecasts for 2014).
14. Create a section of important ratios and growth rates that will help analyze important trends (e.g., ROIC, revenue growth, margins) and potentially spot accounting yellow flags discussed in Exhibit 14.1.

Benefits of "Quarterizing" Two Years Forward

Sell-side analysts almost always forecast the upcoming year on a quarterly basis, and forecast all periods beyond then on an annual basis. This holds true for many buy-side analysts, but some only forecast on an annual basis due to time constraints or because their fund has a very long time horizon.

Generally, those analysts who "quarterize" their models (i.e., break out their annual estimate into four distinct quarters) tend to do so for the upcoming fiscal year just before the year begins or right after it has begun (i.e., before or after the late January earnings season). It can be a painful process because the annual numbers need to be divided over four quarters, adjusting for seasonal or one-time issues, all with the expectation that the full-year total shouldn't be far off the previous annual estimate.

I discovered a solution to this pain midway through my career by quarterizing models a year in advance. I believe this change ultimately helped me to rank higher than my competition in earnings estimate accuracy polls and led to a few additional good stock recommendations. This isn't to say that analysts need to share their quarterly estimates with colleagues or clients for periods beyond a year, but the data and assumptions should be broken out into separate quarterly columns in the financial model.

By having the financial model quarterized for the next two years, as a company reports its quarterly results, the analyst can go into the corresponding quarter of the *next year* to make all of the necessary adjustments for unusual items or trends that occurred in the quarter just reported. This ability to adjust for unusual items one year out can be a *major competitive advantage*. When using the more typical approach of quarterizing as the year is beginning, analysts need to recall all of the unusual things that have occurred over the past 12 months, for each individual quarter and for all of the companies in the assigned universe, which is almost impossible.

The second benefit is that the analyst has a leg up on the rest of the Street going into the late January fourth-quarter earnings season. Companies typically provide their first-quarter guidance at that point, but many analysts haven't quarterized their models, and so they don't know what to make of the number. This confusion by the market can provide a near-term trading opportunity. For my sector, during any other time of year, there would be 10 to 20 brokerage firms contributing to each company's upcoming quarterly consensus estimate. But because most analysts don't have a first-quarter estimate until February, the first-quarter consensus in January would often be wildly skewed by just one or two estimates. Many shops trade on the direction of consensus, and so if my forecast was substantially different than consensus, it was an opportunity to recommend a trade in advance of the company providing guidance during its fourth-quarter earnings release or before the rest of consensus started to publish first-quarter estimates in early February.

And the final benefit is that it can improve the accuracy of valuation. When valuing a stock using 12-month forward earnings or cash flow, most analysts use a percentage of the current full-year estimate plus a percentage of the upcoming year's full-year estimate (e.g., in early October, they use 25 percent of the current year's and 75 percent of the next year's). This poses a problem when the company has a terrible first half of the year, because it weighs down the 12-month forward estimate even though the period has passed. Analysts who have their forward two years quarterized can always be using the upcoming four quarters, which eliminates this problem and creates a more accurate valuation.

Chapter 18

Forecast Scenarios for the Most Important Critical Factors

Introduction

There are many different ways to be successful in almost every profession, but there's usually one factor that sets apart the good from the great. For financial analysts, *discovering alpha-generating ideas* is arguably the most important skill to master, but it's followed closely by *accurately forecasting future earnings*, especially for sell-side analysts. Research shows that abnormal stock returns are earned when following the recommendations of sell-side analysts who are among the top quintile of *accuracy in forecasting earnings*. If you're on the buy-side, the recommendation here is to find the sell-side analysts who have the most accurate forecasts and if you're on the sell-side, do your best at forecasting earnings. Based on my experience, I suspect the connection between earnings forecast accuracy and generating alpha is not the result of more complex financial models (although it can help at times), but rather an analyst's ability to *find insights surrounding critical factors*, which is important to both activities.

When I started in the business in the early 1990s, sell-side analysts provided earnings estimates, but it was rare to see price targets in writing or in client discussions. As the Internet age emerged, allowing buy-side clients to more quickly and easily access all of the underlying fundamentals of a sell-side analyst's work, they began requesting price targets, which eventually became commonplace by the time the Internet bubble started expanding. But after the bubble burst, analysts and PMs began questioning if single-point price targets were the best way to do business. After all, stocks don't trade at one point over an extended period of time.

In 2006, Juan Luis Perez, Morgan Stanley's global director of research, was at the forefront of the effort to move analysts toward thinking about modeling scenarios in order to provide a range of earnings estimates *and* price targets. The concept became unofficially dubbed *open platform* within the firm, because it was intended to get analysts to open up their thought process, thus allowing buy-side clients to use these scenarios for *their* investment process. The initiative was intended to get the firm's analysts to explore factors that wouldn't normally be considered, by stretching their thought process to consider more extreme possibilities. He would tell analysts to "think big both ways, potential upside and downside." After all, *it's what you don't know you don't know that usually creates the biggest surprises.* (The things you know you don't know can be investigated through research, but if it's not anywhere in your gray matter, it can't be something to look out for.) It's also important to appreciate that all analysts have biases in their models, thus causing them to confirm their view (confirmation bias is discussed in Chapter 21). Some of the confirmation bias can be eliminated (or at least recognized) by forecasting scenarios. This concern is held by the director of research of a large hedge fund who said, "Too often new analysts think they know the answer because they are overly confident in their models. Their mind can't comprehend where they could be wrong."

It would be impractical to change every model assumption for each scenario, because it would take an inordinate amount of time and make a relatively small difference compared with simply modifying the two to four most important factors. After all, if your base-case scenario is, a company earns $3.00 per share next year, it's more important to determine that the bull case is $4.00 or $5.00, than it is to fine-tune the $3.00 estimate to the nearest penny.

In a perfect world, you'll routinely uncover critical factors that: (1) have a large impact on a stock, (2) are likely to occur, and (3) are not in consensus. Unfortunately, many critical factors that you come across will fall into only two of the three categories, which leaves you with little to offer your portfolio manager or clients. Experienced buy-side analysts routinely tell me that successful sell-side analysts need to come up with only one or two good ideas per year to have a successful franchise. In general, buy-side firms require more from their analysts, but most don't expect more than a handful each quarter. Don't beat yourself up if you don't have a great new stock call every week, but also occasionally reflect to ensure that you're periodically offering recommendations that generate alpha.

Sell-side analysts as a group are often viewed as too optimistic compared with their buy-side counterparts, which was reinforced by Richard Bilotti, an analyst with 27 years of experience on the buy-side and sell-side, when he expressed, "The buy-side focuses as much if not more on the bear-case scenario than base-case whereas the sell-side focuses on the bull-case scenario." Looking more closely at the bear-case scenario will help the sell-side analyst have a more balanced view and better appreciate the needs of buy-side clients.

To build scenarios, start by listing all of the critical factors for a stock identified earlier. If there's more than four, you probably have too many to realistically research; you can have dozens of factors that may someday drive a stock, but you want four or fewer on your critical factors list, which are those that you think can move the stock substantially during your investment time horizon. Think about stocks that you've seen skyrocket or collapse. The cause of the substantial movement isn't usually a litany of critical factors but one, or occasionally two. It could be better-than-expected pricing, product sales, or cost cutting, but it's not usually all three. You're not trying to identify everything that could impact a company's stock, but rather those that are likely to have the *largest* impact. Remember, much of your job is about managing your time wisely—specifically, knowing where to hunt. This process should narrow down the hunting field.

It's also been demonstrated that it's possible to have too much information. Mauboussin has shown there is a disproportionate number of high-performing funds outside of New York and Boston, despite being the first two places company management and sell-side analysts go to tell their stories (Mauboussin, 2008).

In Chapter 8, I attempted to quantify if a factor impacted the financials by a specific threshold (in my example I used 5 percent), which required some research. Now I take that a step further in order to more accurately quantify the likelihood that a catalyst will occur and cause the critical factor to become part of the consensus. For example, earlier I determined that a coal company's stock will be substantially impacted by changes in coal prices if the company hasn't locked up its production under long-term contracts. Now, I need to determine how much production is not under contract, and the sensitivity earnings have to change in the spot price of coal. Too often analysts don't take this additional critical step to research their thesis. Adam Longson, a Morgan Stanley analyst, holds this philosophy in stating analysts should "dig into the key drivers of the model and ask why. Don't just assume pricing will be up 4 percent next year."

In building scenarios, don't forget about the age-old trade-offs companies make between factors such as price and market share or reinvestment rates and future growth. Even a bullish scenario will look unrealistic if the company is taking up pricing more than any of its competitors and also growing its volume faster than historical trends. For this to occur, something very significant must be happening. Too often, the best-case scenario doesn't consider resources for growth, such as hiring more employees or increasing research and development (R&D).

The next step in the process is to assess upside, downside, and base-case scenarios in terms of the impact on the stock and the likelihood that each scenario will occur. There's an art to this step; if you had five experts in the room they would probably quantify the likelihood of each scenario differently. It's critical to identify a base-case scenario as the one that's most likely to occur. In the coal case, you might want to use the 10-year spot rate for coal prices as your most likely long-term future scenario, or make adjustments to factor in current market dynamics, such as tight supply due to production problems or expanding supply due to new mines being opened. It's also critical to ensure that your upside and downside scenarios are within the realm of reasonableness; you shouldn't routinely model once-in-a-century events. For example, if western U.S. coal prices have ranged between $7 and $10 per ton for the past 15 years, you probably don't want to assume that your upside scenario comes in at $15 per ton or your downside is $5 per ton unless you've done a lot of work to show why you're likely to break a 15-year trend. While there are no hard-and-fast rules about this, a general rule of thumb should be that your base-case scenario has a 50 percent chance of occurring, while there is a 25 percent chance your upside and downside scenarios will occur. Some factors are either/or; for instance, a company will either get FDA approval for a new drug or it won't. In this case, you may have only two scenarios, and they don't need to be split right down the middle, each with a 50 percent probability.

The process of building scenarios should help analysts think about potential future inflection points, something done too infrequently on Wall Street. Dennis Shea, former chief investment officer and head of global equity at Morgan Stanley Investment Management, said, "One of the best lessons I have learned from my years on the Street is not to extrapolate. For all the high-priced analysis and sage commentary, most people seem to project the current trend into the future."

Record a quantifiable figure for each scenario and each critical factor, which you'll need when speaking with information sources and eventually for financial modeling. If you have developed a view about a critical factor that will impact more than one company in your sector, record your scenarios in a *sector* workbook, which will be linked to the company workbooks. This is important because you don't want to enter your new view on coal pricing in every coal company's financial model, and you definitely don't want to later discover that you've updated one company and not another (which I've seen occur with other sell-side analysts).

Assuming you're picking up 10 new stocks and have discovered 3 critical factors for each, you've just had to quantify 90 scenarios (3 scenarios for each factor), which can take up plenty of time. It's a lot of up-front work, but once you have the factors identified and quantified, it makes your research so much easier because *you're not wasting time on factors that you've deemed not critical*. It's also worth mentioning that this isn't a destination, but rather a journey. You'll feel more comfortable with some of your scenarios than others based on your preliminary research, which you'll refine over time as you learn more about your companies and sectors. This is reinforced by Mike Vitek, CFA, senior director, Fiduciary Management Associates, who recommends analysts to "constantly reassess your thesis and question if the world has changed." (Creating and managing scenarios in Excel is explained in Exhibit 18.1.)

Now comes the hard part: determining if your base-case scenario is similar to consensus thinking. As highlighted by a highly ranked sell-side analyst, "An analyst's job is to determine where could consensus be wrong, especially a few years out." Financial pundits are quick to complain that consensus is stale or too optimistic, but the reality is that it's more often right. So don't be surprised if, after all of your work, you discover the consensus view is also your most likely scenario. And when I speak about consensus, I'm not just referring to the consensus estimate of earnings per share or cash flow, but the entire market psychology about a stock. We've all seen situations where a company falls short of the consensus estimate for the quarter, but the stock goes up because the company exceeded the "whisper number," which was in effect the current consensus thinking. This topic is explored in more detail in Chapter 20.

Exhibit 18.1   Best Practice (Skills): Creating Forecast Scenarios in Excel*

Creating forecast scenarios in Excel financial models allows the user to choose one set of assumptions over another by clicking one button. Excel has a built-in scenario manager, but I find that it's not robust enough to meet the needs of most financial analysts because it's limited to only 32 changeable cells and the assumptions driving the multiple scenarios are not visible in one place.

As such, I've developed a process that meets this need. In this example below, the user is creating three sets of assumptions in Excel: one for the base-case, upside, and downside scenario.

1. It's assumed, prior to this process, that all of the initial assumption variables for the model (presumably the base case) are in one worksheet, which should be named *Assumptions Inputs* (see the section Unconventional Thoughts in Chapter 16 for details). The inputs in this worksheet (such as revenue growth rate or margins) are linked to the rest of the model, so changes in these cells drive the changes in the output (e.g., EPS, cash flow).

2. When setting up the time periods (e.g., quarters) in the Assumptions Inputs worksheet, it's ideal to have the columns correspond to those with the same time period in the financial forecast (if column AB in the model is the second quarter of 2012, column AB should be the same time period in the Assumptions Input worksheet).

3. In the Assumptions Inputs worksheet, copy the entire set of assumption inputs to an area below, keeping the corresponding columns consistent. Do this once for each scenario. It's a best practice to leave spare rows between each set of assumptions, which can be done by starting at rows that are divisible by 100 (e.g., base case starts at row 100, upside starts at row 200, and bear case starts at row 300).

4. At this point there should be four identical sets of values in the worksheet. Label each as follows:
   a. The first one: *Values Currently Driving Model Output.* (This area will eventually contain formulas.)
   b. Second: *Base-Case Scenario.*
   c. Third: *Upside Scenario.*
   d. Fourth: *Downside Scenario.*

5. In the Assumptions Inputs worksheet, find a cell location that is free of any other variables and can be seen clearly, such as A1. Enter the number 1, which will be for scenario 1.

(Continued)

---

* I'd like to thank Bob Jones of Murray Hill Associates for his help with this Best Practice.

6. Clear all of the cells that contained the original variables in the *Values Currently Driving Model Output* section, and replace the upper left most assumption cell with a formula that uses Excel's CHOOSE function to select the variables from one of the scenarios below. For example: =Choose(A1, C100, C200, C300). (Pressing F4 while editing a formula inserts the $ characters for absolute reference.)

7. Copy this formula to all the cells in the *Values Currently Driving Model Output* section. They should all contain a CHOOSE function that substitutes a value from the sets below into the formulas, which in turn drive the model. When the number in cell A1 is changed from 1 to 2, all the assumptions from the second scenario should appear in the Values Currently Driving Model Output area.

8. Format font colors so that the cells in the *Values Currently Driving Model Output* are black (or the chosen color for formula cells), and the lower cells in each scenario are the chosen color for input cells. It would be a good idea to protect the top set of cells after this step.

9. At this point, it's time to make changes to the three sets of scenario inputs. Even though all of the assumption inputs are available in each scenario, the analyst should focus on modifying just the two to four critical factors for the company. (There's not enough time to fine-tune each scenario with variables that aren't going to substantially move the stock.)

10. You can hide multiple rows so that only the two to four critical factor assumption inputs are viewed for each scenario. Excel has features that make it quick and easy to hide and unhide multiple sets of rows all at once. They include:
    • Custom Views.
    • Data Group and Outline.

11. Change the assumption inputs for the critical factors in each scenario as desired.

12. To switch scenarios and more clearly see which scenario is currently being used, create a Group Box with the Option button. In version 2003, open the Forms Toolbar, whereas in version 2007 click the Office button, Excel Options button, Customize choice and ensure the left pull-down menu reads "All Commands". Double click the "Group Box tool (Form control)" and "Option button tool (Form control)" icons to add them to the Quick Access Toolbar (directly above the worksheet).

13. Click the Group Box tool and draw a rectangle in a clean area at the top of the Assumptions Inputs sheet; it should be about the size of a business card. Change the caption on this object from *Group Box* to *Switch Scenarios*. As long as each Option button is built inside this Group Box, a

click on an Option button will change a value on the sheet (the first built will change the value to 1, the second to 2, etc.).

14. Click the Option button tool, and then click inside the Group Box near the top. Change the caption on this object from Option button to Base Case.

15. Right click the edge of the Option button and click Format Control. On the Control tab, click in the Cell link and identify the sheet and cell where the original switch was set (='Assumption Inputs'!A1).

16. Clicking the first Option button created should place a 1 in cell A1; when the second one is built, it will automatically place a 2 in the same control cell, because it was the second one built inside the same Group Box. The third one created will produce a 3 when it's clicked, and so on.

17. To keep the Option buttons associated with the Group Box, click the outside edge of the Group Box and hold the Ctrl key while also selecting each of the Option buttons. When all are selected, right click one of the objects and group them together. This Group Box with its Option buttons can be copied anywhere within the model. Since the links in all copies refer to the correct control sheet and the control cell, a click on a choice in any of the copies of the Group Box will change cell A1 in the control sheet, which in turn will result in changes throughout the model. It's also very valuable as a visual indicator of which scenario is in place at any given time.

PART 4

MASTERING PRACTICAL VALUATION AND STOCK-PICKING SKILLS

All of the best practices discussed to this point have been assembled to help analysts pick stocks better than their competition, which is the focus of this section.

Given that valuation is often the foundation for stock picking, I start the section by highlighting the benefits and shortcomings of the most common valuation methods. They can be distilled into two camps: *single-period multiples* and *multiperiod cash flow*. There are pros and cons to both, but in the end, single-period multiples are more widely used by practitioners, which is why they receive the bulk of my discussion. I also review identifying the historical valuation parameters for the companies in an assigned universe, an important exercise for anyone picking up a new sector. I conclude the valuation chapter with best practices for building a comp table.

Valuation leads into the next, and arguably most important, best practice of all: overcoming the typical challenges to becoming a great stock picker. I discuss these challenges and then provide the FaVeS™ framework to highlight that all good stocks calls must possess a unique view toward at least one of the following: *financial forecast, valuation,* or *sentiment.* In addition, all good stock calls must have an identifiable *catalyst* in order to ensure that the analyst's unique view becomes widely accepted by the market during the investment time horizon. I conclude that chapter by highlighting some very valuable lessons learned by experienced stock pickers.

Stock picking isn't just about the numbers; there's an emotional element as well. For this reason, the next chapter attempts to help analysts become more aware of the most common psychological pitfalls that impact professional investors, with the hopes of avoiding them as much as possible.

I end this section with an introduction to technical analysis, with the objective to use valuable information gleaned from the approach, such as trend, support, and resistance, in order to help improve fundamental analysis.

Chapter 19

Understand the Benefits and Limitations of Common Valuation Methodologies

Valuation is easy. The tough part is fundamental analysis.
—Phil Friedman, former Morgan Stanley Portfolio Manager,
John Levin and Co. CIO, and Perella Weinberg Partners
Hedge Fund Manager

Introduction

As highlighted above, some analysts overcomplicate valuation. While it's a critical tool for stock picking, many analysts forget that it's just a tool and not a panacea. When analysts make shaky stock calls, they often confuse challenges in valuation with the real problem, which is assessing the probability, timing, and magnitude of the critical factors—elements that can only be better assessed with more thorough fundamental analysis.

The topic of stock valuation is a large discipline, as evidenced by 10,000 results coming back from a book search of the term on Amazon.com. Given its complexity, I can't explore all of its dimensions, but I can focus on the best practices that equity research analysts use to derive sound valuations for their stocks. Here are some of the broad steps they use when conducting stock valuation:

- They have full command of *historical* valuation parameters for their stocks, or classes of companies, specifically those with similar financial characteristics, which is critical for understanding the valuation levels likely to be afforded in the future.
- They are diligent in understanding why the market values their stocks at *current* levels.
- They appreciate the limitations of the most traditional valuation methods, such as price-to-earnings (P/E), price-to-free cash flow (P/FCF), price-to-book (P/B), price-to-earnings growth (P/EG), and discounted cash flow (DCF).

Selecting a Valuation Method

The first tangible steps in valuation should include acquiring the following knowledge:

- For every stock in the assigned universe, identify the valuation method(s) currently being used and any methods used in the past.
- If more than one, identify the catalyst(s) that caused it to change.
- Determine if there are similar catalysts that could cause investors to look at a new valuation method over a reasonable investment time horizon.

The best way to get these answers is by speaking with individuals who trafficked in the stock in the past. (Elements of this were recommended in Chapter 8, as part of a preliminary step to determine "what's in a stock.")

Most stocks are valued by the market at any point in time by only one valuation methodology. While it's helpful for analysts to use more than one valuation method to get other perspectives, they should be hesitant to use a *change in the valuation method* as the primary reason for making a stock recommendation. Occasionally, analysts are convinced a stock is cheap because the market is using the wrong valuation method, only to discover a year later that the market is still using that "wrong" method. As discussed later in the stock-picking best practice, valuation methodologies can change when industries go through major transformations or are in need of a floor valuation during a sudden collapse (which often differs from the ceiling). However, this doesn't occur often, and therefore should be used sparingly as a stock recommendation rationale. On this topic, Matt Ostrower, an analyst with 15 years of buy-side and sell-side experience, believes, "If you're using a valuation methodology that differs from most market participants, you need to be prepared to quickly tie your methodology back to theirs."

Benefits and Limitations to Most Common Valuation Methodologies

Which valuation method is the best? The more widely used valuation methodologies fall into two camps: *single-period multiples* and *multi-period cash flow*. The former is primarily used to evaluate stocks *relative* to their peers, whereas the latter is used to identify *absolute* values for stocks (i.e., intrinsic value). In theory, money management firms that attempt to generate excess returns for their clients relative to a benchmark (e.g., most mutual funds) should be using relative valuation methods, while firms with the goal of achieving absolute returns (e.g., many hedge funds) should be using absolute valuation methods. For example, just before the tech bubble burst, most mutual fund managers were still expected by their clients to be fully invested in equities, which would have been difficult to achieve had the managers been using a DCF method for valuation. With that said, in practice, many firms allow their analysts to use both valuation types.

Research shows that substantial improvements in price target accuracy occur when analysts use more rigorous multiperiod valuation techniques (e.g., DCF), rather than a simple heuristic such as the P/E ratio. The stock picking performance is even better for the population of analysts who are shown to have the most accurate earnings forecasts (Gleason, et al., 2008).

From an *academic* perspective, DCF appears to get the highest marks, because it measures future free cash flows of the firm, which are the core to almost every valuation methodology.* From a *practitioner's* perspective, the basic P/E ratio is most revered for its simplicity. Studies have shown that even though sell-side analysts use DCF in their research reports when discussing valuation, they rarely use it to justify a price target (Imam Barker & Clubb, 2008). According to that same study, here are the valuation methodologies that sell-side analysts rank as most important (ranked in order of importance):

- P/E
- DCF
- Enterprise value-to-earnings before interest, taxes, depreciation, and amortization (EV/EBITDA)
- P/CF

It took me a good part of my career to conclude that even the most intelligent money managers want to keep things simple. I contend it's for this reason that the vast majority of valuations are conducted using single-period multiples-based methodologies, driven by easily defined forecastable metrics like earnings, cash flow, or book value. These methods aren't elegant or overly complex, but that's what makes them so enduring to portfolio managers, who are ultimately at the top of the industry's decision-making pyramid. (They influence everyone's salaries,

---

* There is good discussion on bridging a connection between multiples-based and cash-flow-based valuation methodologies in Chapters 7 and 8 of *Damodaran on Valuation*, Second Edition. Hoboken: John Wiley & Sons, 2006.

even the sell-side's.) But these methods have their shortcomings, which is why I recommend using a multiperiod cash flow valuation as a reality check for a single-period multiples-based valuation. When they differ substantially, it should cause the analyst to dig more deeply.

There is no methodology that prevents biases from influencing outcomes. (Even when left completely to the discretion of a computer, the biases of those people directing the programmer are somewhere in the code.) For this reason, it can be helpful for analysts to use their firm-wide valuation framework, which may only ask for a financial forecast in order to derive a price target. The output shouldn't be blindly followed, but rather should serve as a reality check to ensure that the analyst's biases haven't been corrupted by his or her own valuation analysis. In the end, analysts can reverse engineer any type of valuation to arrive at or near their desired price target. The challenge is to remain intellectually honest in the process. Creating a range of scenarios, using different valuation methods or different levels of valuation multiples, can help illustrate potential shortcomings in the thought process not apparent when a single valuation method with a single-point multiple is used.

The primary benefit of multiples-based valuation methods is that they are relatively simple and quick to perform. Every market data service provider has a screen that provides these types of valuation multiples. The problem is that there is no uniform agreement in terms of the time frame for the denominators, such as earnings, cash flow, and sales. When I started my career in the 1990s, most services could only provide these multiples based on *trailing* or *prior year* results, which was of no value, because stocks trade on *forward* expectations. Many more services are now using forward consensus in computing the multiples, but again, there is a difference between next year, rolling 12-month forward, and the next four quarters. This may seem minor, but I've seen this difference cause valuation multiples to move by a full point, which can be a 10-percent difference for a slow-growth value stock.

It's critically important when researching *historical* valuation ranges to determine whether the vendor who collected the denominator (financial data) captured consensus at that point in time or actual results for that year. Given that sell-side analysts are generally more bullish about future earnings than the figures companies actually report, the difference between the two data series can be substantial. For example, if an analyst is digging up the historical P/E ratio for a stock back in January 2002, it may have been 10 times *forecast* earnings for full-year 2002 (the consensus at the time) but 12 times the *actual* 2002 reported earnings (because consensus tends to be more optimistic than the results that a company eventually reports). Clearly, using a 12 times P/E ratio to derive a future price target would be high, because the stock isn't going to trade on actual results. (It will trade on consensus expectations.)

The biggest drawback to multiples-based valuation methods is that they don't explicitly capture a company's long-term growth rate or risks, which are core elements to a DCF analysis. After all, a valuation ratio is typically based on earnings or cash flow no more than 12 to 18 months out. If an analyst has a P/E comp table for the 20 stocks within a sector, the degree to which each stock is influenced by long-term growth rate expectations and risks is not clearly evident. For example, two stocks could command a similar P/E ratio for many years, with one company offering a faster growth rate than the other, offset by a higher level of execution risk; these factors could be more clearly identifiable in a DCF analysis. The P/EG ratio is the one multiple-based exception to this rule, but it tends to be simply the growth of next year's earnings over this year's (or possibly two years out), which is not as rigorous as a multiperiod DCF analysis. With that said, growth rates and risks are usually captured *implicitly* in multiples-based valuations, namely, higher growth rates and lower risks result in richer ratios, when all other things are equal. There have been efforts to compute P/E ratios based on a company's growth rates, such as with Ben Graham's formula for growth company valuation: Value = Current (Normal) Earnings ×(8.5 + 2 × expected annual growth rate) (Graham, 1985: 158).

Price-to-Earnings

Among the multiples-based valuation methods, the P/E ratio is the most widely used, because consensus earnings are available for almost all companies and are often viewed as a reasonable proxy for free cash flow. The shortcoming is that earnings are not free cash flow, and therefore just because a company has strong earnings growth doesn't mean that it's throwing off an impressive level of free cash. Also, companies tend to have more flexibility to manage earnings than cash flow, which can make the P/E ratio less reliable than a cash-flow-based methodology.

Price-to-Free Cash Flow

A P/FCF ratio is the multiple closest to the DCF valuation method, but it's shortcoming is that it only covers one period. Furthermore, capital expenditures can be lumpy from one year to the next, which can substantially skew the free cash flow for a given year. Also, some analysts include changes in working capital, while others exclude it.

Price-to-Book

A P/B ratio is used in a limited number of industries where the assets are liquid or easy to compute, such as banking and brokerage firms. But in those cases, analysts must be able to trust that book value is stated correctly. Firms such as Countrywide and Bear Stearns sold themselves at prices far below stated book value, suggesting their most recently reported book values at the time were not realistic. For most companies, book value is not current market or replacement costs, but is based on historical costs. Even for two companies with similar growth and risk characteristics, their book values may be incomparable if either has conducted any significant M&A.

Price-to-Sales

P/S is a poor valuation method, because a given amount of sales rarely produces the same amount of free cash flow across multiple companies.

But this may be the only valuation method available for companies that have no earnings or cash flow (e.g., the airlines for a number of years over the past decade); it can also provide a floor value for companies going through trouble.

Multiperiod Cash Flows

Shifting to multiperiod valuation methodologies, DCF is the primary method, while residual income (RI) comes in as a distant second (Imam et al., 2008). These methods capture a company's potential ability to generate free cash flow over time, which puts the focus on returns from incremental capital spending. This focus on return on invested capital (ROIC) is important for many funds, because it has a high correlation with changes in stock prices. These methods are also superior because they can help an analyst identify when a stock is cheap or expensive on an *absolute* basis, offering the opportunity to get out of an overheated market or get into one that's oversold. The biggest problem with these methods is that some of the inputs, such as the equity risk premium, terminal growth rate, and incremental returns on future capital, are often subjective measures difficult to support with research. Furthermore, a minor change to one of these variables can potentially affect a large change to a price target, thus putting the method's validity into question. And finally, as the underlying inputs to the valuation become more complex, there is a greater likelihood of errors developing. Some of the highest-profile valuation mistakes I've witnessed in my career were found in complex DCF models. The subjectivity allowed in DCF models also creates more chances of analyst manipulation. This is echoed by Dr. Aswath Damodaran, a professor of finance at the Stern School of Business at NYU and author of a number of insightful valuation books, when he said, "Our analysis indicates that analysts see DCF in part as a useful tool for more accurate fundamental valuation but more generally as a flexible device for 'reverse engineering' valuation estimates based on multiples models and/or subjective judgment."

Exhibit 19.1 Best Practice (Knowledge): Benefits and Limitations to the Most Common Valuation Methodologies

Method	Pros	Cons
All multiples-based methods (e.g., P/E, P/B, P/Sales)	• Relatively simple and quick to perform. • Easy to understand.	• The multiple may not be computed in the same manner by all market participants, namely, the underlying financial data can be *trailing*, *forward*, or *current year*. • Rarely includes financial forecasts beyond the next 18 months. • Unlike DCF, a company's expected growth rates and risk are not explicit inputs to the valuation (except for growth in the PEG ratio), making it difficult to compare companies on these dimensions.
P/E	• Understood by all because it's the most commonly used valuation method.	• Company management has more flexibility to manipulate earnings than cash flow. • Does not capture cash available to shareholders.
PEG	• Incorporates earnings growth rate (preferably over multiple future periods), which makes comparisons among companies and, potentially across sectors, more plausible (but not perfect).	• Earnings growth is not the same as the more important free cash flow growth. • If using consensus estimates, may be difficult to find reliable long-term growth forecasts.
P/FCF	• Incorporates free cash flow, which is the best measure of value.	• Considers only one time period. • Methodology can vary for reasons mentioned above as well as in estimating level of capital expenditures (maintenance vs. forecast).
P/S	• Can be helpful if there are no earnings or cash flow.	• Sales do not automatically result in free cash flow, which is the true measure of value.

(Continued)

Exhibit 19.1   Best Practice (Knowledge): Benefits and Limitations to the Most Common Valuation Methodologies *(Continued)*

Method	Pros	Cons
P/B	• For a select number of industries that have liquid assets, book value may be a good proxy for measuring a firm's equity value.	• For most sectors, book value rarely equates to the company's market value of equity. • Book value can be subjectively influenced by interpretation of accounting rules, which can make comparisons between companies meaningless.
Dividend yield	• Can be helpful to measure a floor when stocks collapse.	• Dividends are not the same as free cash flow, although they often move in tandem. • Difficult to forecast when management will cut a dividend.
DCF and RI	• Capture a company's ability to generate free cash flow over the life of the enterprise, which is the best measure of value. • Helps to place the focus on the level and returns from incremental capital spending (ROIC). • More likely to identify overheated and oversold stocks and markets than multiples-based methods.	• Can be highly sensitive to minor input changes for factors difficult to quantify, such as the equity risk premium and terminal growth rate. • Input variables can more easily be manipulated to reverse engineer an outcome. • More time consuming because multiple periods are required for forecast. • Complex models are prone to mistakes. • May be times when there are no attractive equity investments. • Added complexity when comparing companies across borders due to measuring non-U.S. "risk-free" rates.

Identifying an Appropriate Multiples-Based Valuation Level

When using a multiples-based valuation methodology, follow the steps found in Exhibit 19.2 to derive a defendable valuation multiple (or range of multiples).

Exhibit 19.2 Best Practice (Skills): Rigorously Develop an Appropriate Valuation Multiple

1. For every stock in the assigned universe, identify the valuation method(s) currently being used by the market and any used in the past.
2. If more than one, identify the catalyst(s) that caused the change. Determine if this catalyst could occur again to cause investors to look at a different valuation method over a reasonable investment time horizon.
3. Be mindful that the favored valuation method for a given stock doesn't tend to change often, and therefore shouldn't be used as the basis for a stock recommendation unless there is a major or transformative event likely to bring the market around to using a new methodology.
4. Start by using the valuation method(s) of potential institutional buyers and sellers of the stock. Research shows (and my experience confirms) the most common valuation methodologies used on the sell-side are:
   - P/E
   - DCF
   - EV/EBITDA
   - P/CF
5. To provide alternative perspectives, analysts should attempt to use both single-period multiple and multiperiod cash flow methodologies.
6. For stocks with multiple years of trading history, collect stock and benchmark data for historical valuation parameters (i.e., weekly or monthly data going back at least 10 years), such as the consensus estimates and prices, in order to derive the forward-looking absolute and relative multiples at any historical point in time. (Avoid using backward-looking data, such as price-to-trailing-earnings ratios.)
7. For stocks with minimal trading history or achieving growth rates not experienced in the past, collect the data above for companies with similar characteristics, preferably within the same sector.
8. Use the historical valuation data to compute peak, trough, and average multiples on an *absolute* and *relative* basis (as previously discussed in Chapters 7 and 8). Look at the valuation ratio as well as its two components

(Continued)

in graphic form to help identify anomalies or periods that should be removed (such as when earnings go negative, there is take-over speculation, or when consensus is influenced by nonrecurring events like a change in accounting or a one-time charge).

9. Review the historical valuation data in order to accomplish the following:

   a) Isolate when significant *absolute* multiple expansion and contraction does not coincide with the benchmark's in order to isolate the causes of *relative* multiple changes. Identify if this is explained by changes in the market's expectation for macro factors such as GDP or issues at the sector- or company-level, such as customer pricing.

   b) Isolate periods when the company's stock price or sector index outperforms and underperforms materially from the benchmark, which will often be when the relative multiple changes. For periods where there is material outperformance or underperformance, the challenge is in isolating how much is due to the *market anticipating consensus revisions* versus the *actual revisions* that take place. It may be that the stock begins to outperform coincidentally with changes in a factor such as GDP, but changes in the consensus figure lags by three months. This will cause the stock's P/E multiple to spike, but as consensus catches up, the P/E comes back down to more normal levels. Scrutinize historical periods of gradual multiple contraction, especially when it's not related to macroeconomics or an obvious miss by the company; it can be the market correctly anticipating slower growth, which eventually manifests as dropping consensus estimates.

   c) Identify the lead or lag time between the outperformance or underperformance and the catalyst, in order to better understand the causes of historical changes in valuations and when investors tend to rotate into or out of a sector.

10. If there is a strong historical relationship between a company's or sector's valuation multiple and measurable factors such as consensus EPS, growth rate, or the company's current ROIC, ensure that the current price target multiple isn't inconsistent with this historical relationship. A common mistake analysts make is in simply applying a historical average multiple to a company's current earnings, even though the company's prospects or returns have changed substantially. If there are no periods in the company's history comparable to present, it's usually helpful to look at the historical and current multiples being commanded by other companies with similar growth and risk prospects, preferably in the same sector.

11. To avoid self-selecting a multiple in order to justify a predetermined stock call, provide the multiple from the steps above (or a range of multiples) to a trusted colleague or stock selection committee to obtain objective feedback on the plausibility of the call.

12. Periodically review a "comp page" of comparable companies (as highlighted in Exhibit 20.3) to determine if the mispricing is isolated to the company or the entire sector.
13. Be mindful of the shortcomings in the most commonly used valuation methods, found in Exhibit 19.1.

Resources

Among the valuation books I've come across, there are two notable titles that even an experienced practitioner will likely appreciate:

Damodaran, Aswath, *Damodaran on Valuation*, Second Edition, Hoboken: John Wiley & Sons, 2006.

Koller, Tim, Marc Goedhart, and David Wessels. *Valuation: Measuring and Managing the Value of Companies*, Fourth Edition. Hoboken: John Wiley & Sons, 2005.

Chapter 20

Overcome Challenges to Creating Discerning Stock Calls

I don't have any trading secrets that guarantee stock-picking success. If I did, I would be selfishly hoarding them on a private tropical island I'd purchase with the windfall. In truth, it's not that I haven't found them, but that they don't actually exist. Through my entire career working with hundreds of sell-side analysts at Wall Street's largest firms to the thousands of clients I've met, I've never come across a low-risk, high-return investment strategy that could be used with consistency. I mention this first because I find some analysts spending more time seeking this Holy Grail than producing high-quality fundamental research.

It's probably worth mentioning that the discussion in this section is limited to stock picking using a fundamental approach; I cover the technical approach later in Chapter 22. Many portfolio managers prefer their analysts not use both a fundamental and technical approach simultaneously, at least not until the fundamental work is done.

Stock picking is one of the few areas where sell-side analysts have it better than buy-side analysts. Both types of analysts are required to make stock calls, but sell-side analysts can have long and rewarding careers even as mediocre stock pickers, because their clients aren't necessarily paying just for stock calls. With that said, sell-side analysts who are good at every other aspect of the job *and* can pick stocks are rewarded for these efforts. The buy-side isn't as forgiving, because stock picking is usually the major component in setting compensation.

Dennis Shea, who spent many years as a highly ranked sell-side analyst and a senior manager of both sell-side and buy-side analysts, has an insightful view about the qualities that make up a great stock picker:

- Dispassionate, namely, they don't allow nonrelevant factors to cloud their judgment.
- Stick to their discipline and strategy over the long-term.
- Self-aware of where they have expertise and where they don't.

Challenges with Stock Picking

It's important not to confuse valuation with stock picking. There were many people by mid-1998 who could clearly show technology stocks were overvalued, but their bearish calls would have been bad stock picks for another 18 months, well beyond the typical institutional investor's time horizon. Stock picking involves art and science. As highlighted in Exhibit I.1, the science part comprises the primary tasks discussed to this point: identifying critical factors, creating financial forecasts, and using valuation to derive a range of price targets. This last phase also has elements of science within it, but in order to truly achieve success, an analyst must learn the *art* of stock picking.

Experienced practitioners know stock picking is the hardest part of the job, in part due to these challenges:

- All of the information needed to make a perfect stock call is rarely available. My work shows that analysts appreciate this concept more as their experience increases. After all, if the information were readily available, it would have already moved the stock. Thorough research helps give an analyst an edge over the broader market, but it's rarely complete or reliable enough to make a stock call with 100 percent certainty.

- As an analyst diligently takes more time to dig deeply into an investment controversy, the early stages of research often become known by the market, thus diminishing the value of the work. Unlike scientists and doctors who can research topics for years, analysts need to balance relative urgency with the need for more thorough research.

- There isn't always a great stock-picking opportunity in an analyst's space. Despite conducting thorough research, there may not be a big call at a given point in time, because the market has reasonably assessed the critical factors that drive a particular stock.

- Some factors that move stocks can't be forecast. Many analysts had well-researched individual stock recommendations in mid-2008 that completely fell apart due to the subprime-led global financial collapse. These "black swans," which can't be forecast, can disrupt what would otherwise be a great stock call.

- Many analysts are so overworked that they don't have time to find unique insights. As discussed earlier, many shops overload their analysts with so many stocks that the analyst only has time to play defensive catch-up, which means there's no time for creative thinking to generate alpha. If an analyst is only digesting information available to the rest of the market, it's going to be tough to beat the market.

- Emotions cloud clear thinking, often causing an analyst to make the wrong decision. This is discussed further in Chapter 21.

Where Do You Differ?

Put simply: *The key to generating alpha is having a more accurate view about a future stock price than the market.* This can only be done on a consistent basis if the analyst has an edge over the market in one of the three areas that compose our FaVeS™ framework:

- Forecast: Financial forecast superior to the market. (This relies on many of the best practices discussed earlier.)
- Valuation: Valuation methodology or valuation multiple superior to the market.
- Sentiment: Forecast of investor sentiment superior to the market. (Sentiment, void of any fundamental changes, is often the only thing that moves a stock or market in the short-term.)

That's it—nothing more. If you don't have an out-of-consensus view in one of these three areas, you don't have a stock call worth making. Unfortunately, this gets lost on too many analysts. Drew Jones, former associate director of research at Morgan Stanley, would tell analysts, "Don't assume you're smarter than the market. If you think the market is wrong, you need to have some proprietary piece of information or thesis that is not understood or known by the market." Given the importance of the three elements of the FaVeS framework, we explore them in more detail below.

Forecast Superior to the Market

Among the three elements of the FaVeS framework, new analysts are more likely to have success in developing a superior financial forecast than the other two components that take more time and experience to master. There are usually a good number of high-quality, experienced analysts who make up the consensus estimate for a company. Therefore, if an individual analyst's forecast is significantly out of consensus, the starting point should be to assume his forecast is wrong. Understanding why an analyst's estimate differs from consensus can be a time-consuming task, but it's required before making a stock call. *It's critical to ensure that the "differentiated" element of a forecast is concentrated in an area of expertise or has been thoroughly researched, rather than being just a more bullish or cautious view.* It's for this reason that analysts should forecast upside, downside, and base-case scenarios before making a big stock call; it allows critical assumptions to be stress tested and forces the analyst to consider the other side of the trade. (See Chapter 18 for additional information.)

When a forecast is out of consensus, it's important to make sure the components of consensus are understood by asking these questions:

- How many analysts make up consensus? For forecasts that cover periods two to three years out, sometimes there are only a few published sell-side estimates, which is hardly a consensus view for most sectors.

- Where is the "informed consensus," which comprises the sell-side thought leaders, relative to the overall consensus? It's well understood in practice and has been proven in studies that some analysts are better at forecasting the future than others. (StarMine has a patented product, SmartEstimate, that places more weight on estimates from analysts with a more accurate forecast record.) How do their views differ from the broader consensus?

- Are the estimates stale? When the sell-side updates estimates after earnings season, it's not uncommon for there to be no major revisions for another two months until the next earnings season approaches. Being in possession of a financial forecast that differs substantially from a stale consensus may be valuable. Or it may be worthless because it's already accounted for in unpublished Street expectations.

- Are there any disagreements about what's in the number? Data vendors are getting better about this, but occasionally there is still a situation where some sell-side analysts are including something in their estimates that's excluded by everyone else.

If the above mechanical questions surrounding consensus are explored, and the analyst still has an out-of-consensus view, the next step is to understand why. A global director of research for a large sell-side firm tells analysts, "If you don't know what's in the price, you can't justify why a stock will move to a new level." This is one of the more difficult parts of the job, usually requiring conversations with individuals who are close to the stock on the buy-side, sell-side, and within the company. (The range of experts to speak with is explored in Chapter 8.)

Another method for assessing consensus expectations is to survey buy-side analysts. The level of formality can range from a web-based survey to simply calling five colleagues. There are a number of buy-side and sell-side analysts who survey buy-side analysts weekly or monthly to gauge what's in consensus in terms of the key assumptions, as well as to assess investor sentiment.

If an analyst has an out-of-consensus estimate, it's important to avoid a common rookie mistake of putting undue faith in companies that have a weak management team, poor track record of achieving success, or unproven success. Henry McVey, a former Morgan Stanley strategist, liked to say, "Avoid the blowups." This may sound like common sense, but it's alarming how many analysts, especially those early in their careers, assume their financial forecast is better than the Street, just because it puts more faith in questionable stories. The more experienced sell-side analysts that make up consensus often give a haircut to their financial forecasts for poorly performing or unproven companies. So, discovering your estimate is well above consensus may not be cause to upgrade a stock. Viewed another way: When faced with questionable stories, swing for singles and doubles, rather than trying to be the home-run hero, especially if you are an analyst early in your career.

Many buy-side analysts don't have the time (or possibly the desire) to develop their own financial forecasts, and instead rely on sell-side analyst's forecasts. For those who follow this strategy, the first goal should be to determine which analysts are the most accurate. This isn't to say that only sell-side analysts with accurate earnings can add value to the buy-side, but rather that buy-side analysts should make sure any analyst they use for financial forecasting has a proven record in this area. This can be done more efficiently through analyst accuracy polls provided by StarMine, Bloomberg, and FactSet. Here are some of the facts to back up this view:

- A well-established study showed that stock recommendations from sell-side analysts who are in the top quintile of *earnings-forecast* accuracy generate almost 75-basis-points-higher returns than a passive index, whereas recommendations from those in the bottom quintile underperform a passive index by over 50 basis points (Loh and Mian, 2006).
- Another study shows that price targets set by *Institutional Investor's* "All American" analysts are achieved 54 percent of the time within 12 months of applying the target (Asquith, Mikhail, & Au et al., 2005). When they exceed the target, they do so by 37 percent.

Buy-side analysts who create their own forecasts without the help of the sell-side may have a reason to share them with the sell-side, but only at the right time. If after thorough, intelligent work, a buy-side analyst discovers that he's found a reason to be out of consensus and his firm has put on the trade, it's perfectly within his right to influence sell-side analysts to understand his perspective so that consensus (and presumably the stock) moves in his direction. This can be through e-mail exchanges and one-on-one dialogue with sell-side analysts.

Valuation Superior to the Market

Developing an out-of-consensus stock recommendation based solely on expectations that a stock's valuation multiple will be rerated or that the market will change its preferred valuation methodology is plausible, but too often used unsuccessfully by inexperienced analysts. Forecasting that a stock's current 15 times P/E ratio is going to 17 times with no clear catalyst should be met with skepticism. Multiples tend to move in the direction of financial forecast revisions (discussed earlier), which isn't the same as the concept of generating alpha by correctly forecasting that the market will afford a stock a new multiple or valuation method. For example, in 2008, telecom analysts were split, with some valuing stocks on EBITDA, while others were defensively using dividend yields. However, the real valuation differentiator should have been focused on their financial forecasts, specifically, each company's ability to refinance its debt.

If an analyst is going to use an out-of-consensus valuation multiple or methodology as the rationale for a stock call, there must be a clear understanding about *why the market has this misperception* and *the catalyst that will correct it*. Conducting historical valuation analysis for established companies or comparing multiples of other companies with similar expected growth rates should help frame the analysis (as discussed in more detail in Chapter 19).

Let's first discuss potential changes in *valuation methodologies* as a catalyst for stock recommendations, as it's a relatively straight-forward concept. As a general rule, the preferred methodology for valuing a stock doesn't change much over time. There are three primary exceptions to consider:

- When the company or sector is going through a major *secular* transformation, such as moving from subpar returns to generating returns well above the cost of capital, or when a growth sector hits a wall because its market has become saturated.

- When the company or sector is at a certain point of the business cycle (e.g., a time of major distress) that leads the market to use a floor valuation, such as price-to-book (P/B) ratio, price-to-sales (P/S) ratio, or dividend yield.

- When the sector goes through changes in accounting (e.g., media companies transitioned from EV/EBITDA ratios to P/E ratios when accounting for amortization went away).

Given that these situations are not routine, often only occurring once in a decade for any given sector, they shouldn't be the basis for many stock calls. As an analyst with extensive sell-side and buy-side experience put it, "Don't change your valuation methodology just because the stock is moving. Do so only if there's a major change to fundamentals." Great calls can be made here, but only if the analyst can accurately predict the impact of one of the major events mentioned above (which is difficult to do, even for experienced analysts).

Discounted cash flow (DCF) is arguably the most complicated among the more commonly used valuation methods and is also favored more in academia than in practice. It's for this reason that new analysts, fresh out of business school, will often fall into the trap of assuming their intricate DCF valuation has found a mispriced stock that the market has missed using its more traditional multiples-based methodologies. This alternative valuation method is helpful in thinking through the long-term drivers to value creation, but it shouldn't be used as the basis for a stock recommendation unless the rest of the market is going to convert to DCF analysis during the typical investment time horizon. In general, don't assume that just because a valuation methodology is more complex, it will correctly forecast a superior price target.

The other area where an analyst can have an out-of-consensus view on valuation is with the multiple, which is more feasible than a change in valuation methodology, because it tends to occur more often. With that said, it is also often misused in poorly constructed stock calls. We use the term *multiple* to refer to the typical valuation multiples, such as P/E and price-to-free cash flow (P/FCF), but also for the assumptions that drive DCF and residual income models.

A common mistake made by inexperienced analysts is to say that a stock's multiple looks cheap without thoroughly reviewing the forecast. For example, if a stock is trading at a 9 times forward consensus estimate compared with its historical 10 times (10 percent below normal), it could be because the consensus estimate is stale and almost certain to head 10 percent lower, which the market may have already discounted in the stock price. So the analyst makes a big call only to discover her estimate (and consensus) needs to be lowered over the following three months, putting her stock multiple right back to where it belongs. *Before an analyst recommends a stock based on a change in the stock's multiple, the financial forecast should be rigorously tested to ensure that it's not likely to soon move in the wrong direction.*

When a company is going through a transformation, such as a major turnaround, there is a justifiable reason to assume that the multiple will expand. But the market isn't likely to pay the higher multiple until earnings start to beat consensus. Recall that having a well-researched, out-of-consensus financial forecast provides a more stable platform for recommending a stock.

Another common mistake in this area is to disregard the current place of the economic or sector's cycle. Cyclical stocks often trade at trough multiples at the peak of the cycle and peak multiples at the trough. When the market concludes that the peak is about to occur, multiples will contract and no well-constructed stock recommendation is going to stop the freight train until the market concludes that down leg is no longer imminent. That isn't to say an analyst shouldn't try to call the end or beginning of the cycle before the market, but fighting the tape in the face of a potential inflection point is usually a losing proposition. *Before an analyst recommends a cyclical stock based on a change in the multiple, an understanding of where the company is in the sector's or economic cycle must be thoroughly appreciated.* This can (and should) be explored by conducting a historical review of valuation multiples compared with the economic and sector factors discussed earlier. For cyclical stocks, when late into the business cycle, compute multiples based on normalized earnings and cash flows to see if they are truly "cheap."

Unfortunately, the most common mistake made in this area is a complete lack of analysis to justify an out-of-consensus *multiple*. It's not uncommon for an analyst to spend dozens of hours building an earnings or cash flow forecast, and then dedicate only a few minutes selecting an out-of-consensus valuation multiple. The research report reads something like this: "We're raising our price target, because we believe the company's better prospects afford it a 2-points-higher valuation multiple." So the multiple is moved from its historical 15 times P/E ratio to a 17 times P/E ratio, providing no historical context or rationale. Why go to 17 times? Why not 18 times? Why not 20 times? This overly simplistic 2-point change just added 13 percent to the company's value, which may go unscrutinized. However, if the analyst had taken up the EPS or cash flow forecast by that much, there would likely have been heightened scrutiny. To avoid applying valuation multiples arbitrarily, follow the process for identifying an appropriate multiples-based valuation level discussed in Chapter 19.

Assess Sentiment Superior to the Market

Among the three primary areas within the FaVeS framework for an analyst to have an out-of-consensus view, forecasting the correct *change in market sentiment* is arguably the most difficult, often requiring years of experience to master. I wish there was a way to teach new analysts how to do this on their first day, but success is often based on experienced gained while watching stocks or sectors move over a career. To be clear, the skill to be mastered here isn't understanding how investor sentiment changes *after* consensus earnings or cash flow forecasts change, but *beforehand*. The psychological factors that drive stocks almost always relate to anticipation of changes to the financial forecast, but they often react too much in one direction, offering a buying or selling opportunity. These opportunities aren't likely to show up in a complex Microsoft Excel spreadsheet, but rather by watching signs in the way market participants behave.

One of the most basic elements for understanding investor senti-ment is to know which types of investors own the stocks in an analyst's assigned universe. Not all stock calls require the stock to change hands between investor styles (value, growth at reasonable price (GARP) growth and momentum), but it can often play a role. For example, if a value fund is buying a stock because it believes the company will be recognized for successfully moving into attractive growth markets, growth investors will need to bid the stock up to a point where the value manager has an attractive exit point. While not every stock fits cleanly into an investment style box, it's often important to know the investment philosophy of the current owner in an effort to: (1) iden-tify the potential owner who will eventually bid the stock higher, or (2) consider which style is the buyer of last resort should the company stumble. Companies that successfully move from value to momen-tum can see their stocks easily rise 30 to 100 percent, but should that momentum slow, there's often nobody to catch the falling knife until it becomes attractive to value investors again. Analysts who understand this concept will be hesitant to recommend a momentum stock that begins to crater until it reaches a level attractive to a new base of value investors.

Experienced analysts who have a better understanding of the direc-tion of market, sector, and stock sentiment often can get into stocks early and avoid staying in too long. Best practices for exploiting flaws in mar-ket sentiment are highlighted in Exhibit 20.1, while Exhibit 20.2 lists a number of factors an analyst can monitor in order to better understand market sentiment.

Exhibit 20.1 Best Practice (Skills): Exploit Flaws in Market Sentiment to Enhance Stock Picking

While some of these strategies work in isolation, almost all should be used to *supplement thorough fundamental research.* (Picking stocks purely on timing market sentiment, without conducting any research, is a dangerous strategy).
1. Increase your urge to sell when everyone loves a sector or stock, and buy when no one wants to own them. A few telltale signs to *sell* are when:
   a. All or almost all sell-side analysts have buys on a stock.

    b. The general view in sell-side reports and the financial press is, "It's different this time," or "Nothing can go wrong."

    c. The stock no longer reacts positively to good news.

    d. Valuation is reaching or exceeding peak levels.

2. Before making a buy recommendation, ensure that near-term market expectations aren't below published consensus expectations. This may seem like common sense, but too often an analyst will recommend a stock based on a long-term catalyst, but fail to appreciate that the stock is going to remain weighed down in the near-term because near-term consensus expectations are too high.

3. For deep value investing, watch for investors to capitulate before building a position.

4. When a stock appears to have dropped too much due to new concerns, avoid waiting for the herd to get greater clarity about the risk, because it will be too late. The lack of clarity creates an opportunity to exploit.

5. Be careful not to panic when investors who are short the stock attempt to over-blow the impact of negative news flow.

6. If a value stock experiences a strong move and no longer looks cheap, identify a realistic catalyst that will attract a new class of investors (e.g., GARP or growth) before assuming the stock will move any higher.

7. Avoid making individual stock calls in isolation of the market's appetite for risk (i.e., resist recommending weaker companies when the market's risk appetite is waning, such as near the end of an economic cycle).

8. Avoid recommending buying a stock before a large management lock-up expires (unless the stock is already cheap due to these concerns); few investors will want to buy a large block in advance of this event.

9. Avoid recommending stocks when the company is going through a CEO change, unless the change is the primary catalyst.

10. Use a short squeeze as a short-term selling opportunity, due to the panic buying. (These tend to be short lived, and as such, shouldn't be used as the rationale for setting a price target.)

Exhibit 20.2　Best Practice (Knowledge): Factors to Monitor to Understand Market Sentiment

- Short interest for each stock in the assigned universe.
- Company insider buying and selling.
- Changes in the types of investors who own the stock.
- Changes in sentiment toward the following topics, in an effort to understand the herd mentality. This can be done by periodically surveying buy-side sentiment about a sector or individual companies (which is done by some of the best sell-side and buy-side analysts).

(Continued)

o The names and types of stocks receiving:
  – The most attention. (Where is everyone spending their time?)
  – The least attention. (Which stocks are forgotten or written off as dead?)
o Biggest investor concerns by company or sector.
o Expectations that are above or below the published consensus.
o General view toward the market and risk (bullish or bearish).

• Sell-side analysts should monitor the investment styles of clients calling with questions (e.g., value, GARP, growth, momentum), and buy-side analysts should ask about this when speaking with sell-side analysts. If investment styles change or a new group of clients begins calling, that's usually an indicator of major changes in investor sentiment.

• Appreciate the market's relative appetite for risk by monitoring:
o Treasury yields.
o VIX.*
o The size of the deal calendar.
o Recent stock performance of:
  – Weak companies versus stable companies.
  – Emerging markets versus domestic markets.
  – Small cap versus large cap.

• Note when bad news no longer makes stocks go down, or when good news no longer makes them go up; it's a sign that market psychology is shifting.

• Note when a stock continually overreacts in one direction to news flow during a relatively short period of time, because it could be a sign of irrational buying or selling.

• Monitor technical indicators, which are discussed in Chapter 22.

*VIX is an abbreviation for the Chicago Board Options Exchange Volatility Index, which is designed to track volatility in the market.

Copyright McGraw-Hill and AnalystSolutions

Need for a Catalyst

As discussed in the FaVeS framework, before making a great stock call, analysts must have a unique edge when it comes to forecast, valuation, or gauging market sentiment. But none of it matters if the market doesn't eventually accept the analyst's out-of-consensus view. A gun can be dangerous, but not if it doesn't have any bullets. The trigger for getting the market to see the world through the analyst's perspective is the *catalyst*. As in science, the stock's price doesn't transition into its new state without a catalyst. Unfortunately, this straightforward concept is often overlooked by analysts, who make a stock recommendation without identifying the key catalyst that will drive the stock to its price target. Expecting a tech company to command a higher multiple due to accelerated unit sales growth is the critical factor, but the catalyst could be beating quarterly earnings or upward earnings guidance by management over the next two to three quarters. For a catalyst to be high quality, it should:

- Pertain to a critical factor, namely, a factor that will materially move a stock. Sell-side analysts are occasionally guilty of publishing sensationally worded reports to discuss a catalyst that pertains to something trivial. For example, telling investors to buy a stock before the company's upcoming analyst meeting is of little value, unless the analyst also identifies a little-known catalyst likely to occur during the meeting that will drive the stock to its price target.
- Be significant enough to lead investors to believe there will be a material change in the market's view about the company's financial results, long-term growth rate, or risk.
- Not be well known or appreciated by the market.
- Be forecasted with some level of certainty. (A recession or an international currency crisis are poor catalysts, because they are almost impossible to forecast.)
- Be likely to occur during the investment time horizon.

If something occurs that reduces the likelihood that the catalyst will occur, it's time for the analyst to rethink the investment thesis. In addition, if the catalyst occurs and the stock doesn't move, the stock recommendation should also be reconsidered.

Successful analysts are always looking for upcoming catalysts within their assigned universe of stocks, especially those that may support or refute their stock recommendations. Some of the more common places to expect catalysts include:

- Company-sponsored analyst meetings and calls.
- Earnings releases.
- The company's annual pricing, volume, or earnings guidance or projection.
- Deadlines for new legislation, regulations, or court case outcomes.
- Prescheduled announcements by the company's customers, competitors, or suppliers.
- New product releases or significant product extensions.
- Interim sales data, for the company or the sector.

When the event has some level of predictability, analysts should put the date in their calendars as early as possible and attempt to have a view on the event if it's likely to include a catalyst that impacts one of their stock recommendations. While an analyst shouldn't waste time chasing market noise, it's often helpful to monitor catalysts even for stocks in the assigned universe that are not currently being recommended. Pay special attention to the larger companies, because they may offer insight on the sector, and a portfolio manager (or client) may have questions before or after the event.

Questions to Answer before Making a Stock Call

The stock calls that become great almost always start off controversial, because they go against the consensus' commonly held beliefs. Making calls like these often creates uneasiness for analysts, especially for those with less experience. Christopher Columbus probably would have been a great stock picker, because he had conviction about something that the general consensus didn't believe was true, and yet he stuck with his conviction despite the controversy. Great stock pickers feel like outcasts when they are making their best calls; that's what makes them the best. David Tepper, co-founder and manager of the hedge fund Appaloosa Management, said, "I felt like I was alone," when talking about generating $7 billion of profits in 2009, betting against consensus as part of the financial market meltdown.

Feeling alone can be a typical emotion when making a great stock call, but that doesn't mean analysts should avoid working with others. Instead, analysts should try to understand how their views differ from the market to ensure that they're constructing a high-quality call. To that end, here are some critical questions to answer:

- What insight is held by the analyst that isn't in consensus, and where does it fall in the FaVeS framework?
  - Forecast: Is the financial forecast *materially* different from published consensus or current expectations?
  - Valuation: For the call to work, does the stock need to be valued using a *new* methodology or a *significantly* different multiple?
  - Sentiment: Will the market sentiment change *materially* based on the expected catalyst?
- Why doesn't consensus have this insight, or why is consensus ignoring it?
- What is the catalyst that will get the market to accept this out-of-consensus view, and when will it occur?
- What could go wrong? What are the most likely things that will derail the investment thesis? (Having an understanding of the inherent risks for a particular call shows that the analyst has done the work.)

The key lesson here is that great analysts don't recommend buying or selling a stock until they understand the answers to these crucial questions. It's an amateur mistake to disregard the current consensus view toward a stock, and just assume it will eventually move to a new fair value. Answering these questions can be one of the most challenging aspects of the job, because there's no universal place to go to understand consensus. This is why the best analysts don't find their answers by building more complex valuation methodologies, but rather by spending more time talking with market participants. Mark Liinamaa, a senior sell-side analyst believes, "Making outgoing calls (to market participants) makes you smarter because you're getting a better understanding of the consensus view." To find the answer to these questions, analysts should speak with the same market players as discussed in detail in Chapter 8 (summarized in the following list), being careful not to tip off the participants with insights that may move the stock before a recommendation is made and a position can be built.

- Experienced buy-side analysts or PMs who currently own or have owned the stock in the fund
- Sell-side salespeople who have interest in the stock
- Sell-side traders who trade the stock
- The company's investor relations contact
- Sell-side analysts (if you're a buy-side analyst)

Conviction Is Icing on the Cake

The best stock calls are made by analysts with conviction. While working in Equity Research management, I conducted a survey of portfolio managers located in financial centers around the world, from which I learned the top request they had for the sell-side was to provide *high-conviction* calls. For some, the conviction level is evidenced by the strength of the analyst's rating on a stock, but often it's difficult for the buy-side to identify truly high-conviction ideas. Analysts shouldn't be shy about telling portfolio managers or clients that even though there's more upside in one stock, it's not their favorite name right now because conviction is higher with another stock. Investors will appreciate that the analyst is providing an assessment of conviction.

There is a big difference between having conviction and being stubborn. In this context, conviction is based on a well-founded belief supported by fundamental research, whereas being stubborn is simply reiterating a view in the face of facts that would suggest otherwise. It's important to distinguish this because too often analysts who make a stock call with a high degree of conviction will disregard information that runs counter to their call. Instead, the analyst should embrace the information, and either explain why it's not relevant to the call or change the degree of conviction. Chris Leshock, equity analyst at Perkins Investment Management, put it well when he said, "Good investing is a peculiar balance between the conviction to follow your ideas and the flexibility to recognize when you have made a mistake."

To some degree, conviction is developed with experience on the job, after an analyst has learned to separate those factors most likely to move a stock from those that won't. In addition, an analyst's level of conviction can be raised through more thorough research on a topic. For example, if the investment thesis is that the market is overreacting to the risk of a legal claim against the company, the analyst could use an expert network to quickly interview five expert attorneys who practice in the area, all in an effort to have greater conviction that the market's perception is overblown.

Considerations for Price Targets

Analysts should avoid setting a single-point price target, and instead set a range of targets driven by their base, upside, and downside financial forecasts (see Chapter 18). As described by a successful sell-side analyst, "The analyst's job is to show the portfolio manager all of the possible paths and then explain why the analyst chose a given path." The goal here is to get analysts to explore factors that wouldn't normally be considered, by stretching their thought process about the more extreme possibilities. Realistic probabilities should be applied to each scenario. Going through this process can be very helpful to portfolio managers or clients, because it helps calibrate opportunity and risk and may even increase understanding of the analyst's conviction level. Some buy-side analysts will use the sell-side's *range* from downside to upside to help in stock selection, such as requiring two times as much upside as downside before considering a recommendation.

Analysts should avoid revising price targets just because they feel better or worse about a stock (because the stock is moving in favor or against them), and instead wait until something has changed in the investment thesis. But there are legitimate reasons for revising price targets:

- If the target is based on comps of the company's peers or relative to a ratio for the overall market, changes to the price target should be made when the peers or market fluctuate materially.

- Similarly, most multiples-based valuations are driven by forward financial forecasts. As time passes, the nearest forecast becomes history, and a new forecast is needed. To avoid abrupt changes, such as switching forward earnings from the current year to the next year (which some firms do in June or July each year), the analyst should strive toward gradual changes, such as using the next four quarters earnings or cash flow.

- If the target is based on a DCF, it should be revised as the risk-free rate, equity premium, or stock's beta change. These tend to move less frequently than multiples-based valuations, but they shouldn't be forgotten.

Sector before Stock

Occasionally, an entire sector becomes in or out of favor, taking all of the individual stocks with it, which can cause a major rerating of the sector. These occurrences are usually difficult to forecast, but it's important to give them your attention before making a ratings change. In 1999, the U.S. economy was growing at a respectable +4 percent pace, which should have benefited railroads, but instead the sector was *down* 24 percent, while the S&P 500 was *up* 15 percent. Looking back, some portion of this could be explained by railroad-specific M&A complications, but even for the carriers not involved, their stocks were miserably underperforming as investors shifted even further into "new economy" stocks at the expense of "old economy" stocks, regardless of sector fundamentals. It didn't matter how good your investment thesis was for owning a particular railroad, you were getting slammed. Over the following two years, as the tech bubble burst (along with other parts of the new economy), the trade reversed, with railroads up 10 percent and the S&P 500 down 20 percent.

I'm not suggesting stock ratings be driven solely by views about sector rotation, as it's difficult to forecast and doesn't occur frequently. However, an analyst shouldn't fight the tape for 6 to 12 months on an intelligent, individual stock call in a sector that is going out of favor. Forecasting when investors rotate into or out of a sector is difficult, but can be done with historical homework and assessing investor sentiment. As discussed in Chapters 7 and 19, make sure to look at how the sector performed relative to a broader index, going as far back as possible. If there are periods of substantial underperformance or outperformance when compared with the broader index, do some work to find the cause. Was it concern about industrial production, inflation, or consumer spending? Could it be that another sector was more in favor and took funds away? Or was there a new risk for the sector that was being digested by the market?

Not all sector rotation is due to *cyclical* concerns; sometimes it can be the result of a *secular* change. These don't occur often, and as such, shouldn't be the basis for frequent ratings changes. But some of the best stock calls include a secular overlay. Two sell-side analysts I had the pleasure to work with, who were both ranked among the top 5 percent of all sell-side analysts during their tenure, made powerful secular calls to help their individual stock calls. David Adelman made a secular call, rightly forecasting that tobacco litigation would not be as risky as the stocks were suggesting at the time, and Doug Terreson made the "Golden Age of Refining" call, which correctly asserted that limited refining capacity would drive the stocks higher.

Set Parameters for Getting Out

As one of my clients used to say, "I don't need help [from the sell-side] getting into a stock . . . I need to know when to get out." In the perfect stock call, the price target is reached within the investment time, which is the rationale for selling the position or downgrading the stock. But it doesn't always work that way. Here are some tips to consider for setting exit thresholds:

- Set a range of exit thresholds in advance of making the call. Doing so will prevent biases from creeping into the decision at a later date, which occurs all too often. These thresholds won't necessarily line up with the base-case, upside, and downside scenario price targets, because they are based on no changes to the base-case investment thesis (in other words, what should be done at various price levels if the base-case scenario remains intact?). Price targets can be set for the following thresholds, which can be absolute or relative to the market:
  - Upside exit threshold to begin selling *some of the position* when it's playing out as expected. (For the sell-side, this would be the point to stop reiterating the call.)
  - Upside exit threshold to sell the *entire position* unless new information materializes. (For the sell-side, this is the point to downgrade the stock.)
  - Downside exit threshold to *reexamine* the investment thesis. (For example, the stock moves 15 percent in the opposite direction of the call.) Notice I didn't say automatically exit the position. It may be that the stock call is going to work but there's been a short-term setback.

- If the stock reaches the downside exit threshold, additional research must be conducted to either confirm the original thesis or exit the position. If a stock is going against an analyst, the rationale being used by the market must be understood. When a piece of information that runs counter to the call cannot be disproven, it should be assumed to be true.
- Document the original investment thesis well enough so that it can be reviewed periodically. If quantifiable parameters such as EPS, ROIC, or number of new subscribers aren't emerging as planned, the stock call should be revisited in its entirety. Treat it as though it's a new call; would the same call be made today?

Don't rule out an about-face if new information comes to light. I can recall a number of times when, in the face of all the publicity associated with a sell-side ratings change, something new was brought to an analyst's attention that rightfully questioned the plausibility of the stock call. In effect, the new information negated the call (e.g., an analyst upgrades a stock that looks cheap only to discover in conversations with clients that a key factor was overlooked). If this should occur, first make sure this new piece of information is validated. If it's likely to impair the stock call, strongly consider an about-face on the recommendation as soon as possible. It's painful, but not as bad as ignoring the new information only to eventually be wrong. Endure the *reputational* pain of admitting a mistake in an effort to minimize the associated *financial* pain. For this reason, do due diligence *beforehand*, because it's quite embarrassing to change the rating soon after the initial call is made.

Focus on Quality over Quantity

It's important to emphasize *quality* over *quantity* when it comes to stock picking. Feedback from the global survey of portfolio managers mentioned earlier, suggests a sell-side analyst needs to come up with one to two good stock ideas per year. Yes, per *year*. I didn't specifically ask about their buy-side counterparts, but it seems like it wouldn't be much higher, except for trading-oriented shops; after all, it's about generating alpha, not trading volume. Based on my experience, many equity research analysts believe they need to be producing a major new stock call every month, or for some, every week, which can be a futile effort. (Are that many stocks in a sector materially mispriced every week or month?) Analysts who have this tendency should instead channel their energy toward finding proprietary information that either confirms or refutes their existing stock calls. By coming back to the portfolio manager or clients with new value-added nuggets of information about their calls, the analysts can provide more value than chasing a new story every few weeks.

Reviewing Valuations Regularly Helps Stock Picking

Analysts should look at the valuation levels of their stocks regularly, preferably on a daily basis, but no less frequent than weekly. (Constructing a valuation comp table that makes this easy is discussed in Exhibit 20.3.) Doing so provides a number of benefits:

- It can be the catalyst for a ratings change and ensures that current recommendations are consistent with the magnitude of risk-adjusted upside or downside potential.
- It helps to prioritize time, namely, to put more effort into places where the most potential alpha exists. If there is one stock in the universe with 15 percent upside compared with only −5 percent to +5 percent for the rest, it becomes clear where to spend time. For that outlier stock, more work should be done to gain greater conviction, or change one of the assumptions in order to get the price target closer to the market price. Spend less time on the stocks where it will be more difficult to generate alpha (e.g., very stable companies that appear properly valued or stocks that are driven almost entirely by factors that can't be forecast with any accuracy).

- It helps to internalize when stocks are approaching desired price targets, and are thus worthy of a potential ratings change. This is especially important on the sell-side, because analysts don't want to reiterate their rating one week and then downgrade the next, unless there's been a major change in thinking or in the stock price. (I was verbally beaten up, rightfully so, by a few salespeople and clients early in my career for this mistake.)
- It helps to understand the psychology about stocks, in terms of when certain stocks or subsectors move based on changes in the marketplace or in critical factors.

Exhibit 20.3   Best Practice (Skills): Build a Comp Page to Identify Stocks with the Most Upside and Valuation Outliers

Comp tables can be built and stored within certain market data providers' applications, but these often offer less flexibility for data availability and manipulation than creating a table in Excel, where data can be pulled from multiple sources. In addition, online applications can be more difficult to integrate into firm-wide or client presentations. For this reason, the following best practice assumes the table is being created in Excel, but other reasonable options are available.

1. Automate as much of the data collection as possible by setting up formulas that will pull in information from third-party vendors (such as the stock price) and the analyst's individual models (such as earnings and free cash flow per share).
2. In most instances, it will be helpful to display valuation multiples using the analyst's expectations in addition to consensus expectations. Exceptions include some valuation methods where there may not be a consensus, or situations where analysts do not have their own estimates. It's often helpful to create valuation multiple columns based on this year's forecast as well as next year's forecast.
3. At a minimum, the following sections should be included in the comp table for each company in the universe:
   a. Financial forecast data used for valuation such as EPS, FCF, or book value. Clearly identify the analyst's and consensus' forecasts.
   b. Valuation multiples as computed using the analyst's and consensus' expectations.

(Continued)

    c. *Historical* forward-looking average multiples, adjusted for anomalies.

    d. Other financial metrics that influence valuation.

4. If the table will be used in presentations, include this additional information for each stock:

    a. Rating or view.

    b. Price target or range of targets (expressed as percent upside or downside from current levels).

    c. Market capitalization.

    d. Date of stock price.

5. Include the following information, possibly in hidden columns if not for use by others:

    a. The analyst's conviction level.

    b. Exit thresholds.

6. Set up formulas to automatically roll over to the next forward period as time progresses. For example, if the P/E ratio is based on the next four quarters of earnings, it should be relatively easy to move to the next period after the current quarter's results are reported. Avoid creating a system that makes an arbitrary cutover, such as moving from this year's numbers to next year's numbers midyear, because it causes an abrupt change to valuation levels. Ideally use the next four quarters, because it will have no past results to contaminate earnings expectations.

7. The "other financial metrics that influence valuation" section should update automatically, and include factors such as ROIC, the past five-year EPS growth rate, and consensus' forward two-year growth rate. (Many sell-side analysts don't develop thoughtful earnings forecasts beyond two years, which is why an analysis based on consensus over a longer time horizon should be scrutinized.)

8. In selecting a list of comparable companies, group companies that:

    a. Are in the same or similar sector or sub-sector.

    b. Have growth and risk characteristics similar to the company being valued.

9. For each group of companies, create a *mean* and *median* for each metric on an equally weighted basis. (If necessary, also create a mean and median for large-cap stocks separate from small-cap stocks.)

10. Use Excel's conditional formatting to highlight:

    a. Stocks with the most upside and downside.

    b. When the analyst's financial forecast differs from consensus by a predefined threshold (e.g., 5 percent).

    c. When the current valuation multiple for a company differs from its historical levels by a predefined threshold (e.g., 5 percent).

> d. When the *median* average valuation multiple for a group of companies differs from the *mean* by a predefined threshold (e.g., 5 percent). Investigate anomalies, because there may be a reason to use one average over the other.
> 11. Ensure that each group of comparable companies can be sorted by the amount of upside or downside to the price target. An analyst's stock recommendations should generally line up with the rankings. There will be times when an analyst may favor a stock that is not ranked with the most upside, but this should be due to higher conviction or less risk associated with the stock.

Avoid Incrementalism

The analyst has a $13 price target on a $10 stock that he moves up to $15 after the stock hits $12. When the stock moves to $14, he raises the target to $18, and when it hits that level he raises it to $20. Instead, it would have been a much better call to have a $20 price target when the stock was $10. Each $2 to $3 price-target raise provided little value to the portfolio manager, because the upside wasn't worth getting into and then out of the stock. Analysts often raise their targets in these small, incremental steps because it feels less risky and they want more information to confirm their investment thesis. It's not as easy to make the big call, but it should be considered when the analyst has conviction based on solid fundamental research.

Lessons Learned from Experienced Stock Pickers

In addition to the discussion above, there are other stock-picking considerations that usually take years to learn through trial and error. Exhibit 20.4 includes some lessons learned and will hopefully help other analysts avoid making the same missteps.

Exhibit 20.4 Best Practice (Knowledge): Appreciate Lessons Learned from Experienced Stock Pickers

- Appreciate:
  - No single investing style will be successful over every time period. Analysts need to have a toolbox full of different approaches and know when to use them.
  - Human emotions cause markets to overreact; they overshoot to the upside on good news and to the downside on bad news. (See a more detailed discussion in Chapter 21.)
  - Stock ideas that appear in the media have been fully disseminated to the market; it's almost impossible to generate alpha at that point unless the analyst has a unique angle that's still not understood by the market. (It may be possible to exploit misperceptions heightened by the media.)
- Beware of:
  - Value traps, because stocks are often cheap for a reason.
  - New valuation methods, because it's not clear they are necessary. The "price-to-eyeballs" method used to justify valuations at the peak of the dot-com era is noteworthy.
  - Hot products or services, because all good things come to an end.
  - Turnaround stories, because they usually disappoint.
  - Roll-ups, because they rarely work. (When they do, it's because the company has made the tough decision to eliminate all but one of the former brands and fire all but one management team.)
  - Stock calls that rely on a single superstar executive, because they are generally more risky than those where the team is well balanced.
  - Companies with substantial related-party transactions, because it implies lax controls.
- Don't trust bad management. Just because a company has an exciting plan doesn't justify buying the stock. I'd estimate that at least three quarters of the bad stock calls I made early in my career fell apart because management didn't execute its plan. There's no easy litmus test to use for evaluating management, but if you don't feel comfortable that the most senior four to five executives at the firm are all buying into the plan and are capable of executing it, you'll want to assign a low conviction rating.
- Don't ignore the bad gut feeling picked up from a nonfundamental factor (e.g., opulent offices, a CFO who regularly works from home, or a CEO who openly acknowledges cheating on his wife, all of which I witnessed in companies that eventually crashed and burned).

- Superior technology or a patent doesn't guarantee success. Companies need highly qualified management to execute a plan to generate shareholder value.
- Market share shifts are usually most pronounced when times are tough, not in the boom era. Look for the strongest players to come out of slowdowns with more share than the marginal players.
- For the most part, unionized labor causes a company to be competitively disadvantaged. The typical balance of the three primary stakeholders (shareholders, customers, and employees) becomes out of balance with strong unions, which ultimately leads to less for the shareholders (e.g., pre-bankruptcy General Motors) or customers (e.g., pre-bankruptcy United Airlines).
- While much less of a problem now than in the 1980s or early 1990s, the term *diversification* should be viewed as *di-worsification*. A company expanding beyond its core competency is usually a problem.
- Being a first mover isn't always a competitive advantage, because it may have the highest investment cost relative to followers who can learn from mistakes of the first mover.
- When possible, monitor fixed income markets for a company to see if they are inconsistent with the equity markets.

Special Considerations for Buy-Side Analysts

Unlike many other best practices discussed in this book where buy-side and sell-side activities are quite similar, their roles can be quite different when it comes to making stock recommendations. Sell-side analysts, who generally cover a narrowly defined sector(s), have the luxury of downgrading one investment-style stock and replacing it with another. This isn't always feasible on the buy-side, where portfolio managers have restrictions based on the fund's mandate. As such, the buy-side analyst should always be cognizant of the investment style of each stock recommendation, so as to pitch appropriate recommendations to each portfolio manager within the fund (e.g., if you're about to downgrade a large-cap value stock, be hesitant to tell your internal constituents to replace it with a small-cap growth stock that has more upside).

Special Considerations for Sell-Side Analysts

Here are some stock-picking considerations unique to sell-side analysts:

- There's no easy answer for the question of how often to make ratings changes, but there are outliers that should be avoided. The frequency of these changes will be dependent on the attractiveness relative to other names in the universe, as well as the size and volatility of the assigned universe. With that said:
    - Not changing any ratings over a 12-month period is too long. Even going 6 months without a ratings change should be questioned.
    - Changing ratings on more than 25 percent of the assigned universe over a given quarter is probably too excessive, unless it's a sector call. Sell-side analysts generally need to give their clients time to build or exit from positions.
    - Some sell-side firms have introduced short-term trading ideas over the past few years. Analysts can ignore the previously mentioned recommendation, as long as it's clearly labeled a short-term trading idea. However, understand that most large funds can't nimbly jump into and out of a stock due to the size of their typical positions.
- As long as the research is fair and objective, don't be intimidated by management threatening to cut you off or treat you differently based on your rating.
    - Clients won't pay a sell-side analyst who can't be objective and have an independent view.
    - Most management respect analysts who do good work and remain objective. (But don't be antagonistic; see the CASCADE™ framework in Chapter 25.)

Exhibit 20.5   Best Practice (Knowledge and Skills): Ensuring Success as a Stock Picker

1. Appreciate that stock picking is challenging because:
   - All of the information needed to make a perfect stock call is rarely available.
   - As an analyst diligently takes more time to dig deeply into solving an investment controversy, the early stages of research often become known by the market, thus diminishing the value of the work.
   - There may not be any attractive ideas in an analyst's space at a given point in time.
   - Some factors that move stocks can't be forecast.
   - Many analysts are so overworked that they don't have the time to find unique insights.
   - Emotions cloud clear thinking, often causing an analyst to make the wrong decision.
2. For a stock call to generate alpha, the analyst must have *differentiated* insights superior to the market in at least one of the following areas (the FaVeS framework). If none exist (or it doesn't differ much from the consensus thinking), then there is no stock call to be made:
   - Forecast of financial results, such as EPS or cash flow.
   - Valuation multiple or methodology.
   - Sentiment of the market toward the stock.
3. When an analyst's forecast is out of consensus, additional work should be done to determine if the consensus is more accurate. This is done by:
   - Ensuring consensus includes many sell-side estimates and is not isolated to just a few who happen to have forecasts for the time period being used.
   - Comparing the informed consensus of the most accurate sell-side analysts with the overall consensus.
   - Ensuring that the sell-side submissions aren't stale and that there is no disagreement in terms of special items that may be in the number.
4. If after this work, an analyst's estimate is still out of consensus, it's critical to speak with market participants, such as portfolio managers, buy-side analysts, sell-side analysts, and company management, to understand why. Some buy-side and sell-side analysts conduct informal surveys of the buy-side on a weekly or monthly basis to ensure that they have their hands on the pulse of consensus expectations.
5. Analysts should avoid a common rookie mistake of having forecasts higher than consensus, simply based on greater faith in an unproven or weak management team.

(Continued)

6. Buy-side analysts who use sell-side analysts for financial forecasting should check with third-party services to ensure that the ones they use have a good track record of high forecast accuracy.

7. If a buy-side analyst is using a proprietary financial forecast and has put on the trade based on the forecast, it is often helpful to inform the most influential sell-side analysts so that consensus (and the stock price) comes around to the buy-side analyst's thesis.

8. Be hesitant to make an out-of-consensus stock recommendation based solely on the expectation that a stock's valuation multiple will be rerated or that the market will change its preferred valuation methodology, because these situations don't often occur without the benefit of a change in the financial forecast first. Changes to valuation *methodologies* tend to occur only when companies or sectors:
   • Are going through a major secular transformation.
   • Are at a peak or trough of the business cycle.
   • Are converting to a new accounting method.

9. When using an out-of-consensus valuation *multiple* as the basis for a stock recommendation, ensure that:
   • The company or comparable companies have been afforded this multiple under similar conditions in the past. Avoid using the average historical relative multiple of the past, without considering changes that have taken place in the company's prospective growth rate and risk characteristics.
   • For growth companies, ensure that the multiple isn't out of line with companies in other sectors with similar growth prospects and risk profiles.
   • When possible, the multiple(s) should be shared with a trusted colleague or investment committee, so as to avoid personal biases from self-selecting a particular multiple.

10. Exploit flaws in market sentiment to enhance stock picking as highlighted in Exhibit 20.1.

11. Monitor factors that help to understand market sentiment as highlighted in Exhibit 20.2.

12. Before making a new stock recommendation, ensure there is a catalyst that meets these criteria:
   • Pertains to a critical factor that's material enough to move the stock.
   • Not currently appreciated by the market.
   • Can be forecasted with some level of certainty.
   • Likely to occur during the investment time horizon.

13. Put dates in the calendar for the following types of events with the expectation that catalysts may occur:
    - Company-sponsored analyst meetings and calls.
    - Earnings releases.
    - The company's annual pricing, volume, or earnings guidance or projection.
    - Deadlines for new legislation, regulations, or court case outcomes.
    - Prescheduled announcements by the company's customers, competitors, or suppliers.
    - New product releases or significant product extensions.
    - Interim sales data, for the company or the sector.
14. Before making a stock call, answer these questions:
    - What unique insight isn't in consensus?
    - Why doesn't consensus have this insight, or why is consensus ignoring it?
    - What is the catalyst that will get the market to accept this out-of-consensus view, and when will it occur?
    - What could go wrong?
15. Individuals who can help answer these questions include:
    - Experienced buy-side analysts or PMs who currently own or have owned the stock in the fund.
    - Sell-side salespeople who have interest in the stock.
    - Sell-side traders who trade the stock.
    - The company's investor relations contact.
    - Sell-side analysts (if you're a buy-side analyst).
16. Attempt to convey the level of conviction associated with each stock call, as it will help portfolio managers and clients better assess the call.
17. When setting price targets, attempt to set a range of targets rather than a single-point estimate.
18. Adjust price target multiples when:
    - The multiples of comparable companies change.
    - Time passes, causing new forward multiples to change.
    - The multiples of multiperiod cash flow models change (such as the risk-free rate and equity risk premium).
19. Understand the factors that have historically caused investors to rotate into or out of the assigned universe of stocks in order to help the challenging task of identifying them in the future.
20. Set a range of exit thresholds in advance of making a stock recommendation, because it will prevent biases from creeping into the decision at a later date, which occurs all too often.

(Continued)

304 • Best Practices for Equity Research Analysts

21. If new information comes to light that derails the elements of a stock call, validate the information, and if it's likely to hold the stock back, do an about-face on the rating as soon as possible.
22. Review valuation levels of the assigned universe of stocks regularly, preferably on a daily basis, but no less frequently than once per week. (Refer to Exhibit 20.3 for a discussion on constructing a valuation comparables table, which makes this easy.)
23. Appreciate the lessons learned from experienced stock pickers, as discussed in Exhibit 20.4.

Chapter 21

Avoid Common Psychological Challenges That Impede Sound Investing

Introduction

You're probably aware that the human mind can deceive even itself, but you're also probably thinking, "It never happens to me." Your belief is justified by the fact that you possess above-average intelligence and are analytical in the way you make decisions. After all, these traits are what make you a great equity analyst. But the reality is that you're not immune. I've seen the most common psychological mistakes occur to some of my closest colleagues, including some of the brightest analysts in the industry. I've been regarded as very logical throughout my adult life (sometimes to a fault), and yet I'll confess that I've made many of these common mistakes myself. So before you go any further, open your mind to the possibility that you could be fallible in this area too.

Understanding how to avoid psychological pitfalls should be a top priority for every equity research analyst, followed closely by understanding how to exploit these mistakes when others make them (often the S in the FaVeS framework). Our mind plays tricks on us, which can lead to bad decisions. Nowhere is this truer than in the investment process. This isn't just my opinion, but a fact that's been supported by decades of academic research. As much as I want to keep this discussion geared toward the practical aspects of equity research, the reality is that academic studies help demonstrate where the human mind stumbles. Modern Portfolio Theory (MPT) assumes that investors are always rational, but any experienced practitioner knows this is nonsense. There is a psychological dimension to all investor decision making, whether it's recommending stocks, revising earnings models, or even writing a research report. Human beings invariably drag their emotions into their decisions, with the cognitive errors discussed below often being the result. No one can escape these; they are systematic and have a direct effect on pricing (Schoenhart, 2008: 4–5). As such, there's no failsafe system to ensure that you'll never fall into a psychological trap, but being aware of the common pitfalls should allow you to know when they're more likely to occur.

Not recognizing or compensating for psychological traps can lead you (or those you compete with) to:

- Be unjustifiably optimistic or pessimistic (Trammell, 2003: 46–47).
- Be overconfident in abilities and prospects, thus lowering the effort spent investigating risks to an investment thesis.
- Subconsciously overlook important information (Schoenhart, 2008: 78), distort facts, or fail to accurately perceive reality.
- Sell or buy with the herd, at the worst possible time.
- Fail to learn from investment mistakes, and thus risk repeating them.
- Fail to recognize how biases can distort earnings forecasts and valuation analyses.

Personality Traits

Based on my experience, and discussions with others in the field, there is no ideal personality type for investing, but there are traits of good investors. As shown in Exhibit 21.1, one framework—the Bailard, Biehl, & Kaiser (BB&K) Five-Way Model—posits that there are two psychological variables for investing: *confidence* and *method of action* (Bailard, Biehl, & Kaiser, 1992: 263–265). While an analyst's confidence level often fluctuates from one investment opportunity to the next, I've found it to be relatively high with all successful stock pickers. (If you're never confident, you won't pull the trigger in time.) The *method of action* asks if an investor is methodical, careful, and analytical or emotional, intuitive, and impetuous. While not scientifically verified, I've found successful value investors to be more in the upper left quadrant (individualist), and growth investors to be more in the upper right quadrant (adventurer). Successful value investing generally attracts individuals who dig deeply to pick over unloved stories, whereas successful growth investing generally attracts individuals who can take a leap of faith that high-fliers will continue their success. Being too expressed along the horizontal continuum can result in a shortcoming. Those who are too careful will lose out on opportunities while they wait for more information; those who are too impetuous will be held back by insufficient or sloppy research.

Exhibit 21.1 Investor Personalities

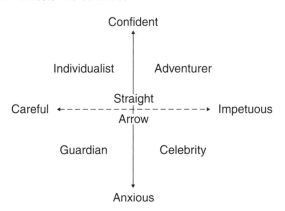

Source: Bailard, Biehl, and Kaiser, 1992

Understanding the Pitfalls

Here are the most common types of pitfalls likely to lead analysts to a bad investment decision, followed by a discussion of how to avoid (or exploit) them.

Confirmation Bias

Holding two conflicting views at the same time makes the human mind uncomfortable, a psychological phenomenon known as cognitive dissonance. Thus, we seek out information that confirms a preestablished view and ignore or reject evidence that contradicts it. Studies have shown that analysts underreact to unfavorable new information in earnings reports, convincing themselves that the situation is only temporary, and the *status quo ante* will soon be restored (Schoenhart, 2008: 40,56; Trammell, 2003: 46–47). Professional investors also preserve their beliefs by interpreting troublesome new evidence as consistent with their preexisting ideas (Schoenhart, 2008: 80).

Overconfidence

Financial professionals tend to be intelligent, often graduating near the top of their classes. While this can provide the extra credentials and confidence needed to land a role as an equity research analyst at a highly regarded firm, it can also lead to shortcomings in investing. A raft of studies shows that about 75 percent of people surveyed rank themselves above average at just about anything: driving a car, playing basketball, betting on horses, getting along with people, being funny, scoring high on IQ tests, completing tasks quickly, and displaying leadership abilities. They also routinely underestimate the probability that they, personally, will be the one to get tagged with bad results (Dremam, 1998: 115; Frick, 2010A; Schoenhart, 2008: 52–57; Zweig, 2007: 86). Jumping from a string of recent successes to the belief that you can't lose is similar to the flawed logic of a poker player after a run of good cards,

who thinks the cards will keep on coming (hot hand fallacy). Overconfidence is a problem, because it prevents the individual from properly assessing the downside or risks of the investment. From my perspective, overconfidence is one of the primary reasons many investment professionals underperform their benchmark. Bill Gross, PIMCO's founder and
co-chief investment officer, put it well when he said, "Becoming overconfident is the spell of doom" (Gross, 2009).

Self-Attribution Bias

Investors will often attribute their successes to personal intelligence and skills, while dismissing their mistakes as not their fault. In reality, some of the wins are just plain luck (the stock moves the right way for the wrong reasons), while some of the losses are the result of poor research. Analysts who fail to appreciate this may undervalue the importance of fundamental research, leading to the same mistake time after time. Nicolosi, Peng, and Zhu (2009) found that, on average, investors increased their number of trades after a good month ("I'm a genius"), but didn't reduce their number of trades after a bad month. Poor results tend to get explained away as bad luck (Schoenhart, 2008: 80; Mangot, 2009: 48). Be hesitant to say, "It wasn't my fault" unless you can categorically prove that it wasn't. Possessing the humility to accept mistakes is often difficult to do, but it's important for long-term success. This is reinforced by Dennis Shea, former chief investment officer and head of global equity, Morgan Stanley Investment Management, who believes, "Markets have a habit of doing the unexpected and making us all look foolish. Our profession is humbling, and the longer you're at it, the more humbled you will feel."

Optimism Bias

Investors tend to be too optimistic about their winners, which causes them to overlook or fail to properly investigate the risks of prospective investments. Bernartzi, Kahneman, and Thaler (1999) surveyed over a thousand investors and found that 74 percent spent more time thinking about potential gains, while only 7 percent focused more on potential losses. Studies have also shown that sell-side analysts tend to be too optimistic. (My experience suggests buy-side analysts also have a positive bias, albeit not as much as the sell-side, but since the buy-side doesn't publish estimates, this can't be validated.)

Recency Bias

Analysts can become overly biased by information or personal experiences that occurred recently, while undervaluing information learned in the distant past. For example, being more positively biased toward a stock because you recently met with the company's management team, as opposed to another stock where you haven't seen management in a while, would show a recency bias that could lead to the wrong investment decision. Related biases include overuse of the first thing that comes to mind (known as *availability bias*) and over-relying on information that gets repeated often (known as a *salience effect*) (Mangot, 2009: 6; Schoenhart, 2008: 80).

Momentum Bias

This is the desire to chase stocks that have already rallied, or believing that market trends will continue (Mangot, 2009). "Don't keep recommending a stock just because it's going up" is a belief held by Alkesh Shah, sell-side analyst at Evercore Partners. I witnessed momentum bias regularly throughout my career, where sell-side analysts would keep raising their price targets each time the previous one was reached, only to watch the stock drop back to prior levels (affectionately known as a "round trip"). Perhaps the ultimate example of wrongly believing market momentum would continue is the bubble of the late 1990s. Young professionals, who hadn't experienced a bear market, overweighted recent information and kept making long bets with little regard to historical valuation parameters. I regularly saw momentum bias on the sell-side, including in some of my own calls. After a stock had unexpectedly rallied 20 percent, you'd see a few analysts get more positive and upgrade the stock, even though it was too late. The mistake being made was obvious to the market, but the analyst was blinded by momentum bias.

Rules of Thumb (Heuristics)

Rules of thumb are mental shortcuts we use to make decisions more quickly, which are important in order to remain efficient in the job. However, they can lead to problems if relied upon blindly (Schoenhart, 2008: 30–32). Constantly relying on the same initial stock screen or one specific valuation metric (e.g., P/E) is likely to limit your opportunities. Research has shown that substantial improvements in price target quality occur when analysts appear to use a rigorous valuation technique rather than a heuristic (Gleason et al., 2009). The investment drivers and risks for a stock are always changing, which means the heuristic about when to buy or sell a particular stock may break down over time (Schoenhart, 2008: 30–32).

Reaching Conclusions Prematurely

Even the most highly rated money managers make investment decisions without 100 percent of the needed information, but this can be taken to an extreme when analysts draw conclusions before completing the necessary research. One mental shortcut that can be abused is representativeness; if item A has some of the characteristics of group A, it must belong to group A (e.g., thinking that all companies in the same sector have similar prospects). Another shortcut is inductive reasoning, which is basing a conclusion on a small, and therefore potentially unrepresentative, sample. This can be seen when a retail analyst makes changes to investment recommendations or financial estimates after visiting one shopping mall.

Familiarity Bias

We have a tendency to prefer the things we're familiar with over those we're less familiar with. The problem in that is, if someone asks you to make a recommendation between a stock you actively follow and one you only know tangentially, you're more likely to recommend the one you know. This might seem like common sense, but the portfolio manager or client who has asked for the advice may not appreciate your familiarity bias, which in turn could lead them to a bad decision (Mangot, 2009: 29–32; Schoenhart, 208: 69–70).

Falling in Love with a Stock

You have a favorite stock, but you can't bear to part with it even though it has reached your price target. Your emotional attachment (Mangot, 2009: 72) might be due to the stock performing well for you over the years or because the CEO treats you like family when visiting the company. But you can't let these factors cloud your view about the stock's future performance. Trees don't grow to the sky. In hindsight, my judgment was clouded in this way more than once, which led to some bad stock calls.

Sunk Cost Fallacy

You spend considerable time researching a stock and then feel obligated to have a strong view, either positive or negative. This is especially problematic for less experienced analysts, who want to impress their boss or clients when initiating coverage on a new sector. It can also be a problem if you've made a considerable investment in a stock, and then something occurs that isn't in your investment thesis. When that happens, ask the following question: Would you still buy the stock? If not, it should probably be sold, but due to all of the effort to get it into the portfolio, it can be difficult to reverse course, especially if the stock was added recently. Dollar-cost averaging and hanging on to positions that have been punished by the market for no good reason can be sensible strategies, but don't follow them just because you've sunk a lot of personal and financial capital into a position (Mangot, 2009: 64).

Snakebite Effect

After having been burned with a particular stock, you say, "Never again." This may be a good strategy in a situation where a company or sector has a long-standing structural problem that isn't going away (e.g., excess capacity such as in the airline sector), but don't let it blind you from giving an old investment a second look. I recommended buying Ryder and Canadian Pacific at different points in my career, both due to a change I saw coming from entrenched management teams. Both calls were met with resistance by experienced investors, because they had been burned by these companies in the past, but both stocks doubled. Research shows that investors are twice as likely to buy stocks they owned in the past that performed well as they are to buy ones that did poorly. You may feel averse to the prospect of touching a previous loser, but don't let that stop you from taking a fresh look when circumstances change (Mangot, 2009: 65).

Anxiety

Being bombarded with daily stock gyrations, especially for a less experienced analyst, can be overwhelming; it can also lead to taking action in an effort to reduce anxiety—action that may be unwarranted. Early in my career, I watched my stocks' daily moves so closely that I found the need to change ratings every two to three months, often missing the longer-term opportunities. Over time, I learned from more experienced analysts to ignore the daily volatility, which substantially reduced my anxiety and helped my stock-picking performance. To help illustrate the risk aversion that occurs when watching your stocks too closely, an experiment with 80 university students found that those who reviewed their returns more regularly were more prone to tilt their portfolio toward a less risky fund than students who reviewed results less regularly (Mangot, 2009: 120). Furthermore, a 2002 study of currency traders found that market moves caused wild reactions in the heart rates and skin valences of less-experienced traders, while the same events hardly caused a blip for the more-experienced ones (Harrington, 2010: 34).

Overreaction

Contrary to the Efficient Market Hypothesis, the market can be quite irrational in the short run, and if you spend too much effort overanalyzing this volatility, it could cloud your judgment or cause you to make the wrong decision. These short-term, often unjustifiable, swings, such as concerns over a potential Fed tightening on Monday, may be completely forgotten when Wal-Mart reports a blowout quarter on Wednesday. Fundamentals generally don't change from one day to the next, and so market moves are often driven by emotion (market sentiment). To this extent, it's not uncommon for the financial markets to overshoot toward the upside on good news and overshoot toward the downside on bad news (Dreman, 1998: 239; Trammell, 2003: 46–47).

- Overreaction is often caused by the two most powerful

emotions associated with investing: fear and greed. The tug-of-war between these two emotions, fear of losing capital and greed in wanting to get a piece of a bull market, caused wild daily swings in the Dow Jones Industrial Average—down 800 points one day and up 600 the next—in the fall of 2008, during the financial crisis. Another example of this conflict is evident in investor sentiment surrounding the overheated tech sector. In February 2000, a month before the bubble burst, 78 percent of Gallup poll respondents thought it was a good time to invest, even though valuations were stretched to 50-year highs. Those who had missed out on some or all of the 20-year bull market were still willing to pile in, because they wanted to get their share. In contrast, only 41 percent polled in March 2003, when the market was reaching a 5-year low, thought it was a good time to invest. The market increased 50 percent over the following 3 years (Statman, 2009). Be mindful that fear and greed are not reliable guides to investment returns.

- Overreaction is often caused by *herding*, the tendency for investors to respond similarly to specific market conditions (Schoenhart, 2008: 88). In a bubble, investors blinded by greed all pile into stocks at the same time. In a panic, they discount stocks for fear, real or imagined, and rush for the exit at the same time. This is probably a good place to remember that *it's impossible to generate alpha if you're following the rest of the herd*. In a study on the topic, subjects were asked to identify if pairs of differently positioned objects placed before them were the same. They were correct 84 percent of the time when answering on their own, but only 59 percent of the time when "peers" (researchers, actually) prompted them with the wrong answer. Brain scans showed that the frontal cortex, the reflective part of the brain, actually dimmed when social pressure was applied (Zweig, 2007: 167). Researchers in similar studies believe that test subjects who answered incorrectly were not merely caving into social pressure, but were actually perceiving things differently (Frick, 2010B). Whether it's social pressure or altered perceptions, the point remains the same: You are susceptible to becoming part of a stampeding herd.

Loss-Aversion

It's been proven in numerous studies that people dislike losing more than they like winning, which is why a stock loss tends to take on disproportionate significance relative to the overall portfolio or universe, when compared with a winner. This can be seen in investors who will avoid selling a stock at a loss, with a hope that it will move back into the black, even if the investment thesis is no longer intact (Schoenhart, 2008: 59, 70). This has been translated into investment advice: Don't hang on to your losers. Since a loser may actually be a turnaround (such as Apple moving from $3 in 1997 to $300 by 2010), a more useful adage would be, Don't hang onto stocks for emotional reasons, just to avoid feeling the pain of regret. If you make a mistake, admit it to yourself and others. The longer you wait, the more painful it may become. This is a common psychological pitfall: not reversing the trade when it's clear that your thesis is wrong. A senior buy-side analyst put it well, "Some of the best things I have ever done in investing, personally and professionally, are cut off small losses before they became big ones."

Avoiding the Pitfalls

While Exhibit 21.2 highlights thoughts on how to avoid the individual pitfalls discussed above, there are a few steps an analyst can take to avoid a broad group of them:

- Document your thought process, and review it periodically.

Even sell-siders who publish reports should keep a private log in their notetaking system to track their investment thesis, price targets, and other key information at the time of a ratings change. This will make it tougher for the mind to revise history at the next stage, evaluating the recommendation.

- Document changes to your financial forecasts. If your investment thesis is all about cost cutting, yet the last three revisions you made to your financial model were to lower margins, the inconsistency suggests that you may have a bias working against you. This doesn't need to be a lengthy process; capture it in your notetaking system or create a worksheet in the company workbook that includes the date and a one-sentence note explaining what was changed in the model.

- Utilize trusted colleagues and investment committees to find blind spots in your investment thesis and prevent you from revising history.

- Create automatic stop-loss triggers (e.g., 15 percent of the purchase price) or other mechanical sell disciplines to take the angst and resistance out of selling losers early.

- Accept mistakes as valuable learning opportunities. I'm not encouraging anyone to make mistakes, but when they occur, consider them lessons learned that will help navigate a better path in the future.

- Periodically review the list of biases to increase your self-awareness.*

- Above all, be thorough before making a stock recommendation. There's no substitute for thorough research when it comes to reducing the likelihood of being wrong.

---

* Cabot Research is a firm that specializes in helping portfolio managers identify their psychological strengths and blind spots.

Exhibit 21.2 Best Practice (Knowledge): Most Common Psychological Pitfalls of Investment Professionals

Psychological Pitfall	Manifestation	Example	Increasing Self-Awareness
Confirmation Bias	Seeking out information that supports your preconceived view and rejecting, distorting, or ignoring information that conflicts with it.	While conducting research on a stock you're recommending, you discover an accounting irregularity but choose to downplay it as insignificant.	• In making recommendations, wait until you've done all of the research before considering the rating. Deciding your rating early in the process will bias you toward finding insights that support your view and rejecting those that conflict with it. • Approach all new information with an open mind, regardless of your current view toward the stock. • Build your base, upside, and downside scenarios *while* conducting the research, documenting, as you go along, which scenarios should be reviewed before making a recommendation. • If you're serious about making a recommendation, ensure that you know the opposing view.
Overconfidence	Assuming you're smarter than everyone else, which prevents you from exploring the real risks or reasons that a stock is not currently at your price target.	After a few good stock calls, you begin to let down your guard in terms of assessing risks for future recommendations.	• Be humble by realizing no professional investor is right 100 percent of the time. • Fully understand the "other side of the trade" before making a recommendation. • Ask a trusted colleague or investment committee to put your thesis under scrutiny.

Psychological Pitfall	Manifestation	Example	Increasing Self-Awareness
Self-Attribution Bias	Taking full credit for wins and placing blame on others for losses.	After a recommended stock goes the wrong way, blaming a colleague (or the sell-side) for conducting shoddy research. (Remember, part of your job is to validate your information sources.)	• When you have a big win, go back to the documents you wrote when you recommended the stock, and see if your thesis really played out. (Or was it some other factor?) • Before placing blame on others, or saying, "The surprise couldn't have been foreseen," ask yourself these questions: ○ Did anyone else see this coming (sell-side or buy-side)? ○ What could have been done to know about this surprise earlier?
Optimism Bias	Being too optimistic about your stock's valuation and future earnings potential.	Modeling a company's EPS growth at a 12% CAGR over the next 2 years, even though it has grown EPS at an 8% CAGR for the past 10 years.	• Research history for your companies and industries, specifically the growth rates and valuation multiples. If you settle on a price target based on factors running well above historical trends, make sure you have a sound reason for doing so. • Spend as much time identifying risks as catalysts. • Examine constructive or negative feedback provided by others. (Don't just internalize the positive praise.)
Recency Bias	Over-emphasizing recent information at the expense of older information.	Having a more positive bias toward a company you've recently met with, compared with one you haven't seen recently.	• When possible, take a long-term view toward investment recommendations. • Before creating a new recommendation or reiterating an existing one, ask if you're over-relying on recent information and/or experiences.

(Continued)

Exhibit 21.2 Best Practice (Knowledge): Most Common Psychological Pitfalls of Investment Professionals (*Continued*)

Psychological Pitfall	Manifestation	Example	Increasing Self-Awareness
Momentum Bias	Assuming recent trends will continue, even if historical evidence and metrics suggest they are unsustainable.	After a recommended stock has rallied to a realistic price target, the analyst raises the valuation multiple or financial forecast to unrealistic levels to justify an even higher price target that ultimately isn't achieved.	• If you've missed a substantial move in a stock, be hesitant to chase it by jumping on the bandwagon. If you are on the same trade as everyone else, ask who's going to drive it up to your price target? • Research history for your companies and industries, specifically, the growth rates and valuation multiples. If your price target relies on one or both being well above historical trends, make sure you have a sound reason for doing so. • When making a change to your thesis, ask where you are in the greed vs. fear spectrum compared with consensus. If you're in the same place, you may be following the herd.
Rules of Thumb (Heuristics)	Overusing a rule of thumb to make investment decisions.	Recommending a stock or a sector every time its P/E ratio drops below 12 times forward earnings, and selling every time it moves above 15 times.	• Useful heuristics should be derived from facts or historical trends that can be substantiated. If your heuristic is key to your investment recommendation, make sure it's backed up with sound logic (and evidence, if applicable). • If someone tells you to follow a simple rule in forecasting or valuation, make sure to validate it with historical analysis.

Psychological Pitfall	Manifestation	Example	Increasing Self-Awareness
Reaching Conclusions Prematurely	Drawing poor conclusions, based on a lack of good information.	In evaluating an initial public offering (IPO), an analyst assumes the company will move toward the same margins and returns of other, more established companies in the sector.	• Conduct thorough research before making an investment recommendation.
Familiarity Bias	Recommending stocks you're familiar with over those you're less familiar with.	When asked for your favorite stock, you reply with the one you're most familiar with rather than the one that may have the most upside.	• Don't make recommendations of stocks you're unfamiliar with, but conversely don't make a suboptimal recommendation, just because you know the stock better than the proposed alternatives.
Falling in Love with a Stock	Becoming so emotionally attached to a stock that it can't be analyzed objectively.	An analyst is hesitant to downgrade a stock that's hit its price target because it's "a franchise name" that the analyst is associated with.	• You're paid to discover alpha, not play favorites. PMs and clients value objective advice. If you find yourself worried about upsetting the company (or your clients on the sell-side) with a ratings change, you may be too emotionally attached. • Ask yourself if you're less likely to downgrade or sell a particular stock than others in your universe. If it's not purely valuation driven, you may have a problem. • When reviewing your comp table, start by looking at only the numbers (hide the company names and tickers) to see if you have a similar view when the names are revealed.

(Continued)

Exhibit 21.2 Best Practice (Knowledge): Most Common Psychological Pitfalls of Investment Professionals (*Continued*)

Psychological Pitfall	Manifestation	Example	Increasing Self-Awareness
Sunk Cost Fallacy	Investing considerable time or capital into a given stock prevents you from looking at it objectively.	When analysts initiate coverage on an entire sector, they may mistakenly recommend many of the names, when in reality only a small number are likely to substantially outperform.	• When conducting extensive research on a topic, periodically ask, "What will I do if I discover nothing new?" It reduces the amount of time sunk into any one effort. • Look at your stock universe based on objective measures, such as percent upside to price target. Resist making changes to your financial forecasts or valuation multiples to "make it work," in an effort to show more upside than you previously expected. • Be willing to reverse your recommendation when you've made a mistake, or your thesis failed to play out. • Periodically ask yourself, "If I was building a new list of stock recommendations today, would they look the same as my current list?" • When mistakes occur, understand why. After beating yourself up, internalize that you've learned a valuable lesson that will make you a better analyst.
Snakebite Effect	Categorically dismissing a stock as a bad investment due to bad past performance.	Telling someone, "I can never own that stock." (At a minimum, there should be a qualifier, such as, "…unless their CEO resigns.")	• While it's important to build on past experiences when conducting research, avoid making any long-term sweeping generalizations about a company, unless there's almost no chance the factor will change (e.g., intense employee unionization in the auto sector).

Psychological Pitfall	Manifestation	Example	Increasing Self-Awareness
Anxiety	Allowing near-term stock volatility to impact your long-term view.	Feeling the need to change your view toward a stock on a weekly or monthly basis, even though fundamentals haven't changed.	• It's important to watch the daily movements in your stocks to understand investor *sentiment*, but don't let stock price movements alter your view about the *fundamentals*. • When uncertainty arises around a key stock call, do more work to either reduce anxiety or lead to a better decision. • When considering a recommendation change, if possible, think about it overnight.
Overreaction	Selling or buying at irrational prices with the herd, which in hindsight, turns out to be the worst possible time.	An analyst downgrades a stock in response to bad news even though his research suggests the concern is being overblown.	• When markets appear to be moving too far too fast for irrational reasons (not based on fundamentals), consider the contrarian view. • Periodically review your stocks with historical peak and trough valuation parameters to see if their moves have been overdone. • Conduct scenario analysis to identify realistic worst-case and best-case scenarios for your financial forecast and potential price targets.
Loss-Aversion	Avoiding selling a stock at a loss even though the upside thesis has failed to materialize.	An analyst looks to find a new rationale to keep recommending a stock that hasn't been performing as well as originally expected.	• Document your thesis for recommending a stock and the price target specifics before you make your recommendation. If key tenets to the thesis fail to play out, reassess your price target and recommendation; you may have to sell at a loss.

Chapter 22

Leverage Technical Analysis to Improve Fundamental Analysis

Typical fundamental equity analysts assume that stock recommendations should be based in part (or entirely) on forecasts of *future* earnings or cash flows, whereas technical equity analysts look at stocks' *historical* prices and volumes. At the extreme, they are as different in philosophy as liberals are from conservatives. But, I'd contend that there is common ground: A fundamental equity analyst can use technical analysis techniques to improve stock picking.

I should begin with two notes of caution. During my research for this book, I met a few portfolio managers who use technical analysis with fundamental analysis, but they were adamant about not wanting their analysts to do the same. They were concerned that it would cloud the fundamental call. So, first, be cautious about walking into a portfolio manager's office to exclaim that your favorite stock looks great on a technical basis. (It's worth noting, there are highly regarded sell-side analysts who include technical analysis with their fundamental work.) Second, it should be understood that, due to space limitations, this discussion is

I'd like to thank Barry M. Sine, CFA, CMT, for his significant contribution to this chapter.

confined to a small subset of the field. Therefore, if you intend to use it as the primary method for making stock recommendations, it should be explored much further.

While technical analysis can also be used as a *screening tool* to identify investment candidates for further analysis, this best practice explores *how to utilize technical analysis after fundamental analysis has been completed.* To do this, I will first introduce some basic concepts of technical analysis, such as chart construction, trendlines, and oscillators.

Objective Data Can Capture Subjective Emotions

Technicians believe in the power of the free market and the wisdom of the crowd. In a freely traded market, a wide variety of participants come together and collectively determine price through bidding and selling. These participants come with a range of knowledge about a subject company; they may be true insiders (e.g., board members or employees) or knowledgeable outsiders (e.g., buy-side or sell-side analysts). One of the inputs market players likely bring to the table is their fundamental analysis, but this is rarely the only input. As discussed earlier in the book, they also bring their emotions. A simplified assumption of fundamental analysis is that investors are cool, logical, rational individuals ignoring their emotions when valuing securities. While this might be true on the Vulcan Stock Exchange, humans are at times highly emotional creatures, and these emotions invade and influence every aspect of our existence, sometimes significantly. The field of behavioral finance is beginning to recognize the impact of irrational behavior. The field of technical analysis provides the tools to analyze it.

Market participants bring all of the above to bear on the markets. When they trade, the end result of their process, whether logical, emotional, or some combination thereof, becomes publicly available in the form of *volume* and *price*. These are the two primary inputs technicians use in their work. Technicians do not consider, or even care about, the inputs traders are bringing to the market, only the end results of price and volume. Technicians believe that the market is all knowing. In the words of Charles Dow, "The market reduces all knowledge to a bloodless verdict." Technicians believe that this verdict will be just, and, in fact, predict future events, such as earnings misses or economic weakness. In recognition of the markets' predictive power, stock prices are one of the 10 components of the U.S. Index of Leading Economic Indicators.

Chart Construction

Technical analysis typically uses daily price and volume data, specifically the high, low, opening, and closing prices, for constructing charts. For the purpose of this discussion, I am using a candlestick chart, which is highlighted in Exhibit 22.1. The high and low price of the day are represented by vertical lines above and below the body, known as *wicks*. The distance from the top of the top wick to the bottom of the bottom wick represents the day's trading range, so extreme volatility is visually apparent. Exhibit 22.2 shows a daily candlestick chart for Apple (AAPL).

Exhibit 22.1 Explanation of Candlestick Chart

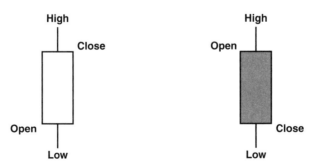

White body means security closed UP
Close > Open

Dark body means security closed DOWN
Close < Open

Exhibit 22.2   Example of Candlestick Daily Price Chart over 12 Months

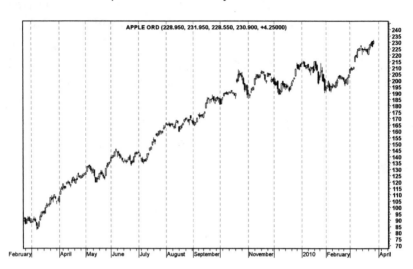

Two other aspects of chart construction are also important to note: periodicity and vertical axis scaling. Any time frame can be used, ranging from less than one minute to years. Each candle represents one time period with the high, low, opening, and closing prices. The same tools and concepts can be used to analyze all charts, regardless of the time frame, which can be seen with a day trader using one-minute increments or a pension fund manager using weekly or monthly increments.

The vertical axis, which is simply the stock's price in a traditional price chart, has been converted to a logarithmic scale, so that each dollar change in price is represented by the same vertical distance. In semi-log charts, one axis—the vertical in this case—is scaled logarithmically, so that each percentage change in price is represented by the same vertical distance.

Finally, volume is often added as a separate column chart below the price chart, represented by the height of the column below the price candlestick. Volume is an important consideration in technical analysis. Technical analysis is used to determine the overall sentiment of the market. Thus, the greater the volume, the more conviction the market has. Price movements accompanied by greater volume are said to have greater significance than those with lower-than-normal volume for the security being analyzed.

Trend, Support, and Resistance

The most important concept in technical analysis is *trend*. Trend refers to the direction that price is moving: up, down, or sideways. An uptrend refers to a security that is moving up in price over time. It indicates that market participants are becoming more favorably disposed toward that security and are willing to pay more for it over time, and/or that sellers are demanding higher and higher prices to part with the security. The reverse is true for downtrends. A security may also remain in a tight sideways price range for some time, meaning the downward pressure on price exerted by sellers is offsetting the upward pressure on price exerted by buyers. It also means that the market has come to a rough consensus on price. Finally, it is also possible that a price chart can look completely random, with no apparent trend discernable. It is important not to try too hard to draw a technical conclusion in such cases, when none is readily apparent.

Trend is indicated on a price chart by drawing trendlines. Uptrends are drawn by connecting the low prices over time, and downtrends are drawn by connecting high prices. An uptrend is defined as prices steadily moving higher, making new highs on each advance, but with sell-offs ending at higher lows. This concept is shortened to *higher highs and higher lows*. A downtrend is characterized by lower highs and lower lows. There are two cautions to keep in mind when drawing trendlines: (1) If a trend is not visually obvious, don't try to force it. (2) Note that it's not possible to call a trend until it is already underway. One of the shortcomings of technical analysis is that technicians often miss the first 5 to 10 percent of a price move.

Another concept associated with trends is *support* and *resistance*. A support or resistance level is a price where market participants in the past have stepped in to end or reverse trends. At support levels (i.e., the floor on a chart after a downtrend), buyers begin to move prices up again or cease their decline following a period of decreasing price. At resistance levels (i.e., the peaks of a chart after an uptrend), sellers begin to move prices down or cease their advance following a period of increasing price. The key concept here is that once a support or resistance level has been established, this price level is expected to serve as support or resistance in the future.

Putting Technical Analysis to Use

Now that you have an understanding of the basic concepts, you can examine how a fundamental analyst can use technical analysis to improve stock selection. Perhaps the best way to start is by taking a longer-term perspective and then moving into shorter time horizons. Look at Apple (AAPL) in Exhibits 22.3 and 22.4. Exhibit 22.3 is a monthly price chart covering 30 years of data, and Exhibit 22.4 is a weekly chart covering 10 years of data. Since AAPL has ranged from $5 to over $200 during this

Exhibit 22.3   Example of Candlestick Monthly Price Chart over 30 Years

Exhibit 22.4   Example of Candlestick Weekly Price Chart over 10 Years

time period, we use a semi-log chart. The weekly chart (also semi-log) shows a basing period for three years (from mid-2000 to mid-2003), followed by a strong rally. From this chart, the analyst would not know AAPL had previously spent a decade in a trading range. The monthly chart shows that its price increased in the mid-1980s, and then spent roughly a decade in a trading range. This resistance level held until 1999, when the shares broke well above their $15 high from 1987.

Moving on to Exhibit 22.5, which is a daily price chart, you'll see that price was in a steady decline until November 2009, when it hit a low of $79. Two months later, in January, the price hit $79 again, and the selling stopped. This tells us that one or more investors had $79 in mind as a buying level, and they had enough capital to buy enough shares to influence the market price.

Following the January $79 low, price embarked on an uptrend. Note that trend, support, and resistance are not readily apparent until after the fact. But once the shares began hitting higher prices in early 2009, while subsequent lows were also higher than prior lows, it became clear that an uptrend was underway. During an uptrend (or downtrend), it may be necessary to redraw the trendline. Again, in

Exhibit 22.5 AAPL's Daily Price Chart with Volume Showing Support and Uptrend

an uptrend, the trendline connects the low price points. This uptrend line also serves as a support level. Should the share price significantly break below the trendline, say by 5 percent or more, and stay there for several days, a technical warning signal has been given that the uptrend is likely over.

It is also useful to take note of volume, and how it changes with price. In this case, note that volume declined significantly during the October through January basing period. This suggested a diminishing of the selling pressure that had driven the stock lower during the second half of 2008. Conversely, the pickup in volume in early 2010 was a bullish signal as buyers stepped in to halt a decline, keeping the uptrend in place.

Incorporating Technicals with Fundamentals

Technical and fundamental analyses are typically conducted separately, but once the work has been done, the results can be compared. Some investors like to look at a chart at the beginning of the analysis process to get a sense of which way the market for a particular security is heading. Others prefer to perform their fundamental work first, so as not to be biased, and then conduct their technical analysis. There are several possible outcomes:

- Technical and fundamental analyses come to the same conclusion.
- Technical and fundamental analyses come to opposite conclusions.
- Fundamentals suggest security is overvalued or undervalued, but no trend is apparent in technical analysis.
- Technicals suggest security looks attractive or unattractive, but fundamental analysis is inconclusive.

Technical and Fundamental Analyses Come to the Same Conclusion

In Exhibit 22.5, the shares are in an uptrend. This is a positive technical indicator, suggesting that they will continue to move higher unless a warning sign, such as the price dropping significantly below a key support level, is given. If the fundamental conclusion is that the stock is undervalued, both technical and fundamental analyses are in agreement. The fact that investors have been steadily bidding up the shares, without significant sell-offs, suggests that the market consensus would concur with this.

Technical and Fundamental Analyses Come to Opposite Conclusions

As discussed throughout the book, the farther your view is out of consensus, the more work you need to do. In the context of using technical analysis, if the trendline was similarly strong to AAPL's in Exhibit 22.5, but you've concluded the stock is significantly overvalued, it warrants much deeper analysis. Appreciate that technical analysis helps illustrate the collective wisdom of a vast number of participants; it's not saying

334 • Best Practices for Equity Research Analysts

they're right, but if there's a significant divergence between your fundamental analysis and the results of technical analysis, you need to know why. Also, don't forget that in both the Internet and real estate bubbles, irrationality persisted in the market for years, and contrarian investors had significant losses (at least on paper), including some who were forced out of their positions before they were proven correct.

No Technical Trend Is Apparent

There are times when the chart shows no apparent trend or is showing sideways pricing action. Cases where a security is trading in the same price range for some time are actually considered positive if fundamental valuation suggests a higher price. A tight trading range suggests a consensus between buyers and sellers of a security. The longer this range persists, the more shares change hands from old holders, who may become discouraged with the company's prospects, to newer, more optimistic investors. A technician would wait for a breakout above prior resistance levels before buying, instead of preemptively buying in advance of the market discovering the security's potential upside. The logic is that it takes buying activity to move a price up, and in the absence of this buying, an undervalued security may remain undervalued. This is an ideal situation for combining fundamental analysis with technical analysis—using fundamentals to identify good potential long or short investments and technical analysis to time the entry into new positions.

Technicals Suggest Security Looks Attractive or Unattractive, but Fundamental Analysis Is Inconclusive

The fourth scenario is one in which the technical indicators are giving a clear reading, but fundamental analysis gives a mixed signal. The best approach in this case is for the analyst to seek understanding about why other investors are collectively bullish (or bearish), and analyze whether this conclusion makes sense. Even if one concludes that the market is wrong, trading on this conclusion can be dangerous since securities trade on perception, which is sometimes different from reality. It also may be the case that while the security was attractively valued at one time, with good prospects and a low valuation, an uptrend may already have taken the security to a level at or above a fundamentally derived fair value. Even in this case, uptrends (and downtrends) tend to have momentum and overshoot (or undershoot, in the case of downtrends) fair-value levels. So, an analyst looking at a security that is fairly or overvalued yet still in an uptrend, should look for technical signals, such as a break in support or an oversold condition (discussed later), before entering into a short position.

Analyzing Investor Sentiment Using Momentum Oscillators

As discussed in Chapter 21, markets are often led by extremely optimistic or pessimistic sentiment, driving securities well above or below fair value. Technical analysis has tools to gauge when sentiment is overdone. A security that has advanced too far, too fast, and is thus likely to experience at least a brief correction, is called *overbought*. An *oversold* security is just the opposite. To determine when a security is overbought or oversold, technicians utilize indicators called *momentum oscillators*. These are constructed entirely from historical price data, presented graphically, and analyzed similarly to price charts. The most commonly used momentum oscillators are the stochastic, moving average convergence-divergence (MACD, pronounced mack dee), and relative strength index (RSI). RSI should not be confused with the concept of relative strength charting, in which the ratio of two securities' prices are charted over time. Many oscillators are calculated so that they remain in a given range, say between 0 and 100, and have predefined overbought and/or oversold levels. For example, a security in which the

RSI oscillator is above 70 is considered overbought and one with the oscillator below 30 is considered oversold. For this discussion, I will explore the momentum oscillator, since it is the simplest to construct. This oscillator is also called the rate of change (ROC) oscillator.

The momentum oscillator can be calculated using one of two methods. The first, which is used in the example in Exhibit 22.6, is:

$$\text{Momentum oscillator} = \frac{(\text{Current closing price})}{(\text{Closing price } n \text{ time periods ago})} \times 100$$

I use $n = 12$ days in the example discussed below. Note: Multiplying by 100 simply makes the numbers easier to work with.

An alternative method is as follows:

$$\text{Momentum oscillator} = (\text{Current closing price} - \text{Closing price } n \text{ time periods ago}) \times 100$$

In the example found in Exhibit 22.6, I have added the momentum oscillator below the price chart. The theory behind this and other oscillators is that a stock's price movement will usually remain in a certain band on the momentum oscillator. This can vary by security, with more volatile securities having a wider band. For securities in an uptrend, the

Exhibit 22.6 Daily Price Chart with Momentum Oscillator

oscillator is usually at the high end of the range, or slightly above average, and the opposite is true for securities in a downtrend. For my example, I added lines at the 80 and 120 levels, as it appears from visual analysis that most price action has remained within this boundary. Situations where the oscillator dipped below this band are called *oversold*. The technical implication of an oversold security is that a sell-off has been too sharp, and a rebound is likely to occur. These corrections need not reverse a long-term trend, but can be short-term in nature and not breach support or resistance levels. On the left side of the exhibit, it appears AAPL was oversold on two occasions, followed by upward price moves. This was followed by three occasions where it was overbought, with a sell-off following on each occasion, although the third sell-off was reasonably modest.

Understanding momentum oscillators is important, because they can lead to an interpretation that is contrary to normal trend analysis. A technician might decide to short a security in an uptrend if it is significantly overbought and if that strategy would have worked in the past. This process can even be computerized and back-tested. For the fundamentally based analyst, using momentum oscillators can decrease the temptation to chase a stock, and encourage waiting for a more opportune entry price point.

Subjectivity and Objectivity in Technical Analysis

Just as in fundamental analysis, certain aspects of technical analysis are objective, while others are subjective. The underlying data used in technical analysis, price, and volume, is objective, as is the construction of charts and calculation of indicators. Beyond that, technical analysis is subjective, just as the analysis of a company's financial statements requires subjective interpretation. These subjective areas include drawing trendlines, calling trends, and considering when a support or resistance level has been sufficiently broken to warrant a trading call. The best way to learn technical analysis is through plenty of practice. What works for one stock or market may not work for another, and what worked in one era may not work in another. So keep an open mind, and be creative.

Additional Resources

Your market data service will likely have a robust menu of technical analysis tools. Here are some options if you're looking for charting on the Web:

- Stockcharts.com
- Yahoo! Finance (charts section)
- Bigcharts.com
- MSN Moneycentral (charts section)
- Google Finance ("Technicals" option in company chart)

Exhibit 22.7   Best Practice (Skills): Blend Technical Analysis with Fundamental Analysis

1. When conducting your fundamental analysis, in addition to reviewing a stock's price chart, routinely look at technical indicators, because they bring the objective, collective wisdom of a vast number of market participants to your analysis.
2. Learn how to quickly chart the technicals for your stocks using your preferred market data service provider. (Call its help desk, take one of its training classes, or read its documentation.)
3. Using these charts, ensure that you can identify and understand:
   a. Uptrends and downtrends.
   b. Support and resistance.
   c. Significant changes in volume. (Price movements accompanied by greater volume generally have greater significance.)
   d. Momentum oscillators.
4. Set up alerts to be notified when your stocks breach an oversold or overbought oscillator threshold.
5. When reaching a new *fundamental* buy or sell conclusion on a stock, check the technicals to see if they:
   a. Confirm your view.
   b. Contradict your view.
   c. Are inconclusive.
6. If your recommendation is in stark contrast to the buy or sell signal from a technical perspective, make sure you understand why the market participants are betting against you.

7. If a stock you're recommending as a buy or sell should break through a trendline in the wrong direction by a preset threshold (e.g., 5 percent or more), do additional work to ensure that your thesis is still intact.
8. If you find value in these basic technical analysis tools, take a course or read a book on the more advanced tools.

Further Reading

Colby, Robert W., *The Encyclopedia of Technical Indicators*, Second Edition, New York: McGraw-Hill, 2002.

Edwards, Robert, and John Magee, *Technical Analysis of Stock Trends*, Ninth Edition, New York: AMACOM, 2007.

Murphy, John J., *Technical Analysis of the Financial Markets: A Comprehensive Guide to Trading Methods and Applications*, New York: New York Institute of Finance, 1999.

Pring, Martin J., *Technical Analysis Explained*, Fourth Edition, New York: McGraw-Hill, 2002.

PART 5

COMMUNICATING STOCK IDEAS SO OTHERS TAKE ACTION

Some analysts might conclude that the end of the section on stock picking is the end of the best practices, because, in their view, getting the stock call right is all that matters. While making great stock calls is the most important skill to master, analysts won't receive credit unless their message has been constructed and delivered in an effective manner. It's for this reason that we dedicate a section to communicating stock ideas.

Unless you own your own firm, you'll need to communicate your ideas to get recognized, and eventually rewarded, for your efforts. Don't assume this section is just for sell-side analysts, because, in addition to buy-side analysts being evaluated on their stock-picking ability, it's important for their ideas to get into the portfolio.

Effectively communicating stock ideas may be more complex than you initially think. It's important to consider the three primary steps, similar to a manufacturing assembly line, which are summarized below and discussed in more detail in each of the subsequent chapters.

Before delving into this process, it's worth distinguishing the difference between assessing the quality of your *content* versus your *message*; content quality is a product of the research conducted, whereas the message quality is evaluated on its effectiveness in influencing the consumer of

STEP 1: **ENSURE CONTENT HAS VALUE** (ENTER™ framework)	STEP 2: **IDENTIFY THE OPTIMAL CHANNEL(S)**	STEP 3: **ENSURE MESSAGE HAS VALUE** (CASCADE™ framework)
• Expectational • Novel • Thorough • Examinable • Revealing	• In-person conversation • Telephone conversation • Leaving voicemail • Presenting, five minutes or less • Presenting, in-depth • Sending an e-mail or text message • Writing a report	• Conclusion-oriented • Appealing • Stock-oriented • Concise • Aware • Data-driven • Easy-to-understand

the message (e.g., portfolio manager). Using the movie-making process as an analogy, think of the content as the original book (or screenplay) and the message as the movie. We've all seen movies where we thought the book was better, suggesting the movie producers had good content but did a poor job conveying the message. The figure below illustrates how an analyst's communication can fall into one of four quadrants, based on the success of creating the content and delivering the message.

Analyst's Communication Quality

Quality of Message (CASADE™ framework)

	Quality of Content (ENTER™ framework)	
HIGH	**Lipstick on a Pig** Analyst ensured the message was delivered effectively, but unfortunately there wasn't any value for the receiver—too much sell-side research falls into this quadrant.	**Reputation Builder** Analysts did high-quality work and took the time to deliver a well-constructed message.
LOW	**Reputation Killer** Analyst didn't do the work or convey the message effectively. These types of communication hurt the analyst's reputation and should never be created.	**Lost Opportunity** Analyst did high-quality research but didn't effectively deliver the message.
	LOW	**HIGH**

Chapter 23

Create Content That Has Value

This step is all about the things analysts should do *before* preparing to communicate their research efforts with colleagues or clients. When analysts fail to create high-quality content in this first step, it inevitably prevents them from conveying a great message, regardless of how much time they spend on steps 2 and 3. With the assembly-line analogy, consider that a small problem with the quality of parts going into the product can mushroom into major problems later in the process.

Content matters—a lot. The more sophisticated the consumers of your message, the easier it is for them to identify great content among the masses of mediocrity. At the risk of stating the obvious, if you're on the buy-side, your primary goal is to *generate alpha*, and if on the sell-side, it's to *help clients generate alpha*. As such, the overwhelming preponderance of your communications should be in these areas, whether it be an e-mail to a portfolio manager or leaving a voicemail for a client. I state the obvious here, because so much of the work done by the sell-side, and to a lesser extent by the buy-side, has no connection to picking a stock. Bill Greene, a Morgan Stanley analyst with more than 12 years of sell-side experience, reinforces this point with, "PMs don't want to hear noise. They want an analyst to build a theme around their industry or a stock and then come back with proprietary research that supports or refutes the theme."

When I came across analysts who struggled to be good stock pickers, they often lost sight of their role as *stock* analysts and, over time, morphed into *company* or *sector* analysts. There's nothing wrong with company and sector analysts, but they are of less value to their firms than stock analysts, especially for buy-side firms. This is one contributor to the plethora of mediocre research out there: *Company* and *sector* analysts are compelled to spew a regular stream of facts and company-sponsored propaganda, all in an effort to feel like they're producing something.

Analysts can make certain the content of their communication is of high value by ensuring it meets the five elements of the ENTER™ framework, regardless of the medium used to communicate the message.* (The framework is further discussed in Exhibit 23.1.)

- Expectational: Provides insights about the *future*, especially catalysts likely to move the market toward the analyst's out-of-consensus view.
- Novel: Answers the question, "What's new or unique that's not already known by the broader market?"
- Thorough: Ensures that the view is backed by sound research, rather than just a hunch.
- Examinable: Provides decision makers with the information used to make conclusions.
- Revealing: Exposes risks, and acknowledges a conviction level.

---

* During my role as global director of product and development for Morgan Stanley's Research Department, I sought to create a universal framework that analysts could use to assess the quality of their research. I would like to thank Vlad Jenkins and Steve Lipmann for their creative talent in devising the first version of this effort, which we called the "ROI Quality" framework (rigorous, open, and insightful).

Exhibit 23.1   Best Practice (Knowledge): Ensure Content Has Value Using the ENTER™ Framework

Philosophy	Put into Action
Expectational. Always be thinking about the *future*, all in an effort to convey how your expectations differ from consensus, and resist the temptation to focus on the past. Understanding historical trends is important, but only in helping pick stocks in the future.	• Ensure that you have a *forward-looking* view of the most important critical factors for each company. • Identify important dates or events that could be catalysts to cause the stock to perform significantly different than its peers or the broader market. • When responding to news flow, such as a company's earnings release, keep asking yourself, "How does this change my *forward* view?"
Novel. Identify the piece of information you have that's not in the consensus view, or if responding to news flow, ask yourself, "How is the market misinterpreting the information?"	• Determine where your information fits into the FaVeS framework for stock picking (see Exhibit 20.5). If it doesn't cover one of those areas or a catalyst, it's probably not worth communicating. • Ask yourself, "Why would an owner of the stock be interested in learning my insight today?" • Avoid the common mistake of communicating information that's not unique. (Telling someone that a stock is at a 12 times P/E multiple, when it should be at a 14 times multiple is not novel.)
Thorough. Ensure that the thoroughness of your research is commensurate with the potential impact on your stock(s) by obtaining insights to accurately forecast critical factors.	• Have more than one source of information to confirm an out-of-consensus critical factor when it's imperative to your stock call. • Create a financial forecast that's detailed enough to test your hypothesis (e.g., if it's a call on product pricing by segment, there should be historical and forecasted segment pricing in the model). • Use management guidance sparingly. (Discuss management guidance to show how it contrasts with your view, not as your primary source of information.)

(Continued)

Exhibit 23.1   Best Practice (Knowledge): Ensure Content Has Value Using the ENTER™ Framework *(Continued)*

Philosophy	Put into Action

Examinable. Exposing your work to decision makers will raise its quality. It's not necessary to reveal proprietary sources, but effort should be made to provide enough depth to show others you have done the work.	• Collect all of the important data points for others to arrive at your conclusion, including upside and downside scenarios.
	• Clearly separate:
	  ○ Your opinion or forecast from . . .
	  ○ Views from others from . . .
	  ○ Undisputable facts
	• Prepare your financial forecast and valuation framework, so that you can provide others enough detail to see the assumptions for your critical factors and price target(s).

Revealing. Identify specific risks not in your base-case scenario, both positive and negative, by determining why the market believes the stock's current price is more correct than your price target. For an out-of-consensus stock call, assess your conviction level to allow others to gauge the risks to your thesis.	• Conduct upside and downside scenarios in addition to your base-case scenario. • Don't identify only general macro risks, such as, "The economy might slow" or "Inflation may accelerate," but include risks to the critical factors where you're out of consensus. • For your own use, write down why you have your current level of conviction, and what it would take to change it.

Copyright McGraw-Hill and AnalystSolutions

Expectational

Just for fun, take this test. Randomly scan 10 to 20 sell-side research reports to identify this one element: Is the report *proactive* or *reactive*? In other words, was the primary purpose to highlight a key catalyst in the future that's likely to impact a stock price, or to highlight something that has occurred in the past? I suspect you'll find over 80 percent are reactive. If you want to be more lenient, scan the first page, and where there is some discussion about future implications derived from a past event, put it into the proactive group. I suspect you'll still find the majority are reactive.

It's tough to forecast the future, especially when you know plenty of other experts are going to be listening (PMs for buy-side analysts and the entire industry for sell-side analysts), but this is what you're expected to do: make a better prediction of the future than the consensus. A well-known internet analyst I worked with liked to say that we need our people to "see around corners." If you aren't comfortable forecasting the future, you're in the wrong profession.

There are times when analysts need to respond to news flow or an event, such as quarterly earnings, but that shouldn't make up the bulk of their idea generation, because it doesn't allow anyone to get in front of a stock. When communicating about events that have occurred prior to this moment in time, the discussion should center around how it is likely to *impact the future*, and specifically, its impact on changing consensus' forward view. To spend time telling others about a company that reported an in-line quarter is a waste of everyone's time, but to assert that the underlying quality of those earnings is likely to change future expectations can be a real gem.

Novel

You're scanning a news service and come across a headline for a story you just read on another news service. Why do you ignore it? Because, there's nothing new. It's a waste of your time. So before you decide to communicate your message, ask yourself, "What do I have to say that is new and insightful?" and "What am I going to say that hasn't already been picked up by audiences through other channels?" Make sure you can answer these questions with a clear message before making noise. Ask if it applies to any of the three elements of the FaVeS stock-picking framework or a key catalyst. If not, it's tough to understand why others need to know this piece of information. Drew Jones, former associate director of research at Morgan Stanley, tells analysts, "Understand what you know that other people don't. Really try to quantify it."

Thorough

While meeting with thousands of analysts and portfolio managers during my years as a sell-side analyst, I learned that there are a lot of very talented people, but there are also a lot of people who don't do their homework. (They aren't necessarily mutually exclusive groups.) It can be easy to tell from a line of questioning whether someone understands a topic. I didn't mind that new clients would ask rudimentary questions, but when I received very basic questions from an experienced buy-side analyst whose firm owned the stock in size, I started wondering about the thoroughness of the analyst's prior research. There may be a group of fundamental investors who outperform their benchmarks without having to be thorough, but I haven't come across them yet. If you have an investment thesis that leads to an out-of-consensus view, it needs to be validated with out-of-consensus data; otherwise, it's just a hunch. Notice that I didn't say it has to be entirely proprietary. It just can't be something widely accepted by the mainstream thinking. This is important, because I believe the buy-side can use publicly disseminated sell-side research to make an out-of-consensus call as long as it's still controversial or somewhat unknown. The bottom line is that someone needs to be conducting a thorough analysis—either you and your team or the individuals you rely on for insights.

The level of thoroughness should be commensurate with how much is on the line. If getting a call wrong is simply going to cost you lunch for the person on the other side of a bet, then back-of-the-envelope is appropriate. But if your firm has 3 percent of its largest portfolio riding on FDA approval for a drug being released by a struggling company, you had better investigate the critical factors with numerous, credible, unbiased sources.

For anyone new to the industry, be advised that shoddy equity research can be spotted fairly quickly; it lacks facts to support the conclusion. Conversely, one of the most compelling aspects of a great stock call is that it's supported with data points. This isn't to say every good analyst has 100 percent of the required information to ensure that a stock call is successful (which is unrealistic), but rather that the basis for the stock call is supported by information that's been thoroughly researched.

Examinable

Rob Krebs, a former CEO of Burlington Northern Santa Fe, would often cite, "The truth will set you free," when discussing why the company would disclose more detail than necessary in its financial statements. At the other extreme, a sell-side analyst at one of my prior firms refused to publish his earnings models or provide them to clients "for proprietary reasons." When pushed, it turned out that he didn't have the models, which wasn't a surprise, because he always seemed behind the curve with his earnings forecasts.

The message here is that if you're not willing to share your analysis with those who are using your recommendations (portfolio managers for buy-side analysts and the buy-side community for sell-side analysts), then there's probably something wrong. I'm not suggesting you post your proprietary industry contact list on the Internet, but rather, provide enough depth to show others you have done work on the subject. If you're not comfortable doing this, then you may not have done enough work. At a minimum, you're going to have a tough time communicating your message without supporting information.

Revealing

Your worst stock calls will come from what you didn't know you didn't know. Even when you don't know all of the particular aspects of a given risk, if you know it's out there, you can monitor it and do some follow-up work. When you make an out-of-consensus call, those relying on your insights want to make sure you're not oblivious to the critical factors or catalysts that can go against you. One of the best ways to achieve this is to create a base-case, upside, and downside scenarios for your stock recommendations. It doesn't have to be a complicated exercise, but you should be able to identify why someone is selling the stock on a day you're recommending buying. If you don't know why, you probably haven't turned over all of the stones necessary to understand the investment. Douglas Cohen, who has spent 16 years at Morgan Stanley as both a sell-side analyst and a portfolio manager focused on utilizing the best ideas from equity research, believes, "Analysts who are 100 percent certain about an outcome likely haven't looked at all of the risks."

Chapter 24

Identify the Optimal Communication Channels

Step 2 of the overall communication process, which is *identify the optimal communication channel(s) to convey your message*, may seem like common sense. However, if you routinely communicate with a wide audience, it's important to select the channel that makes the best personal connection without consuming too much of your time. Exhibit 24.1 helps illustrate the ongoing challenge of communicating stock ideas: staying close to your colleagues and clients, while minimizing the amount of time required to do so. Finding the right balance is critical, especially as the number of people you need to influence (portfolio managers or clients) grows. If you're a sell-side analyst with the hopes of getting 150 firms to give you a strong broker vote or a buy-side analyst trying to impress 10 portfolio managers, you'll need to operate in many of the boxes below. As a general rule, you need to invest more personal time with someone early in your relationship in an effort to develop trust, before moving to less personal channels of communication.

Notice how research reports and presentations can be high in terms of time-spent-per-message-recipient, and relatively low in terms of personal-connection-with-recipient. In general, you don't want to invest significant time in either, unless you'll likely impact the majority of your target audience. There are exceptions, such as a new analyst initiating coverage for the first time (a lot of time spent, but likely few clients or

Exhibit 24.1 Communication Channel Trade-Offs When Presenting Stock Ideas

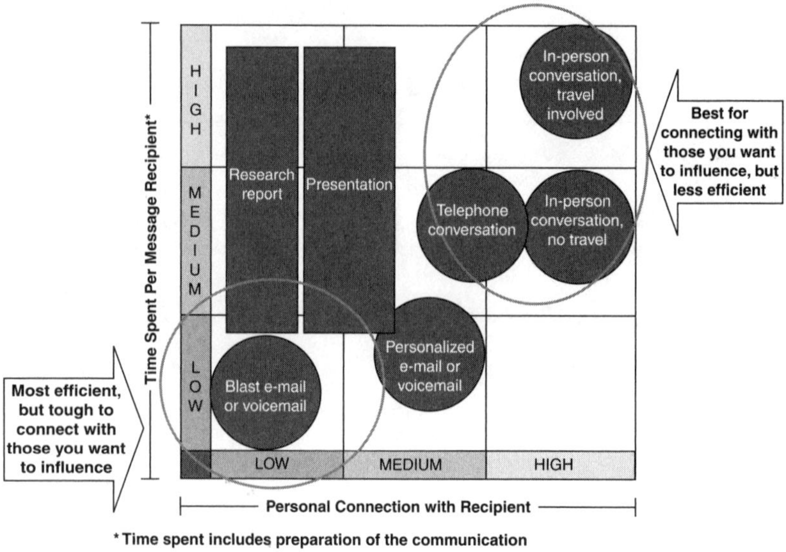

*Time spent includes preparation of the communication

Copyright McGraw-Hill and AnalystSolutions

colleagues reading the message), but in general, research reports should be created sparingly, especially long ones.

The primary reason that professionals prefer one-on-one conversations over all other forms of communication is, they can ask questions. Think about the last time your computer wasn't working properly. Did you want to reference the FAQ section of the company's website, or have a live conversation with someone who could help? It's for this reason that you want to make yourself available to the individuals you want to influence the most. Often, it's not how much you tell the person, but simply offering to be there to answer questions. Think of it as being the volunteer fire department that's always on call, but rarely gets activated. I'm not suggesting you should just sit at your desk waiting for your portfolio managers or clients to call, but don't feel like you need to be in their face 24/7 to add value. When one of the sell-side firms I worked for conducted buy-side client surveys, they found clients highly valued access to the sell-side analysts, but they didn't necessarily want proactive inbound calls.

Exhibit 24.2 highlights the pros and cons of each communication channel. Some of it may appear intuitive, but it's important to fully

Exhibit 24.2 Best Practice (Knowledge): Delivery Channel Pros and Cons for Communicating Stock Ideas

Communication Type	Most Often Used for:	Pros	Cons
In-person conversation	• Sell-side analyst conveying information to a buy-side analyst • Buy-side analyst conveying information to PM	• Can answer questions • Can read body language • Can check for understanding • Can customize discussion to meet both individuals' needs	• Not scalable (time consuming) • May require travel, especially when speaking to those outside of your firm
Telephone conversation	• Analyst collecting insights from information source	• Can answer questions • No travel required • Can check for understanding • Can customize discussion to meet both individuals' needs	• Can't read body language • Not scalable (time consuming)
Leaving voicemail	• Sell-side analyst leaving blast voicemail (BVM) for buy-side • Buy-side analyst leaving voicemail for PMs	• Fast • BVMs are scalable	• Can't check for understanding • Can't answer questions
Presenting, five minutes or less	• Analyst speaking on firm's daily call among other analysts also presenting	• Fast • Often scalable (presenting as part of a larger meeting) • Captive audience	If the meeting time is limited: • Can't provide supporting detail • Can't check for understanding • May not be able to answer questions

(Continued)

Exhibit 24.2 Best Practice (Knowledge): Delivery Channel Pros and Cons for Communicating Stock Ideas (*Continued*)

Communication Type	Most Often Used for:	Pros	Cons
Presenting in-depth	• Sell-side analyst presenting to buy-side analysts or PMs • Buy-side analyst presenting to PMs or investment committee	• Can provide details • Can check for understanding • Can read body language • Can answer questions • Often scalable (broadcast to multiple audiences) • Captive audience	• Participants may be at a range of knowledge levels • Time consuming to prepare
Sending an e-mail or text message	• Sell-side analyst conveying information to a buy-side analyst • Buy-side analyst conveying information to PM • Analyst collecting insights from information source	• Fast • Scalable for those that are not customized and personal for those that are • Allows user to respond with follow-up question	• Can't check for understanding without getting a reply • Difficult to convey tone of message such as conviction level • May get lost with hundreds of other e-mails and text messages
Writing a report	• Sell-side publishing report for buy-side usage • Buy-side analyst conveying information to PM or investment committee	• Usually provides the most detail of any form of communication • Scalable (can be read by many) • Can be stored for reference by others	• Can't check for understanding • Can't answer questions that may come from reading report • Time consuming to create and read • May not be read due to volume of other available reports
Creating a PowerPoint slide deck	• Sell-side or buy-side analyst conveying information to buy-side analysts or PMs	• Convey concepts in a user-friendly manner • Scalable (can be read by many) • Can be stored for reference by others	• Can't check for understanding • Can't answer questions that may come from reading presentation • Lacks detail of a report • Bullet points and exhibits may be difficult to understand without accompanying narration

understand that you're making a strategic decision based on the type of communication channel you use. For example if you're a buy-side analyst at a large shop and routinely leave voicemails for PMs with thoughts on your stocks, you can feel comfortable that you're being efficient, but you won't know if they understand your points or if they have any interest. Specific best practices for using each communication channel are highlighted in Chapter 26.

Chapter 25

Convey the 7 Critical Elements of Stock Recommendations

As part of the overall communication effort, I've already discussed producing a piece of high-quality content (that meets the ENTER™ standards) and choosing the optimal communication channel(s). Now comes step 3, delivering the message. Think of it this way: You're producing a Broadway play. You've already written a fantastic script and found the perfect cast. Now, you need to deliver the performance.

This chapter focuses on the seven elements of the CASCADE™ message-delivery framework, which is intended to help analysts with all types of messages. Chapter 26 then explores special considerations for delivering messages using each of the most popular channels.

Messages conveying information to make stock recommendations or trading decisions should strive to have the following elements:

- Conclusion-oriented (starts with conclusions)
- Appealing (has a hook)
- Stock-oriented (talks about stocks)
- Concise (brief as possible without excluding supporting information)

- <u>A</u>ware (acknowledges alternative views and avoids attacking people)
- <u>D</u>ata-driven (supported with data)
- <u>E</u>asy-to-understand (can be understood by almost any practitioner)

The ENTER framework, discussed in Chapter 24, is designed to help analysts ensure their *content* has value, while the CASCADE framework is designed to help ensure that the *message* has value. Don't confuse the two tasks, because they are very different. When analysts have trouble communicating their stock calls, it is very often because of a shortcoming in only one of the two areas. Exhibit 25.1 highlights each of the seven elements of the CASCADE framework.

Exhibit 25.1 Best Practice (Knowledge): Ensure That the Message Has Value Using the CASCADE™ Framework

Element	Put into Action	Examples
Conclusion-oriented Starts with conclusions	Start your stock communications with conclusions. You may feel naked by exposing your conclusion before supplying the supporting data, but it's necessary to draw in the consumer of your message.	Start with conclusions such as: • We recommend buying or selling the stock because . . . • This event is positive or negative (quantify EPS and cash flow impact if possible) because . . . • We're more bullish or bearish about XYZ due to . . . • We believe the stock will or will not react to this because . . . [Insert your unique view not found in the press or supplied by company management.]

Element	Put into Action	Examples
Appealing Has a hook	Communicate in a manner that pulls others in. Anecdotes and stories are some of the most powerful types of communication and should be used when time or space allow.	We were speaking with one of XYZ's largest customers, who said he's had two of XYZ's largest competitors in his office over the past month, because they're now offering 10% to 15% discounts to achieve their year-end sales quotas.
Stock-oriented Talks about stocks	Ensure that your communication helps a PM understand if you're more or less favored toward a stock than beforehand. (Should they be buying or selling?) Avoid the temptation to discuss company or sector issues, unless they relate directly to your concurrent discussion of a stock.	What *not* to say: We recently attended an industry trade show where we saw a number of products that were interesting, but not likely to have any impact on the companies we follow.
Concise Brief as possible without excluding supporting information	Provide the minimum required to understand your view and supporting data. Many analysts make the mistake of explaining everything they've done, even if it doesn't impact a stock price. Each concept (spoken word or paragraph in writing) should be supported with independent insights. If not, ask yourself if it's just fluff.	See Easy-to-understand below.

(Continued)

Exhibit 25.1 Best Practice (Knowledge): Ensure That the Message Has Value Using the CASCADE™ Framework *(Continued)*

Element	Put into Action	Examples

Aware
Acknowledges
  alternative views
  and avoids
  attacking people
	Demonstrate that you're not oblivious to those taking the other side of your recommendation (by addressing views driving the scenarios you've chosen not to take). Acknowledge how your view has changed, if it is significantly different from your past position. Also, have awareness of management's needs by not attacking personalities, but rather highlighting their actions or the stock price.	We're downgrading XYZ to underweight, because consensus expectations about the company's customer pricing appear too optimistic. Our bearish pricing view is refuted by others who cite a strong order book, but our work suggests that there is double-ordering taking place. In our view, pricing will be challenged to increase more than 2%, while consensus is between 4% and 5%.

Data-driven Supported with data	The data prepared earlier, in an effort to be thorough, examinable, and revealing, should make its way into your communication. Don't overwhelm your audience with tons of data up front, but make sure to incorporate facts to support your key points.	Our view is supported by our quarterly survey of large industry customers, where the average price increase for new contracts is only 1.5%, the lowest level in at least 4 years, which is critical because over 50% of XYZ's customer contracts roll over this year.

Element	Put into Action	Examples
Easy-to-understand Can be understood by almost any practitioner	Have a clear message by ensuring your content has already met the requirements of the ENTER framework (expectational, novel, thorough, examinable, and revealing) along with the elements of this CASCADE framework. For most presentations and reports, start with an outline to ensure clarity in the final product.	We are lowering our 1Q estimate for ABC (from $0.62 to $0.50), as our discussion with sector players regarding construction delays suggests production capacity will be delayed by at least six months. Should this continue, our downside scenario suggests the stock could be down 15% from here. At current levels, we recommend not owning the stock.

Conclusion-Oriented

Ensure that your opening statements, verbal or written, include a conclusion, preferably one that's expectational, about a stock, and unique. Rather than say, "We had a good meeting with a number of XYZ's customers yesterday . . .," it's much more powerful to say, "We continue to recommend purchasing XYZ, as our view was further validated by a meeting yesterday with its customers." It takes effort to communicate like this, but it's worthwhile, because the majority of those consuming your message (PMs for the buy-side and clients for the sell-side), want you to link your new insight to a stock conclusion. Your conclusions should illustrate that you understand the big picture, rather than simply discuss a factor in isolation of the stock or company.

Appealing

Why do motorists slow down when there's an accident, even when it's on the other side of the road? You want to create this same type of intrigue in your communication by identifying a hook that draws them in. Here are some tools to use:

- Position your message to answer questions already in the marketplace. If everyone is worried about downward margin pressure, and you've done some work that is closely linked to margins, make sure to communicate this angle even if the intended conclusion ultimately leads the discussion into another element of the story.

- Tell a story that helps illustrate the eureka moment that led to your unique investment thesis. ("I was sitting at my desk last night, after spending considerable time in the model, and it hit me that if these pricing trends continue, the stock could be up 25 percent.")

- Provide a real-life anecdote pertinent to supporting your view. ("We had lunch with the staff that helps regulate our sector, and they sounded very concerned about the lack of competition that's developing.")

- Be enthusiastic when you're presenting live or having a discussion, because most people equate energy level with conviction.

- Don't be boring. The consumer of your message (PM, client, etc.) is likely to be very intelligent, which creates challenge, because these people tend to get bored quickly. While you don't want your message to be way over their heads, go fast enough that they need to work to keep up. It could lead to questions, but it will keep everyone engaged.

Stock-Oriented

Talk about stocks, not just companies and industries. Should investors be buying or selling? If the majority of your message isn't about implications for a stock, you're probably off course. Surprisingly, many of the sell-side's reports are about companies, but they fail to discuss stock implications (other than a rating label on page 1). It's much easier to write about company or sector fundamentals than the stock price, because they lack the all-important forecast of a future stock price. Take the extra step, and tie your work back to stocks.

Concise

"If I had more time, I would have written you a shorter letter." This quote, attributed to a number of established authors, illustrates the challenge of conveying an idea concisely. If you don't set time aside to prepare your message, it will not be communicated with maximum impact. David Adelman, a Morgan Stanley analyst with 20 years of sell-side experience and co-head of the firm's North American stock selection committee, reinforces this point when telling his firm's new analysts, "Be concise— distill the most important points down to an understandable format."

If you're reading this thinking, *I'm not verbose*, you're probably among the majority of analysts who think they're above average on this count. Unless you find that your presentations consistently end before the allotted time and your written work is shorter than most of your peers, there's probably room to tighten up your thoughts.

If you've spent 20 hours working on an investment idea, don't budget 15 minutes to prepare your communication. The amount of time budgeted will depend on your firm's requirements, with smaller buy-side shops more likely to encourage informal communication, while large sell-side firms require more time for the documentation to be prepared and reviewed by management. When possible, prepare your communication at least a day before you intend to make it, so that you have a night to sleep on it. When you look at it the next morning, you're bound to have refinements that could make it more concise.

For brevity's sake, distill your key message down to two pitches:

- Fifteen-second elevator pitch: You unexpectedly meet a PM on the elevator who says, "Do you have any new thoughts on XYZ?" and you have 15 seconds to provide your new insight.
- Sixty-second (or less) phone pitch: You get a call about your work (PM, client, salesperson, etc.), and the person asks, "Do you have any new thoughts on XYZ?" (You have an extra 45 seconds here, because the person called you, but don't blabber on with a 5-minute answer until you've heard their reaction to your 60-second or less pitch.)

When considering the written word, remember that PMs receive 200 to 600 e-mails per day, and so, if you can't convey your message in the first few lines of the e-mail or first two bullets of your report, your message will not likely be read. Start by considering how you would convey your message using Twitter's 140-character limitation.

Avoid being verbose by asking yourself, "How quickly could I convey this information if my career depended on it?" If your answer is 5 to 6 minutes, but you are presenting at a meeting that allows you 15 minutes, make the 5- to 6-minute presentation and then ask the individual or group, "What other elements of this topic would you like to discuss?" If there are no requests, discussion over; you'll be applauded for being concise. If there is genuine interest in the topic, they'll ask questions from which you can expand the discussion. For written communication: If you can convey the concept in three paragraphs rather than three pages, choose the former. Nobody will ever punish you for being too brief or concise, unless your work lacks the facts to support your thoughts. In that case, no amount of stylistic changes will yield a high-quality message.

Another option to improve brevity is to use a picture because it can replace a thousand words. A senior sell-side analysts tells his team, "Be concise — use exhibits to tell the story rather than text."

There will be times when you'll need to provide background information, but try to be as concise as possible. If your message is that Apple is likely to take market share from its competitors, you don't need to offer a history on the IT sector. Occasionally, there is a place for more lengthy background discussions and reports, but only when your consumer is asking for it. The best analysts get recognized for their stock calls, not by how much background information they provide others.

Don't communicate fluff. Every thought (spoken sentence or written paragraph) should be supporting your view, with facts. Here are some examples:

- Poor: We like IBM because of its superior products and talented management. (This reads like a company press release; where's the value add?)
- Good: We like IBM's cost-cutting efforts, as demonstrated by the 8,000-employee downsizing announced last month.

Avoid repetition. Don't discuss the company's pricing early in your communication, and then bring it up again later. (Creating an outline will help with this.)

While numbers are paramount for supporting your thoughts, don't put too much into the text, when it could be more clearly explained in an exhibit.

- Poor: We're raising our 2012 EPS estimate for XYZ by $0.05 and our 2013 estimate by $0.25, putting us at $5.25 and $6.25, respectively, which compares with consensus at $4.75 and $5.75, respectively, which moves our price target from $72 to $75.

- Good: As shown in the exhibit below, we're raising our EPS estimate, putting us 9 to 11 percent above consensus over the next two years. Our new $75 price target is 10 percent above Tuesday's close.

	Former	New	Consensus	Difference
2012E EPS	$5.20	$5.25	$4.75	11%
2013E EPS	$6.00	$6.25	$5.75	9%
Price target	$72.00	$75.00		

Aware

Be aware of alternative views about the stock and of the recipients who will be receiving your communication. To understand alternative views, when conducting research, make sure to ask market players, "Why do you like or dislike this stock?" Don't lose sight of the fact that your buy recommendations are essentially saying that the market participants selling the stock are wrong. Every good out-of-consensus stock idea has an opposing view. Some of the best research reports are those that go through the objections to their call, refuting them one-by-one with a thoughtful and unique perspective. If you can answer objections when they arise, it demonstrates that you've explored all aspects of your call, not just the ones that support your view. You're also more likely to win over cynics if they see you've considered their opposing view. Much of the content for this element of the message will come from a good scenario analysis.

The other element of being aware is to understand the recipients of your communication outside of your firm, an issue more applicable to the sell-side than buy-side. Company managers take criticism of their company personally, as do the PMs of the stocks they own. So, if you're about to be very negative (or less positive) toward a stock in a public forum, anticipate losing some goodwill with them. (Even though buy-side analysts don't publish reports, they run into this problem when a company discovers that the fund has sold its position in the company.) By keeping your views directed at *facts* rather than *personalities;* you'll help reduce friction. Great analysts can convey their view without antagonizing the rest of the market participants; nothing is gained by being antagonistic. Clients won't pay more for it, and company management won't reward the antagonistic analyst with better access.

Don't misread this to suggest that analysts shouldn't be critical; they just need to be skillful in how they deliver a message. The financial community is a small place, and as such, there's no need to unnecessarily burn bridges you may need in the future. Rather than say, "The CEO is a deadbeat who should be fired," put the focus on the facts with something like, "Three years of declining margins suggests a change in strategy and possibly individuals within management are warranted."

Some would say there is a fine line between a sell-side analyst being promotional and sensationalistic. With over 2,000 sell-side analysts in North America alone, they need to craft their message in a unique manner to be heard, but they shouldn't communicate in a way that misleads or is destructive. Sell-side analysts who are about to communicate a message that may cross this line should run it by a trusted colleague or compliance officer in order to ensure that something isn't said that will be regretted.

Data-Driven

One of the fastest ways to identify bad research is to see if the conclusions are based solely on opinion. Great analysts do work to ensure that their out-of-consensus views have a reason to be that way. Make sure to showcase this work without divulging proprietary sources of information. All of your underlying data doesn't have to be proprietary, but if it's easy to obtain and analyze, ask yourself, "Why isn't this already priced into the stock?" Also, don't ask the consumer of your message to go find important information in other places; if it's critical, find the information yourself, include it in your work, and cite the source. Use phrases like, "We forecast" or "We believe" to clearly distinguish your view from those of others and from facts. Provide supporting data as an attachment to an e-mail or at the end of a presentation or report.

Easy-to-Understand

Of all the areas of communication, this one is the toughest to master quickly, because there isn't an objective checklist you can follow to ensure that your work is easy to understand. (Even the most unclear communication probably didn't appear that way to the person creating it.) Here are a few tips to ensure that your work is easy to understand:

- Start with an outline (or create an outline in your head) for important communications, even if it's only a one-minute pitch you're making to a PM. As you're conducting your research on a topic, create an outline that includes the content elements found in the ENTER framework and the message delivery elements found in this CASCADE framework. *Don't move to communicate your message until you're comfortable with the outline.* (Microsoft Word has a great outline feature that can be used by simply creating a new document in the "View," "Outline" mode, which can then be used as the basis for a report or PowerPoint presentation.)
- Before creating the final message, ask at least one trusted colleague to review your outline and provide feedback. *It's 10 times more difficult to modify a poorly written presentation or report than a poorly constructed outline.* And for verbal communication, it's tough to go back and improve perceptions if you botched your first attempt at the message, either live or via voicemail.

Belong to the Club

Have you noticed that police officers and military personnel often communicate using terms that would never be used in everyday conversation? Just hearing them speak a few sentences immediately tells you they belong to a unique profession. The vocabulary of a profession is very powerful; if mastered, an individual is allowed to enter the club of others who speak the same way. If you want to belong to the club of financial analysts, you'll need to ensure that you've mastered the language. Knowing the jargon for your sector(s) is also important, and it can take time to master. If you're not familiar with a term you hear or see regularly, make sure to learn it.

It's unrealistic to think this chapter can cover jargon for every sector, but some best practices for communicating to other financial analysts or PMs are provided in Exhibit 25.2.

Exhibit 25.2   Best Practice (Knowledge): Terms and Phrases Used by Practitioners

Recommendation	Examples	Why
Write in the active voice rather than passive, and be specific when possible.	Passive: "Expectations are not likely to be met this quarter." Active: "We don't expect the company to meet our $0.40 EPS for the quarter."	It strengthens your message, and shows you've done the work.
Don't pretend to have a level of precision that doesn't exist.	"We expect XYZ to earn $7.03 in 2013 by achieving operating margins of 8.37%"	It conveys the image you rely too much on your financial model output, without thinking through the big picture.
Avoid media-based words or phrases that appear sensationalistic.	"The stock is poised for a break-out due to a revolutionary new product." or "This never-before-seen turnaround by management makes this stock a screaming buy."	It will send a signal to your reader that you're inexperienced, which may cause them to question your judgment or the quality of your work.

(Continued)

Exhibit 25.2 Best Practice (Knowledge): Terms and Phrases Used by Practitioners *(Continued)*

Recommendation	Examples	Why
If you're referencing management's view, always include yours first.	"We expect the company's margins to reach 10% next year, which compares to management's guidance of 9.5%.	It shows you're a thought-leader by highlighting how management's views compare with yours.
When referring to your view, try to use words that convey research has been done, rather than just conjecture: • Best: "We forecast . . ." • Acceptable: "We expect . . ." or "We believe . . ." • Poor: "We think . . ."	"We forecast the company's earnings to grow 10% next year."	*Think* is used for informal situations more than the others. You might say, "I think I'll go get a beer." But you wouldn't say, "I forecast I'll get a beer."
Unless it runs counter to your firm's style, refer to yourself in your work as *we* and *our*, rather than *I* or *my*.	"We believe the stock is overvalued, because our work suggests consensus EPS is 10% too high next year."	It sounds more humble. You likely haven't arrived at the conclusion solely on your own. At a minimum, you've had training from others to understand how to conduct your job.
Refer to companies and management as *it*, rather than *they*.	"Management held its quarterly call where it debuted its new outlook."	This is an industry standard.

Chapter 26

Special Considerations for the Most Important Delivery Channels

This chapter builds on the communication message principles discussed in Chapter 25 by providing specific considerations for the most common types of stock communications, specifically:

- In-person conversations, presentations, and telephone calls
- PowerPoint presentations
- Marketing handouts
- Voicemails
- E-mails and text messages
- Research reports

Conveying Research Insights via In-Person Conversations, Presentations, and Telephone Calls

Most stock-based communication contains an element of influencing. Specifically, the analyst generating the stock idea wants the recipient to act on the idea and then reward the analyst for the idea. The most personal forms of communication, such as in-person conversations, presentations, and phone calls, offer a better opportunity to influence others than less personal forms of communication, such as e-mails, voicemails, and reports. In addition to building trust, which is critical to the influencing process, being live also allows the other person to ask questions. Keep in mind that this two-way street can only be achieved if the analyst is a good, active listener. When meeting others or making presentations to a small group, especially with people you meet infrequently, analysts should identify the following from the participants:

- Determine what they would like to get from the interaction (preferably beforehand, but at the beginning is acceptable).
- Periodically ask if they have any questions.
- If there are only one or two participants, ask about their background or current situation (e.g., what's your role, how's your performance, how's your firm?).

For relationship building, make sure to keep track of their responses, either mentally or in a database. If they show concern about XYZ's margin erosion, make sure to bring this up next time you're discussing the stock with them. And it doesn't end with just the professional stuff; if they tell you they're about to have a baby, make sure to ask about the baby the next time you speak with them. It helps to build a stronger bond.

If it's an important interaction and you don't know the participants very well, prepare by getting information about them so you can better convey empathy for their position or concerns. When sell-side analysts are asked to call or visit a client, they should always first have a dialogue with the client's salesperson to identify key concerns or work styles. This helps the analyst understand the needs of the client.

It's easier to influence if you start with their position and build toward yours. For example, start a meeting by asking for the portfolio manager's view on the economy. Based on the reply, begin to pitch stocks that will play well. (I'm not suggesting changing your views to meet those of the PM's.)

Exhibit 26.1   Best Practice (Knowledge): Specific Tips for Presenting to Others

Appear confident	Prepare your thoughts by creating an outline in your head or on paper. (If using PowerPoint, utilize the notes section.) Rehearse if you're unfamiliar with the topic. If it's a critically important presentation, record your rehearsal so you can review it (audio or video).
Speak at an appropriate speed and volume	In general, speak at the maximum speed that will be understood by most of the participants. Slow down to make important points, and speed up to convey enthusiasm (Johnson & Eaton, 2002: 59). If in a larger group, make sure the people in the back of the room can hear you well. If speaking into a microphone, make sure that you're close to it and that it's turned on. Lower the tone of your voice to demonstrate confidence (Johnson & Eaton, 2002: 59).
Convey the right body language	If in person, convey the right body language. (Research has shown that as much as 65% to 93% of the message being delivered can be nonverbal [Dent & Brent, 2006: 40].) The objective is to appear in control (relaxed and confident). • Be energetic. • Make good eye contact. • Maintain good posture. • Don't cross your hands or legs. • Smile, if appropriate. • Stand up if presenting to more than five people.

Conveying Research Insights via PowerPoint Presentations

There are two primary uses of PowerPoint for equity analysts:

- Presenting a stock recommendation(s)
- Providing insights through a marketing handout (generally, the sell-side only)

They each serve very different purposes. The former is a concentrated discussion about a stock, highlighting the current rationale for buying or selling, whereas the latter is intended to support all of the work that a sell-side analyst could be asked to discuss during a client meeting (including all of the content likely to come up in as many as 30 separate one-on-one meetings during a sell-side analyst's marketing road show). Viewed another way, the single-stock idea is a "push" presentation, because the presenter is pushing his or her idea to the audience. In contrast, the marketing handout tends to be a "pull," where the client requests the sell-side analyst to delve into a topic in greater detail. This is important, because a push presentation should have less information per slide than a pull presentation.

One of the most common problems I see made by research analysts (especially on the sell-side) is that their slides are too dense, lack insight, and include outdated elements. The motto should not be, "He who has the thickest slide deck wins," but rather, "He who concisely conveys the most insights, supported with data, wins."

The phrase *death by PowerPoint* is so widespread in our society that it has its own Wikipedia entry.* Exhibit 26.2 has best practices for creating PowerPoint presentations that I've picked up from others or learned on my own.

Exhibit 26.2   Best Practice (Skills): Specific Tips for Creating PowerPoint Presentations

- Before launching PowerPoint to create your first slide, have an outline for the content that includes as much of the ENTER (see Exhibit 23.1) and CASCADE (see Exhibit 25.1) frameworks as possible.
- Use the same header, footer, and font throughout, including on all exhibits. If creating your first presentation, check to see if your firm or department has a preferred PowerPoint style template.
- If one or more slides requires data that changes daily, set it up to automatically link to a market data feed, instead of updating it manually. This can be a big time saver, but requires that the analyst review the slides before each presentation to ensure the data updated correctly and isn't inconsistent with the text.

---

* Alexei Kapterev has a good presentation on the topic that can be found by searching the Internet for his name and "Death by PowerPoint."

- Make sure the font size is easily readable for everyone in the room (or for viewing online).
- Have no more than five lines of text per slide.
- Break up your text with *relevant* exhibits, while avoiding animation. (Include a video if it's critical for conveying your point, but understand that it adds complexity, which raises the odds of a technical glitch.)
- Avoid graphics that are not critical to the message (e.g., clipart, stock photos).
- If others in your firm may find value in the slides, save the presentation on a company network.
- When presenting, keep in mind that the human mind can read faster than the typical person can speak. So by the time you get halfway through reading the slide aloud, everyone else is finished, allowing their minds time to wander. In order to avoid this problem:
  - Don't read slides verbatim. Instead, use the slides to accentuate or support your points.
  - Don't use your slides as a lazy man's speaker notes. Notes should be separate; PowerPoint has a notes feature, where the author can review notes for each slide that the audience cannot see.

Sell-Side Only: Best Practices for Marketing Handouts

When visiting one-on-one with a client, sell-side analysts often feel naked without their marketing handout, because it's critical for conveying the message. A well-constructed marketing handout will be one the client marks up, and even rips apart, to use as future reference. (The more the client defaced my marketing handout during our meeting, the better I felt about its quality.) Exhibit 26.3 includes some best practices for creating a sell-side marketing handout.

Creating a great marketing handout may seem like an easy task, but here's some feedback I received from conversations with buy-side analysts about consistent problems with sell-side handouts:

- Too technical, full of data but no insights.
- Minimal support for the analyst's key points.
- Outdated material or conclusions.

Exhibit 26.3   Best Practice (Skills): Specific Tips for Marketing Handouts

- When data changes frequently, create a dynamic link back to the original document to avoid manually updating the handout. Review the data from these links before printing for client presentations, because you don't want to be surprised by a failed link during your meeting.
- Include a comp table with all the stocks in your universe, with the details highlighted in Exhibit 20.3.
- Include an overview page for each sector covered, listing your favorite and least favorite stocks.
- Include one page for each company (snapshot or SWOT-type analysis):
  - Focus on the critical factors and how you differ from consensus. (You may agree with consensus on a number of your stocks.)
  - Provide your upside, downside, and base-case scenarios, preferably in graph form but a table will do.
  - Highlight key catalysts and risks.
  - If valuation is critical to understanding the upside/downside, include a more thorough exhibit (e.g., showing why the valuation gap will close soon, or why you think your valuation is superior to the consensus view).
- Supporting data is good, but keep in mind that you should:
  - Turn large tables of numbers into easy-to-read graphs, when possible. (If a table is required, circle the most important numbers and annotate.)
  - Avoid using more than two graphs per slide.
- Approximately 24 to 48 hours before leaving on a marketing trip, review every slide and make updates as necessary.
- At least once per quarter (preferably a week after earnings season, when all of your models should be up to date), review the entire marketing handout and ask yourself, "Does it answer the most pressing questions I'm getting from clients?"
- Always have at least one unmarked copy of your marketing handout with you when traveling, as you never know when you might run into a client who wants to discuss your stocks.

Copyright McGraw-Hill and AnalystSolutions

Conveying Research Insights via Voicemail

If you're an equity research analyst, the odds are fairly high that you'll go to voicemail when attempting to share or get information. Don't imagine that this is less prevalent for industry veterans, because even the most senior analysts are met with voicemail for at least 75 percent of their outbound calls. For this reason, mastering the art of leaving a good voicemail message is important. Exhibit 26.4 highlights best practices for leaving voicemail:

Exhibit 26.4 Best Practice (Skills): Specific Tips for Leaving Voicemails

Make sure to include the following elements in every voicemail:
- Identify yourself. (You may think a person knows you, but if the recipient is going through 30 voicemails in an inbox, he or she may not quickly associate your voice with your name.)
- The purpose of your call.
- The action you want the person to take, if any.
- The best time to call you back.
- The best phone number to call. (Speak slowly enough for the recipient to write down the number.)

Other considerations:
- Try to keep it to under 30 seconds. If you're well scripted, and the message is packed with good content (e.g., "Here are the 5 things I learned at the meeting"), it can go 60 seconds. Beyond that, you'll lose your listener.
- If your message is too complex for a 60-second voicemail, tell the person that you will be following up with a more detailed e-mail.
- Try to use a landline telephone. If a mobile phone is your only option, find a quiet place with a strong signal.
- Try to avoid saying "today" or "yesterday," and instead say the day of the week. Your recipient may not pick up the message for a day or two.

If leaving a stock idea:
- Include as much of the ENTER and CASCADE frameworks as possible.
- Describe where you differ from consensus, specifically in one of these three areas: financial forecast, valuation, or sentiment about the market (the FaVeS framework).
- Say the company name at the beginning, and mention the ticker throughout. (If you only mention a ticker at the beginning, and your listener misses it, he or she will have no idea which company you're referring to throughout the rest of the message.)
- Mention the title of a report or subject line of an e-mail that contains more information.
- Encourage the person to call you back if he or she has questions.

You may think it's impossible to get all of this jammed into 60 seconds, but if you prepare your thoughts, they can include most of these elements. It's unrealistic to include all of the potential scenarios and risks in a voicemail. Therefore, refer the recipient to an e-mail or written work that includes more information.

If you're leaving the message for more than one recipient, either through a blast voicemail (BVM) or multiple calls to PMs or clients throughout the day, write out a script. If you're a sell-side analyst at a firm with a policy of not allowing BVMs to clients until your report has been released in the morning, create your script the night before you make the big call. As you speak with clients and salespeople throughout the next day, keep fine tuning your script. (If you keep getting recurring questions, make sure to update your script to proactively answer them.) If you do this throughout the day, by that evening your script is ready for that night's BVM.

Here is an example script that attempts to include the key elements discussed above:

Hello, this is Tim Smith of Golden Bull Advisors, with thoughts about the Always Best Corporation, ticker ABC, which we upgraded from equal weight to overweight on Tuesday morning. Our one-year price target is $50, which is 18 percent above Monday night's close. We're at $4.00 per share for next year, while consensus is at $3.50. We have three reasons for the upgrade:

- *First, our survey of 75 of its customers confirms our view that they are upgrading to ABC's new product line much faster than consensus believes.*
- *Second, based on recent interviews with experts in Washington, we believe ABC will benefit from legislation likely to be passed later this year; and*

- *Third, historically, ABC sees a 50-basis-point improvement to margins each time it opens a more modern facility, something it's doing later this year, and yet consensus is calling for weakening margins next year.*

Others have concerns about competitors growing into ABC's market, but our recent survey showed very little impact. Even in our downside scenario, we see the stock flat to up 5 percent. There are more details in our report from Tuesday morning, titled "Upgrading ABC on Likely Margin Expansion." If you have any questions, please call me at 212-555-1212.

Conveying Research Insights via E-mails and Text Messages

We use e-mails and text messages to communicate with our family and friends, which is probably why so many people consider these forms of communication informal, even in the workplace. Unfortunately, for anyone who works for a company that's licensed by the securities industry, the reality is that regulators and litigators can request your written communication, including e-mails and text messages, which can then be used any way they deem appropriate. Avoid these problems by assuming that every message you write is being viewed by others outside your firm. If you have something sensitive to communicate, which could be misinterpreted if taken out of context, do it in person or over the phone. Also, it should go without saying that you shouldn't forward anything that would be considered inappropriate by others. I mention this because I know of two senior analysts who separately lost their jobs over this issue. Exhibit 26.5 includes some best practices for conveying research insights via e-mail and text messages.

Exhibit 26.5 Best Practice (Skills): Specific Tips for E-mails and Text Messages

- E-mail can't convey the tone in which something is written, and so don't try to be humorous or lighthearted. Adding LOL or a smiley face might help, but if the recipient is not in the right frame of mind, she or he may not understand your perspective. (Also, jokes don't always transcend cultural boundaries.)
- Don't send e-mails when you're upset. Drafting them often helps to let off steam, but don't press the send button until you've had a night to sleep on it.
- Don't attack people. If you need to be critical, challenge the idea rather than the person, and offer a solution to show that you want to be constructive.
- Try to keep e-mails to no more than half a page. If they go any longer, you probably need to make a call or hold a meeting on the topic. (If it takes you 20 minutes to draft a lengthy e-mail, and it takes 20 minutes for your respondent to interpret the e-mail and reply to you, you could have had a 10-minute call and saved time for both of you.)
- Before starting to write:
  - Attach any files you're going to discuss.
  - Put the recipient(s) name in the *to* field, and be sure to double-check the recipient list again before pressing send. (I knew a manger who thought he was sending an e-mail to another manager, concurring they should fire an analyst, but inadvertently sent it to the analyst.)
- Write the subject line *after* drafting the e-mail, and make sure it's descriptive so that the recipient will be more motivated to open it.
- Don't reply to a previous e-mail if you are starting up a new thread of discussion.
  - The subject line won't make sense.
  - One of you may forward the new thread to someone pertinent to the topic, not realizing the person now has all of the text from your other discussion.
- If sending to multiple recipients who don't know one another, consider using the BCC function, so that you respect the privacy of each recipient's e-mail address.
- If you need someone to take action (e.g., respond by a certain date), underline it. (Many analysts and portfolio managers get 200 to 600 e-mails a day, and so they may spend only five seconds scanning your e-mail.)
- If you want to make it easy for others to reach you, make sure to include a signature file with as many contact details as possible.
- Check with your IT department to ensure that your e-mails are being backed up and are in a place that is included in your desktop search feature.

Conveying Research Insights via Reports

As a general rule, sell-side analysts tend to write more frequently and produce more pages than buy-side analysts, but there are exceptions. The typical sell-side analyst's mission is to disseminate a stock recommendation to the widest audience possible, whereas the buy-side analyst often is only conveying the key conclusions to an immediate team of colleagues and portfolio managers. While it's clear that the reports are serving two different purposes, there are many overlapping best practices, regardless of the intended audience. I highlight best practices for writing research reports for both types of analysts, which are based heavily on the CASCADE framework discussed previously, followed by specific considerations for sell-side reports.

What Readers Want

During my role in research management, I conducted research to identify the items in sell-side research reports that portfolio managers value the most. (It included interviews with over 40 portfolio managers in New York, London, Tokyo, and Singapore.) While much of the discussion was about sell-side research, some of it also applies to the buy-side as well. Their views are as follows:

- Most inbound e-mails to buy-side clients that include a report are deleted before they are reviewed. Of the rare few that catch clients' interest, they spend 5 minutes on a typical report, but up to 45 minutes for an in-depth report on an important topic (which doesn't occur often).
- In general, sell-side analysts produce too many:
  ○ Short reports that have no insights or impact, especially post earnings.
  ○ Reports that are too long or not well constructed.

- Sell-side analysts don't produce enough:
  - Thematic sector pieces that compare companies or illustrate competitive advantages and/or disadvantages.
  - Explanation of valuation multiples.
  - Historical perspective of valuation multiples.
- When asked about the ideal maximum number of pages of text for a report, the average response was:
  - For non-in-depth reports: 2.3 pages
  - For in-depth reports: 13 pages
- In terms of typical sell-side report qualities, portfolio managers find the greatest value from a "forward-looking view," and the least value from an "actionable call." (This means that they want to understand the thought process more than the conclusion.) (See Exhibit 26.6.)
- Among the standard components of sell-side research reports, they find the greatest value from the financial forecast and the least value from the stock rating (see Exhibit 26.7).

Exhibit 26.6   Value of Report Qualities

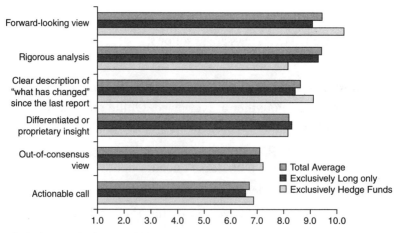

Ranked on a scale of 1 to 10 with 10 as "most important"

Source: Morgan Stanley

Exhibit 26.7   Value of Report Components

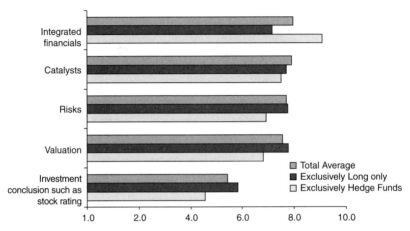

Ranked on a scale of 1 to 10 with 10 as "most important"

Source: Morgan Stanley

Anatomy of a Great Research Report

As a refresher, the key considerations discussed earlier for all forms of investment communications also apply to research reports. Among the elements of the CASCADE framework, the most important to the early stages of the report-writing process is *easy-to-understand*, because the report won't be clear if it's not organized well. Follow these guidelines to ensure that the report is organized in a manner that will lead to clear communication when read by others:

- Create an outline *before* writing a report that includes the content elements found in the ENTER framework and the message delivery elements found in the CASCADE framework.
- Don't start writing the report until you're comfortable with the outline. If possible, ask at least one trusted colleague to review the outline and provide feedback. *It's 10 times more difficult to modify the final version of a poorly written presentation or report than a poorly constructed outline.*

Exhibit 26.8 uses the CASCADE framework to highlight the key elements unique to research reports. With the previous discussion in mind, don't use it as a checklist *after* you've written the report, but rather as a guide when drafting a preliminary outline.

Exhibit 26.8 Best Practice (Knowledge): Special Considerations for Writing Research Reports

Use this as a checklist when drafting your preliminary outline. (It's very tough to go back and include these elements after the report is written.)

CASCADE Framework Element	Specific Considerations for Reports
Conclusion-oriented (Start with conclusions)	• The title should include your conclusion. • Page one should clearly indicate a view toward adding or reducing a position in the stock at its current price.
Appealing (Have a hook)	• Write the title and bullets in a persuasive manner to draw in the reader without sensationalizing or hyping.
Stock-oriented (Talk about stocks)	• At least one stock should be mentioned in the first two bullets. • Try to include the company's name or ticker in the report title, if isolated to one company.
Concise (Be as brief as possible without excluding supporting information)	• Write in bullet points to keep message succinct. • Use exhibits to tell the story; if done correctly, one exhibit can replace three to four paragraphs. • Showcase key points in the first two pages; most PMs and clients won't read past page two unless it's an in-depth report covering a very important topic. Anything past page two should be considered an appendix to support your new insights.
Aware (Acknowledge alternative views)	• To illustrate that you've looked at other perspectives beyond your own, include an exhibit that shows upside, downside, and base-case assumptions and price targets. • Comments attacking people are slow to die; avoid them at any cost, especially on the sell-side, where messages are widely disseminated.

Data-driven (Support view with data)	• Try to include at least one supporting fact per paragraph or bullet. (If it doesn't include facts or data, ask yourself, "What purpose does it serve?") • Include a financial model, with at least a two-year forecast. • Include historical valuation discussion and charts if critical to investment thesis. • Cite all sources of data or facts critical to the investment thesis. (Keep proprietary sources anonymous.)
Easy-to-understand (Can be understood by almost any practitioner)	For clarity, page one should include the following information: • How your forward-looking view differs from consensus. • The future catalyst(s) that will bring consensus into your way of thinking. • The new insight(s) that was the genesis for the report. • Numbers to support price target (valuation and key elements from your financial forecast). • Risks. • Conviction level. • Exhibits that are clear. (Avoid using large tables of numbers; annotate or use a graph of just the key information.)

For sell-side only	• Don't hesitate to write about why you were wrong, because clients like to see humility and understand why a stock call failed.
	• Create templates for quarterly earnings reports:
	  ◦ Bullets prepopulated before earnings with prior period numbers.
	  ◦ Variance table.
	  ◦ Place to discuss any changes in the forecast.

Considerations for the Sell-Side Only

From the buy-side survey discussed earlier, PMs said that sell-side analysts need to publish only 1.4 times per quarter to remain in their "top three" position, presuming that the analyst does good work and is available to the portfolio manager when requested. Sell-side analysts typically publish more in a week than a portfolio manager expects in a quarter, and so there's a clear gap. Nobody would discourage an analyst from publishing a comprehensive piece of work to justify a major ratings change or to support a current recommendation, but these types of reports don't tend to come along regularly. Instead, much of the published research goes unread. The debate about what constitutes unwanted research often includes a discussion about *maintenance* research.

Throughout my career, I heard clients and research management telling sell-side analysts to "stop producing maintenance research." I was one of the most prolific writers within my firm, including some work focused on very short-term, tactical trends. Was it "maintenance"? Since I didn't know how to define maintenance, I included it as part of my interviews with portfolio managers. Here's what they said about maintenance research:

- Maintenance research is bad when there is:
  - Nothing new or nothing has changed.
  - No stock-specific insight.
- Maintenance research is acceptable or good when it:
  - Revisits a good long-term call with periodic data points.
  - Is an earnings write-up that is very brief (two or three bullets), highlighting how the results provide new insights about the *future*.
  - Highlights key takeaways from a firm-sponsored event like a conference or company visit.

Not every message you write will be about a 25 percent upside stock call, but conversely, avoid writing about the minutia. (If it doesn't have most of the elements of the ENTER framework, it's probably not useful maintenance.)

Creating periodicals (e.g., a weekly, monthly, or quarterly) can help build and promote a sell-side analyst's franchise, but the time commitment should be weighed against the benefits. They have their own momentum; once they get started, they're difficult to stop, which can be either good or bad. Before starting a periodical, ask yourself:

- Is there more than one competitor already publishing a similar periodical? If so, ask clients if they read it. If not, what would they look for in a periodical? If so, what do they like and dislike the most about the competitor's product(s)? Unless there is a resounding need from a wide client base, don't publish a periodical.

- How could you ensure that there are *forward-looking investment-significant insights* you'll discuss on page one of *every* future periodical you publish? If the periodical (such as the weekly or monthly release of sector data) doesn't create new catalysts that change views or conviction levels toward stocks, it will be tough to get readers to find it insightful.

- If you're set on publishing a periodical, could you create synergy by copublishing with a colleague who follows a related sector (e.g., airlines and aircraft manufacturers) or the same sector in another region (to provide a unique global perspective)?

PART 6

MAKING ETHICAL DECISIONS

Under pressure to increase a portfolio's performance or to look better among fellow colleagues, analysts may be tempted to cut ethical corners. These ethical lapses can cost the analyst a job, client relationships, or professional credentials, and can even lead to lawsuits. This best practice presents a process to help analysts appropriately resolve ethical dilemmas.

Chapter 27

Identify and Resolve
Ethical Challenges

Identifying the Ethical Dilemma
Is the First Step

The first step in making the appropriate ethical decision relies on identifying the potential dilemma. This may seem obvious, but it can be difficult to see when an analyst is deeply entrenched in his or her research. Ethical dilemmas can come from many aspects of the analyst's role, but they almost always fall into one of two categories:

- Misconduct by the analyst for personal or professional gain.
- Conflicts of interest between two or more parties that rely on the analyst for an objective investment recommendation.

To help spot these potential ethical challenges, here are some of the most common types of misconduct by analysts seeking personal or professional gains:

- Going beyond building the mosaic by seeking out or requesting material information that the analyst knows or suspects is nonpublic

- Omitting risks or relevant facts from an investment recommendation that were:
  - Known, but downplayed in order to make the investment appear more attractive
  - Not properly assessed due to insignificant research conducted on the topic, even though the general risk was understood early in the process
- Relying solely on company management to provide an assessment of risk for an investment.
- Misrepresenting the thoroughness of research conducted, proactively or in response to a question
- Not clearly identifying an opinion, which could lead others to interpret it as fact
- Modifying a financial forecast or valuation multiple solely to justify a predetermined price target
- Covering up a mistake that could lead others to make an impaired investment conclusion
- Plagiarizing others' work
- Misrepresenting past performance or qualifications
- Sell-side only: Sharing material non-published information about a stock or recommendation with a client before it has been published or widely disseminated to all of the firm's clients

Unlike the misconduct mentioned above, even if an analyst has the best of intentions, *conflicts of interest* can't be entirely avoided. For equity research analysts, these conflicts most commonly hinder their ability to provide objective investment advice. To help spot these potential ethical challenges, I've identified some of the most common types of conflicts of interest. (Note that many are not unethical acts like those above, but rather conflicts.) Most of these are related to the sell-side, due to the nature of the sell-side analyst's role, which often involves serving more than one constituent:

- Being asked or influenced by a client or portfolio manager to make a recommendation change solely to help the person's position.

- Being asked by a trader or client for an objective analysis of a stock when the analyst is in possession of information that can't be disclosed to the party (e.g., an impending ratings change or proprietary information that hasn't been disseminated).
- Being less than objective with a stock recommendation because the analyst has received information, either directly or indirectly, that the firm could lose an investment banking transaction if she doesn't have a positive rating.
- Being biased to write favorably about a company's stock because the company has provided the analyst special access to management, superior information, or gifts such as tickets to a sporting event.

Some professionals believe that disclosing a conflict of interest is sufficient for resolving it, but this misses an important element of conflict resolution. The research analyst has an obligation to maintain objectivity and independence, regardless of whether the directly affected parties are comfortable. Analysts shouldn't assume that they can fully self-assess their ability to remain objective. Professionals in all fields, including equity research, can be particularly vulnerable to overestimating their ability to withstand the ethical pressures that conflicts of interest create. Just as most people believe themselves to have above-average intelligence (a statistical impossibility), many professionals believe themselves to be exceptionally able to ignore temptation and act independently despite conflicts of interest. This is why it's particularly important to consider not only how well you believe you can rise above the conflict, but also whether others would be likely to agree.

Guidelines for the Right Course of Action

When an analyst has identified that an ethical dilemma likely exists (or is beginning to emerge), it's imperative to take the right course of action. Each situation will have its own unique elements, but in almost every instance, the analyst's course of action should meet these criteria:

- Legal
- Consistent with the analyst's firm's rules
- Transparent
- Protective of others' legitimate interests
- Prudent
- Consistent with the CFA Institute guidelines

Legal

Analysts aren't expected to be lawyers, but they should know the pertinent regulations and laws that apply to their work. Ask your manager or compliance officer for help in becoming familiar with the laws that cover your role and for advice when faced with an ethical issue that may have legal implications.

Consistent with the Firm's Rules

Many firms have internal codes of ethics that their employees are required to follow. These ethical standards that analysts working for the firm are expected to meet can become compelling evidence during litigation. When joining a new firm, ask if there is training to help understand the firm's policies. If so, make sure to participate so that you're not caught by surprise. If not, ask to meet with your compliance officer to discuss the most common problems incurred by other analysts, so that you're aware of the likely land mines.

Transparent

If you cannot easily or comfortably explain to others why you are considering a particular course of action, you may be contemplating unethical conduct. Ethical behavior is usually simple to explain and readily accepted by third parties. When considering how you would describe a particular course of action to a third party, imagine that you're talking to someone who is not an equity research analyst and who may not be as knowledgeable as you are on the topic at hand. It can be all too easy for professionals to think, "We've always done it this way." A mindset like that can distort their view of reality; someone from outside the industry does not suffer from this bias. Keep that person in mind as you consider how you would explain your behavior. It should be fairly clear if your actions are transparent, but if you're unsure, use the tests discussed later.

Protective of Others' Legitimate Interests

There are at least two parties in almost every financial transaction, and each one has legitimate interests. (For the purposes of this discussion, a legitimate interest is one that is lawful, reasonable, and transparent.) Before taking any ethically questionable action, it's important to thoughtfully identify parties whose legitimate interests could be harmed. Make sure to keep a mental list of individuals and organizations that could be harmed by unethical behavior on your part, so that you choose a course of action that protects, rather than damages, their interests.

If you decide to move forward when a conflict of interest exists, it's imperative to disclose the conflict. Disclosure may be as simple as telling a client you have information that can't be disclosed, and thus prevents you from providing an objective response. It could also entail further action, such as notifying your compliance department of a conflict. Moving forward without disclosure is setting yourself up for a bad outcome that may ultimately upset one of your key constituents or even lead to an investigation.

Prudent

Making stock recommendations isn't an exact science. Bad stock calls are an accepted part of the job, even for the best analysts. These bad calls should be the result of factors that could not have been foreseen or where the analyst's sound research led to a different outcome, rather than sloppy or insufficient research. In making recommendations, it's important to strike an appropriate balance between optimism and realism, in order to fully disclose the risks associated with an investment and to avoid encouraging others to make overly risky investments in the hope of obtaining unrealistically high returns. When considering whether a particular course of action is prudent, it usually helps to establish a long-term perspective. Ethical mistakes are often driven by a sense of urgency to achieve short-term financial goals or meet tight deadlines. Think past the immediate time constraint that tempts you to cut ethical corners, and choose a course of action that makes good sense for you and the other parties involved over the long haul.

Consistent with the CFA Institute Guidelines

The CFA Institute's published Code of Ethics and Standards of Professional Conduct codifies the ethical responsibilities of members and candidates in the CFA Program, as do the Best Practice Guidelines Governing Analyst and Corporate Issuer Relations. These rules explain how our profession expects analysts to behave. Not surprisingly, they emphasize the importance of integrity, independence, and objectivity to promote ethical practices. Even if you're not a CFA, the actions you take should be consistent with the CFA's rules.

Test Your Decision

If your conscience causes you to reflect on a potential decision because your actions may not be completely ethical, take a moment to test it before taking action. Here are several tests that can be helpful:

The TV Test

Before you act, imagine how you would feel if, the following day, all of detailed elements of your actions were reported on television worldwide. This test is particularly useful to help you imagine how people who are not in your profession would judge your behavior. Would you be proud or embarrassed by what you think the press would say? How would people close to you—family, friends, and professional colleagues—react to the story? What consequences would result from your actions being made public? If you would not be comfortable by the press's likely portrayal of the event, choose another course of action.

Discipline Committee Test

Before you act, imagine being called upon to explain your decision before the senior management of your department or the CFA Institute's Disciplinary Review Committee. This test is particularly useful to help you imagine how your peers would judge your behavior. Could you readily explain your conduct? Could you point to provisions in your firm's or the CFA Institute's rules to support your actions? Would your professional peers understand and agree that what you did was appropriate? If you are uncomfortable with the idea of presenting your actions to your peers, make a more ethical choice.

The 10-Year Test

Before you act, try to envision how your actions might affect your circumstances 10 years from now if fully understood by others. This test is particularly useful to offset short-term thinking that can cloud your ethical judgment. Will you have lost anything—a job, a client, a promotion, your professional reputation—because of your actions? If you take an ethical shortcut, will the benefits even matter 10 years from now?

The Exemplar Test

You may have seen bumper stickers or t-shirts that ask the question, "What would Jesus do?" This test is particularly useful to depersonalize an ethical dilemma, and while it certainly can be faith-based, it doesn't necessarily need to be. Think of someone whose integrity you greatly admire. It can be a religious leader, an historical figure, a professional mentor, a family member, or anyone else you respect. Try to imagine that person in your situation, and ask yourself whether he or she would follow the course of action you have chosen. If you can't imagine that person doing what you have in mind, come up with a different solution.

Act on Your Choice

Once you've tested your proposed course of action and believe that it's an ethical choice, resist the temptation to delay. The longer you wait to do the right thing, the more likely you'll be put under additional pressure to do something unethical. Ideally, do something that will make it impossible for you to lapse into unethical conduct. For example, if you've been tempted to cover up a mistake, tell a respected colleague so that it's no longer possible for you to deny it. Quick, irreversible action is usually the best way to make your ethical choice a reality.

In the case of a conflict of interest: If you determine that the conflict will undoubtedly bias your investment advice, then it's time to find a graceful exit strategy. For the more difficult situations, such as those that impact your clients, trader, or boss, you'll need to be diplomatic. In my experience, if you provide them with your assessment of the situation, they tend to understand why you see a conflict and are choosing to step away from the situation. They may be disappointed that you didn't sway to their influence, but they'll know in the future not to put you in the situation. Taking the more ethical route could potentially have a short-term negative impact on pay, promotion, or standing with these constituents, but in the long run, it will provide assurance that your career path won't be derailed due to a bad decision.

Special Considerations for Sell-Side Analysts

Sell-side analysts are often faced with conflicts of interest that arise in investment banking transactions. Their firm wants an opinion about a company to determine if it should be involved in the deal, but if the analyst has a negative view, it could result in millions of dollars of lost business for the firm. Remember that the investment banking department's clients are the companies, whereas the typical sell-side analyst's clients are the potential investors in the companies; there is a significant conflict of interest here that should be fully appreciated. Here are some thoughts about working with investment banking, especially in the initial public offering (IPO) process:

- When communication is required, use the proper legal channels (often through a chaperone). When having an authorized conversation, follow up via e-mail for clarity, using the proper legal channels.

- Make all requests for information and due diligence sessions with management and industry sources as early in the process as possible. (More than 75 percent of the problems I witnessed between research and investment banking could have been mitigated if analysts had spoken up early to request information or object to an issue.)

- Build financial forecast and valuation as soon as possible to avoid last minute surprises.

- Quickly move up the chain of command if the data needed to evaluate and value a company is not being made available. If it's still not available after more than one request, use the proper channels to notify investment banking, in writing, that there may be a delay for Research's view due to a lack of information.

- Don't argue with bankers over valuation. Conduct a thorough, detailed valuation, as though for a major buy-side client, that offers upside, base, and downside scenarios. It should be the same one that will be published in your first report on the company. Ultimately, the market will set the price for the deal, not the analyst.

- Don't let the bankers do any of the work that will impact valuation on the stock, such as making accounting adjustments or selecting the comparable companies.
- Be willing to say no if a deal looks bad. (As a sell-side analyst, your primary asset is your reputation.)
- Avoid changing earnings estimates or valuation between the internal presentation to the salesforce and publishing a report on the stock, unless there's been a major change in the market or with the company.

Exhibit 27.1 Best Practice (Skills): Follow Ethical Practices to Make the Right Decisions

1. In order to make the right ethical decision, it's imperative to spot ethical dilemmas as they emerge. Most of these dilemmas occur as:
   - Misconduct by the analyst for personal or professional gain, such as:
     - Seeking material, nonpublic information.
     - Omitting risks or relevant facts.
     - Relying solely on company management to provide an assessment of risks for an investment.
     - Misrepresenting the thoroughness of research conducted.
     - Not clearly identifying an opinion, which could be interpreted by others as a fact.
     - Modifying a financial forecast or valuation multiple solely to justify a predetermined price target.
     - Covering up a mistake that could lead others to make an impaired investment conclusion.
     - Plagiarizing others' work.
     - Misrepresenting past performance or qualifications.
     - Sharing material, non-published information about a stock or recommendation with a client before it has been published or widely disseminated to all of the firm's clients.
   - Conflicts of interest between two or more parties that rely on the analyst for an objective investment recommendation such as the following situations:
     - Being asked or influenced by a client or portfolio manager to make a recommendation change solely to help the person's position.

- Being asked by a trader or client for an objective analysis of a stock when the analyst is in possession of information that can't be disclosed to the party (e.g., an impending ratings change or proprietary information that hasn't been disseminated).
- Being less than objective with a stock recommendation because the analyst has received information, either directly or indirectly, that the firm could lose an investment banking transaction if she doesn't have a positive rating.
- Being biased to write favorably about a company's stock because the company has provided the analyst special access to management, superior information, or gifts such as tickets to a sporting event.

2. Make sure your actions are:
   - Legal
   - Consistent with the analyst's firm's rules
   - Transparent
   - Protective of others' legitimate interests
   - Prudent
   - Consistent with the CFA Institute guidelines

3. If you're struggling with a decision because it could result in unethical behavior, run it through these tests:
   - The TV Test
   - Discipline Committee Test
   - The 10-Year Test
   - The Exemplar Test

4. Once you've decided on the ethical path to take, move forward with that course of action as soon as possible to avoid the temptation to back away from your ethical decision.

5. If you've determined that a conflict of interest will potentially bias your investment advice, disclose it to all parties involved, and if the conflict prevents you from rendering an objective view, exit the situation gracefully.

Works Cited

Asquith, Paul, Michael B. Mikhail, and Andrea S. Au, "Information Content of Equity Analyst Reports," *Journal of Financial Economics*, 2005: 75, 245-282.

Bailard, Thomas, David Biehl, and Ronald Kaiser, *Personal Money Management*, Sixth Edition, New York: Macmillan Publishing Company, 1992.

Benartzi, Shlomo, Daniel Kahneman, and Richard H. Thaler, "Optimism and Overconfidence in Asset Allocation Decisions," Morningstar.com, http://www.behaviouralfinance.net/optimism/ Morningstar_com%20Optimism%20and%20Overconfidence%20 in%20Asset%20Allocation%20Decisions.htm, April 23, 1999.

Clement, Michael, "Analyst Forecast Accuracy: Do Ability, Resources, and Portfolio Complexity Matter?," *Journal of Accounting and Economics*, 1999: 27, 285-303.

Cohen, Daniel A., and Paul Zarowin, "Accrual-Based and Real Earnings Management Activities Around Seasoned Equity Offerings," *Journal of Accounting and Economics*, 2010: 50, 2-19.

Damodaran, Aswath, *Damodaran on Valuation*, Second Edition, Hoboken: John Wiley & Sons, 2006.

Demirakos, Efthimios G., Norman C. Strong, and Martin Walker, "What Valuation Models Do Analysts Use?," *Accounting Horizons*, 2004: 18(4), 221.

Dent, Fiona Elsa, and Mike Brent, *Influencing*, Hampshire, UK: Houndmills, 2006.

Dreman, David, *Contrarian Investment Strategies: The Next Generation,* New York: Simon & Schuster, 1998.

eFinancial Careers, "Firms Use Intelligence Officers, Skills to Pierce Deception," Review of *Broker, Trader, Lawyer, Spy: The Secret World of Corporate Espionage,* by Eamon Javers, March 1, 2010, http://news.efinancialcareers.com/newsandviews_item/newsItemId-24045.

Frick, Bob. "Don't Trust the Crowd", Kiplinger, http://www.kiplinger.com/magazine/archives/dont-trust-the-crowd-.html, September 30, 2010A.

Frick, Bob. "How Poker Can Make You a Better Investor," Kiplinger, http://www.kiplinger.com/features/archives/how-poker-can-make you-a-better-investor.html?kipad_id=×, January 7, 2010B.

Gleason, Cristi A., W. Bruce Johnson, and Haidan Li, "Valuation Model Use and the Price Target Performance of Sell-Side Equity Analysts," paper, Tippie College of Business, University of Iowa, October 30, 2009, http://ssrn.com/abstract=930720.

Goman, Carol K., *The Nonverbal Advantage: Secrets and Science of Body Language at Work,* San Francsco: Berrett-Koehler, 2008.

Gordon, Nathan J. and William L. Fleisher, *Effective Interviewing and Interrogation Techniques,* Amsterdam: Elsevier Academic Press, 2006.

Graham, Benjamin, *The Intelligent Investor: A Book of Practical Counsel,* New York: Harper & Row, 1985.

Gross, Bill, CNBC, October 28, 2009.

Harrington, Cynthia, "Mind Games," *CFA Magazine,* January/February 2010.

Imam, Shahed, Richard Barker, and Colin Clubb, "The Use of Valuation Models by UK Investment Analysts," *European Accounting Review,* 2008: 17(3), 503–535.

Integrity Research Associates, *Custom Survey Research.* New York: Integrity Research Associates, 2009.

Johnson, Roy and John Eaton, *Influencing People*; New York: DK Publishing, 2002.

Loh, Roger, and G. Mujtaba Mian, "Do Accurate Earnings Forecasts Facilitate Superior Investment Recommendations?," *Journal of Financial Economics*, 2006: 80, 455–483.

Mauboussin, Michael J., *More Than You Know*, Updated and Expanded Edition, New York: Columbia University Press, 2008.

Mangot, Mickäel, *50 Psychological Experiments for Investors*, Singapore: John Wiley & Sons, 2009.

Mills, Terence C., *Time Series Techniques for Economists*, Cambridge: Cambridge University Press, 1991.

Myring, Mark, and William Wrege, "Analysts' Earnings Forecast Accuracy and Activity: A Time-Series Analysis," *Journal of Business & Economics Research*, 2009: 7, 88-95.

Nance, Jef, *Conquering Deception*, Kansas City, MO: Irvin-Benham, 2000.

Navarro, Joe, and Marvin Karlins, *What Every Body Is Saying: An Ex-FBI Agent's Guide to Speed-Reading People*, New York: HarperCollins, 2008.

Nicolosi, G, L Peng, and N Zhu, "Do Individual Investors Learn from Their Trade Experience?," *Journal of Financial Markets*, 2009: 12(2), 317–336.

Occupational Information Network (U.S. Department of Labor), Detailed Report for Financial Analysts, O*Net Online, http://online.onetcenter.org/link/details/13-2051.00, October 5, 2009.

Pease, Barbara, and Allan Pease, *The Definitive Book of Body Language*, New York: Bantam Books, 2006.

Ramnath, Sundaresh, Steve Rock, and Philip Shane, "A Review of Research Related to Financial Analysts' Forecasts and Stock Recommendations," paper, University of Miami, Department of

Accounting; University of Colorado at Boulder, Department of Accounting; and University of Colorado at Boulder, Leeds School of Business, June 30, 2008, http://ssrn.com/abstract= 848248.

Robinson, Joe, "E-mail Is Making You Stupid," *Entrepreneur*, March 2010.

Schoenhart, Michael, *Behavioral Finance and Market Anomalies: An Academic Review*, Saarbrücken, Germany: VDM Verlag, 2008.

Statman, Meir, "The Mistakes We Make—And Why We Make Them," *Wall Street Journal*, August 24, 2009, R1.

Stine, Robert E. and Dean Foster, *Statistics for Business: Decision Making and Analysis*. Boston: Addison Wesley, 2010.

Trammell, Susan, "Are Analysts Just Human, After All? How the Pitfalls of Investor Psychology Can Catch Analysts Off Guard," *CFA Magazine*, September/October 2003.

Vovici, 7 Habits of Highly Successful Surveys, http://www.vovici.com/forms/signup-wp-7habits-web.aspx?lst=surveySoftware, September 30, 2010.

Zweig, Jason, *Your Money & Your Brain—How the New Science of Neuroeconomics Can Help Make You Rich*, New York: Simon & Schuster, 2007.

Index

About the Author

James J. Valentine, CFA, is the founder of AnalystSolutions, which provides best practices, training and career advancement services for equity research analysts. He has held a number of analyst roles at four of Wall Street's largest firms, including most recently Morgan Stanley, where he was the Associate Director of North American Research as well as Director of Training for the firm's global Research department. He was also an established research analyst where, for 10 consecutive years, he was ranked by the major Wall Street institutional investor polls as one of the top three analysts within his sector. In 2006, *Forbes* named him one of the top three Wall Street analysts among all 2,000 U.S. sell-side analysts that year. He has been recognized for his stock picking, earnings forecasts and client service from the *Wall Street Journal, Thomson Reuters, Institutional Investor,* and *Greenwich Associates.* He holds a Master's degree in finance from the University of Iowa and the Chartered Financial Analyst (CFA) designation. He lives in a Connecticut suburb of New York City with his wife and three children. Contact details can be found at jamesvalentine.com.